Red Hat® Linux®
FOR
DUMMIES®

Red Hat® Linux®
FOR
DUMMIES®

by Jon "maddog" Hall and Paul G. Sery

IDG
BOOKS
WORLDWIDE

IDG Books Worldwide, Inc.
An International Data Group Company

Foster City, CA ◆ Chicago, IL ◆ Indianapolis, IN ◆ New York, NY

Red Hat® Linux® For Dummies®

Published by
IDG Books Worldwide, Inc.
An International Data Group Company
919 E. Hillsdale Blvd.
Suite 400
Foster City, CA 94404
www.idgbooks.com (IDG Books Worldwide Web site)
www.dummies.com (Dummies Press Web site)

Library of Congress Catalog Card No.: 99-67158

ISBN: 0-7645-0663-3

Printed in the United States of America

10 9 8 7 6 5 4 3

1B/RZ/RR/ZZ/IN

Distributed in the United States by IDG Books Worldwide, Inc.

Distributed by CDG Books Canada Inc. for Canada; by Transworld Publishers Limited in the United Kingdom; by IDG Norge Books for Norway; by IDG Sweden Books for Sweden; by IDG Books Australia Publishing Corporation Pty. Ltd. for Australia and New Zealand; by TransQuest Publishers Pte Ltd. for Singapore, Malaysia, Thailand, Indonesia, and Hong Kong; by Gotop Information Inc. for Taiwan; by ICG Muse, Inc. for Japan; by Intersoft for South Africa; by Eyrolles for France; by International Thomson Publishing for Germany, Austria and Switzerland; by Distribuidora Cuspide for Argentina; by LR International for Brazil; by Galileo Libros for Chile; by Ediciones ZETA S.C.R. Ltda. for Peru; by WS Computer Publishing Corporation, Inc., for the Philippines; by Contemporanea de Ediciones for Venezuela; by Express Computer Distributors for the Caribbean and West Indies; by Micronesia Media Distributor, Inc. for Micronesia; by Chips Computadoras S.A. de C.V. for Mexico; by Editorial Norma de Panama S.A. for Panama; by American Bookshops for Finland.

For general information on IDG Books Worldwide's books in the U.S., please call our Consumer Customer Service department at 800-762-2974. For reseller information, including discounts and premium sales, please call our Reseller Customer Service department at 800-434-3422.

For information on where to purchase IDG Books Worldwide's books outside the U.S., please contact our International Sales department at 317-596-5530 or fax 317-596-5692.

For consumer information on foreign language translations, please contact our Customer Service department at 1-800-434-3422, fax 317-596-5692, or e-mail rights@idgbooks.com.

For information on licensing foreign or domestic rights, please phone +1-650-655-3109.

For sales inquiries and special prices for bulk quantities, please contact our Sales department at 650-655-3200 or write to the address above.

For information on using IDG Books Worldwide's books in the classroom or for ordering examination copies, please contact our Educational Sales department at 800-434-2086 or fax 317-596-5499.

For press review copies, author interviews, or other publicity information, please contact our Public Relations department at 650-655-3000 or fax 650-655-3299.

For authorization to photocopy items for corporate, personal, or educational use, please contact Copyright Clearance Center, 222 Rosewood Drive, Danvers, MA 01923, or fax 978-750-4470.

is a registered trademark under exclusive license to IDG Books Worldwide, Inc. from International Data Group, Inc.

About the Authors

Jon "maddog" Hall is the Executive Director of Linux International, a vendor organization dedicated to promoting the use of the Linux Operating System. He has been in the computer industry for over a quarter century (somehow that sounds more impressive than just "twenty-five years"), the past eighteen years of which have been spent using, programming, and admiring the UNIX Operating System. Currently, Jon works for Compaq Computer Corporation, where he is helping to shape Compaq's strategy with respect to Linux. Previously, Jon was the Department Head of Computer Science at Hartford State Technical College, where his students lovingly (he hopes) gave him the nickname "maddog" as he tried to teach them operating system design, compiler theory, and how to live an honorable life.

While working for Digital Equipment Corporation in May of 1994, maddog met Linus Torvalds, and was intelligent enough (his critics say maddog was just lucky) to recognize the potential of the Linux Operating System. Linux changed his life, mostly by providing him with twenty-two hour work days. Since maddog has started working with Linux, however, he has also started meeting more girls (in particular his two godchildren). You can usually find Jon speaking at various Linux conferences and events (maddog just barks) and he has also been known to travel long distances to speak to local Linux user groups.

Paul G. Sery works for Sandia National Laboratories in Albuquerque, New Mexico. He's a member of the Computer Service Unit, Special Projects, which specializes in managing and troubleshooting UNIX and Linux systems.

When Paul is not beating his head against systems administration problems, he and his wife Lidia enjoy riding their tandem in Rio Grande valley. They also enjoy traveling throughout Mexico. Paul is the author of *LINUX Network Toolkit* and *Red Hat Linux 6 in Small Business* (both published by IDG Books Worldwide, Inc.). Paul has a bachelors degree in Electrical Engineering from the University of New Mexico.

ABOUT IDG BOOKS WORLDWIDE

Welcome to the world of IDG Books Worldwide.

IDG Books Worldwide, Inc., is a subsidiary of International Data Group, the world's largest publisher of computer-related information and the leading global provider of information services on information technology. IDG was founded more than 30 years ago by Patrick J. McGovern and now employs more than 9,000 people worldwide. IDG publishes more than 290 computer publications in over 75 countries. More than 90 million people read one or more IDG publications each month.

Launched in 1990, IDG Books Worldwide is today the #1 publisher of best-selling computer books in the United States. We are proud to have received eight awards from the Computer Press Association in recognition of editorial excellence and three from Computer Currents' First Annual Readers' Choice Awards. Our best-selling *...For Dummies*® series has more than 50 million copies in print with translations in 31 languages. IDG Books Worldwide, through a joint venture with IDG's Hi-Tech Beijing, became the first U.S. publisher to publish a computer book in the People's Republic of China. In record time, IDG Books Worldwide has become the first choice for millions of readers around the world who want to learn how to better manage their businesses.

Our mission is simple: Every one of our books is designed to bring extra value and skill-building instructions to the reader. Our books are written by experts who understand and care about our readers. The knowledge base of our editorial staff comes from years of experience in publishing, education, and journalism — experience we use to produce books to carry us into the new millennium. In short, we care about books, so we attract the best people. We devote special attention to details such as audience, interior design, use of icons, and illustrations. And because we use an efficient process of authoring, editing, and desktop publishing our books electronically, we can spend more time ensuring superior content and less time on the technicalities of making books.

You can count on our commitment to deliver high-quality books at competitive prices on topics you want to read about. At IDG Books Worldwide, we continue in the IDG tradition of delivering quality for more than 30 years. You'll find no better book on a subject than one from IDG Books Worldwide.

John Kilcullen
Chairman and CEO
IDG Books Worldwide, Inc.

Steven Berkowitz
President and Publisher
IDG Books Worldwide, Inc.

VIII WINNER
*Eighth Annual
Computer Press
Awards 1992*

IX WINNER
*Ninth Annual
Computer Press
Awards 1993*

X WINNER
*Tenth Annual
Computer Press
Awards 1994*

XI WINNER
*Eleventh Annual
Computer Press
Awards 1995*

IDG is the world's leading IT media, research and exposition company. Founded in 1964, IDG had 1997 revenues of $2.05 billion and has more than 9,000 employees worldwide. IDG offers the widest range of media options that reach IT buyers in 75 countries representing 95% of worldwide IT spending. IDG's diverse product and services portfolio spans six key areas including print publishing, online publishing, expositions and conferences, market research, education and training, and global marketing services. More than 90 million people read one or more of IDG's 290 magazines and newspapers, including IDG's leading global brands — Computerworld, PC World, Network World, Macworld and the Channel World family of publications. IDG Books Worldwide is one of the fastest-growing computer book publishers in the world, with more than 700 titles in 36 languages. The "...For Dummies®" series alone has more than 50 million copies in print. IDG offers online users the largest network of technology-specific Web sites around the world through IDG.net (http://www.idg.net), which comprises more than 225 targeted Web sites in 55 countries worldwide. International Data Corporation (IDC) is the world's largest provider of information technology data, analysis and consulting, with research centers in over 41 countries and more than 400 research analysts worldwide. IDG World Expo is a leading producer of more than 168 globally branded conferences and expositions in 35 countries including E3 (Electronic Entertainment Expo), Macworld Expo, ComNet, Windows World Expo, ICE (Internet Commerce Expo), Agenda, DEMO, and Spotlight. IDG's training subsidiary, ExecuTrain, is the world's largest computer training company, with more than 230 locations worldwide and 785 training courses. IDG Marketing Services helps industry-leading IT companies build international brand recognition by developing global integrated marketing programs via IDG's print, online and exposition products worldwide. Further information about the company can be found at www.idg.com. 1/24/99

Dedication

Jon "maddog" Hall: To Mom & Pop (TM), whose aversion to things electronic is well known, and who still call their son Jon rather than maddog.

Paul G. Sery: To my wife Lidia Maura Vazquez Sery.

Publisher's Acknowledgments

We're proud of this book; please register your comments through our IDG Books Worldwide Online Registration Form located at http://my2cents.dummies.com.

Some of the people who helped bring this book to market include the following:

Acquisitions, Editorial, and Media Development

Project Editor: Jade L. Williams

Acquisitions Editor: Laura Lewin

Copy Editors: Kim Darosett, James H. Russell

Technical Editor: Eric Butow

Media Development Editor: Marita Ellixson

Associate Permissions Editor: Carmen Krikorian

Media Development Coordinator: Megan Decraene

Editorial Manager: Leah Cameron

Media Development Manager: Heather Heath Dismore

Editorial Assistant: Beth Parlon

Production

Project Coordinators: E. Shawn Aylsworth, Amanda Foxworth

Layout and Graphics: Amy M. Adrian, Kate Jenkins, Barry Offringa, Jill Piscitelli, Brent Savage, Jacque Schneider, Maggie Ubertini, Erin Zeltner

Proofreaders: Laura Albert, Arielle Carole Mennelle, Marianne Santy, Charles Spencer

Indexer: Sharon Hilgenberg

Special Help
Red Hat Software, Inc.

General and Administrative

IDG Books Worldwide, Inc.: John Kilcullen, CEO; Steven Berkowitz, President and Publisher

IDG Books Technology Publishing Group: Richard Swadley, Senior Vice President and Publisher; Walter Bruce III, Vice President and Associate Publisher; Joseph Wikert, Associate Publisher; Mary Bednarek, Branded Product Development Director; Mary Corder, Editorial Director; Barry Pruett, Publishing Manager; Michelle Baxter, Publishing Manager

IDG Books Consumer Publishing Group: Roland Elgey, Senior Vice President and Publisher; Kathleen A. Welton, Vice President and Publisher; Kevin Thornton, Acquisitions Manager; Kristin A. Cocks, Editorial Director

IDG Books Internet Publishing Group: Brenda McLaughlin, Senior Vice President and Publisher; Diane Graves Steele, Vice President and Associate Publisher; Sofia Marchant, Online Marketing Manager

IDG Books Production for Dummies Press: Debbie Stailey, Associate Director of Production; Cindy L. Phipps, Manager of Project Coordination, Production Proofreading, and Indexing; Tony Augsburger, Manager of Prepress, Reprints, and Systems; Laura Carpenter, Production Control Manager; Shelley Lea, Supervisor of Graphics and Design; Debbie J. Gates, Production Systems Specialist; Robert Springer, Supervisor of Proofreading; Kathie Schutte, Production Supervisor

Dummies Packaging and Book Design: Patty Page, Manager, Promotions Marketing

◆

The publisher would like to give special thanks to Patrick J. McGovern, without whom this book would not have been possible.

◆

Contents at a Glance

Cartoons at a Glance

By Rich Tennant

page 299

page 9

page 109

page 195

page 31

page 245

page 279

Fax: 978-546-7747 • E-mail: the5wave@tiac.net

Table of Contents

Introduction

O ther books about Linux contain fascinating information for UNIX system administrators as well as long lists of unpronounceable commands with confusing options. *Red Hat Linux For Dummies* is different. The fascinating information is for you, and the descriptions and directions are written in plain English.

Use this book as an entertaining and informative reference to Linux. Or buy a whole stack of them and use them to press flowers. (Hey, you can still use the top one as a reference for Linux.)

About This Book

This book is designed to be a helping-hands reference. It provides a place to turn to for help and solace in those moments when, after two hours of typing *xstart* fruitlessly and reloading X Window System twice, your 5-year-old tells you that the *x* goes at the end of the word.

We tried our hardest to fill this book with the things that you need to know, such as:

- Installing Red Hat Linux
- Installing the X Window System
- Issuing important commands
- Working with files and directories
- Using Applix Words and other applications
- Getting online and building a firewall
- Finding help

You'll see troubleshooting tips throughout the book. It's not that Linux is all that much trouble — we just want your experience to be as trouble-free as possible.

Foolish Assumptions

You know what they say about people who make assumptions, but this book would never have been written if we didn't make a few. This book is for you if:

- ✔ You have a Linux operating system. Surprise — one is on the *Red Hat Linux For Dummies* CD-ROM in the back of the book.

- ✔ You have an x86 PC-compatible computer with at least a 2x CD-ROM drive.

- ✔ You want to put the Linux operating system and the computer together, and using duct tape hasn't worked.

- ✔ You don't need to become a Linux guru — at least not yet.

Conventions Used in This Book

At computer conventions, thousands of computer people get together and talk about deep technical issues such as:

- ✔ Is Coke better than Pepsi?
- ✔ Are Tim-Tams the ultimate junk food?
- ✔ What is the best hardware for running Linux?

But these aren't the types of conventions we're talking about in this section. Our conventions are shorthand ways of designating specific information, such as what is and isn't a command or the meaning of certain funny-looking symbols.

Typing code

Commands in the text are shown like this. Commands not in the text, but set off on lines by themselves, look like this:

```
[maddog@shamet maddog]$pwd
/home/maddog
```

When you see stuff in boldface, it means it's something you should type. The non-bold stuff is text that the computer displays. So, in the preceding example, when you type **pwd** (and press Return), the computer displays /home/maddog.

Well, not quite. Notice the [maddog@shamet maddog] in the preceding shaded area. You won't see that on your system, unless you're my doppelganger, that is. But you will see something similar. The same goes for /home/maddog; the maddog is replaced with the directory name on your system.

Now for some further complications. Check out the following:

```
[root@shamet /root]# passwd <name>
```

<name> is *italic*. That means you should replace <name> with a name. In this case, you replace <name> with your logon name. How are you supposed to know that? Don't worry, we tell you so in the text.

Here's a rundown of the command syntax in Linux:

- ✔ Text inside brackets [ ] is optional.
- ✔ Text inside angle brackets < > must be replaced with appropriate text.
- ✔ Text inside braces { } indicates that you must choose one of the values that are inside the braces and separated by the | sign.
- ✔ Text *not* surrounded by [ ], { }, or < > must be typed exactly as shown.
- ✔ An ellipsis (. . .) means *and so on* or to repeat the preceding command line as needed.

Don't concern yourself with this too much now. For most of the book, you don't need to know these particulars. When you do need to know something about a particular syntax, come back here for a refresher course.

Keystrokes and such

Keystrokes are shown with a plus sign between the keys. For example, Ctrl+Alt+Delete means you should press the Ctrl key, Alt key, and Delete key all at the same time. (No, we don't make you press any more than three keys at the same time.)

You also see something like this from time to time:

```
[maddog@shamet maddog]$ vi quagmire
a
echo Report of login names and users on the Linux system
date
echo ========================================
cut -f 1,5 -d: /etc/passwd | sed -e 's/:/ - /'
<ESC>
:wq
```

Now, you know from the "Typing code" section that the stuff in boldface needs to be typed as shown. But when you see a key in angle brackets, such as <ESC>, in code, it's telling you to press the Escape key, not to type the E S C characters.

How This Book Is Organized

Like all proper *For Dummies* books, this book is organized into independent parts. Well, that's not quite true. This is an almost proper *For Dummies* book. If you don't have Linux installed, you really have to go through Part II before you can do much with Linux, aside from framing the CD or using it as a neat Frisbee.

For all other parts, you can read them in any order. Heck, try reading them backwards for a real challenge. In this section, we tell you what each part contains.

Part I: Introducing Linux

In Part I, you find out about the birth of Linux and about the different types of Linux out there, including the one on the *Red Hat Linux For Dummies* CD-ROM. You also get some tips on which one is right for you.

Part II: Installing Linux

In Part II, you get your answer to the age-old question: How the heck do I install Linux? We give you detailed, step-by-step instructions. You also get lots of help installing the X Window System, the graphical part of Linux. You may want a double espresso or a can of Jolt soda (Twice the caffeine!) by your side for this one.

Part III: Just the Basics

Linux isn't a high-maintenance operating system, but it does need some care. (Chocolate helps, too.) In Part III, you discover how to manage the Linux file system, which is the biggest part of caring for and feeding Linux. You also get some hints on writing simple programs with Linux scripts and adding new software with RPM. Vroom. Vroom.

Part IV: Using Red Hat Linux

In Part IV, you get the glorious particulars on actually doing something with Linux. We'll take you through the X Window System and the GNOME desktop windows environment by moving, resizing, hiding, and closing windows, as well as using the file manager and much more. We also introduce full-featured desktop productivity suites such as Applixware and StarOffice, and show you how Linux can now be used in the front office as well as the back office.

Part V: Going Online

Everyone is online these days, and Linux users are no exception. In Part V, you find out how to contact an Internet service provider (ISP) to get an account for accessing the Internet, how to set up Linux to interact with that account, and how to use the Netscape Navigator Web browser with that account to ski the Web. We also give instructions for setting up a simple but effective firewall to protect your valuable information.

Part VI: The Part of Tens

A *For Dummies* book just isn't complete without a Part of Tens, and that's Part VI. You find ten all-important resources in Chapter 19. And in Chapter 20, we provide answers to the ten most bothersome questions people have after installing Linux. (The folks at Red Hat Software provided these questions.)

Part VII: Appendixes

Finally, the appendixes. In Appendix A, instructions are given for using the de facto Linux text editor vi. We list all the hardware that we know that's compatible with Linux in Appendix B. In Appendix C, you find out all you need to know about the Linux man pages, while Appendix D gives you instructions for using fdisk to partition your hard disk. And in Appendix E, we'll tell you where in the book you can get information on installing the applications on CD-ROMs.

What You're Not to Read

Heck, you don't have to read any of this book if you don't want to, but why did you buy it? (Not that we're complaining.) Part I has background information. If you don't want it, don't read it. Also, text in sidebars is optional, although often helpful. If you're on the fast track to using Linux, you could skip the sidebars and the text with a technical stuff icon. But we suggest instead that you slow down a bit and enjoy the experience.

Icons in This Book

This is particularly nerdy, technical information. You may skip it.

This icon flags discussions that relate to the CD-ROMs. The first CD-ROM (CD1) is a copy of the Red Hat Publishers Edition V6.1 distribution, the latest distribution available at publishing time.

Don't let this happen to you! We hope that our experiences in UNIX and Linux will help you avoid the mistakes we made.

Other uses for CD-ROMs

Where computers and computer programmers abound, lots of CD-ROMs arrive in the mail or as part of the software that someone bought. Eventually, these CD-ROMs become obsolete or are never installed — that's the case with software products that arrive as unwanted advertisements. What can ecologically-minded programmers do with these CDs so that they don't fill up landfills?

Some use them as coasters for drinks. Others make mobiles out of them. (The sun shining off of a CD-ROM makes wonderful rainbows on the wall.) Still others use the CD-ROMs as clocks, by purchasing inexpensive quartz-crystal clock motors (complete with hands) and using the CD-ROM as the face of the clock. We have four of these clocks made out of Windows NT CD-ROMs — hey, can you imagine a better use for Windows NT?

More exotic uses require high heat to melt a CD-ROM around the base of a water tumbler, creating either a nice flowerpot or, with the hole plugged, an ashtray. As you can imagine, this causes some consternation among management at these facilities, particularly after they find out that one of the more expensive programs they've purchased has ended up at the bottom of a flowerpot.

For right now, please keep your *Red Hat Linux For Dummies* CD-ROMs in a safe place, such as the sleeve in the back of the book, when you are not using them. The first CD (CD1) gets your computer running Linux, and also contains the software that comes with Red Hat Linux. The second CD (CD2) contains the source code for the Linux kernel, for those who want to take a crack at Linux hacking.

Nifty little shortcuts and timesavers. Red Hat Linux is a powerful operating system, and you can save unbelievable amounts of time and energy by utilizing its tools and programs. We hope our tips show you how.

Where to Go from Here

You are about to join the legions of people who have been using and developing Linux. Maddog has been using UNIX for more than 20 years and Linux for more than 6 years. We've found Linux to be a flexible, powerful operating system, capable of solving most problems even without a large set of commercial software. The future of the Linux operating system is bright. The time and energy you expend in becoming familiar with it will be worthwhile. Carpe Linuxum.

Part I
Introducing Linux

The 5th Wave   By Rich Tennant

Look, all I said was, "FTC for Mr. Gates," and this nerdy guy with big glasses comes out and tells me he's not afraid of me, I can investigate him all I want, and he'll see me in court with his attorneys.

Flying Turkey Courier

Microsoft

In this part . . .

Check out this part if you want to know what Linux is all about. First, we delve into a little history (not nearly as much as we'd like to). Then you find out why Linux is faster, smaller, less expensive, and prettier than other systems. You also get a few pointers on the different ways you can use Linux.

In the next chapter, we tell you about the different Linux varieties (*distributions* in Linux lingo) so you can better decide which one's right for you. You also get some examples of programs that are useful with Linux — some come with Linux and others you have to buy — to show what great things you can do with the operating system.

Chapter 1

Linux and You

*I*n 1991, Linus Torvalds, an undergraduate student at the University of Helsinki in Finland, got a brand-new IBM 386 PC. Dissatisfied with the operating system that came with the hardware, he wanted to run the UNIX operating system instead. UNIX, however, was too expensive. So Linus started his work and later recruited a team of talented programmers to tackle the daunting task of creating a new version of UNIX. They created a core operating system, or *kernel,* named Linux.

As mentioned, Linux kernel development began in 1991. By the early spring of 1994, the first real version of Linux (Version 1.0) was available for public use. Even then it was an impressive operating system, running at amazing speeds in less than 2MB of RAM on Intel systems. This free system included the following features found in operating systems costing hundreds of dollars:

✔ Multitasking (that is, running more than one job simultaneously).

✔ The ability for multiple users to work at the same time.

✔ Linux uses *demand page virtual memory,* which stores unused portions — pages — of a program on disk when there is not enough memory to hold the entire program. Using demand page memory allows you to run programs that are much larger than the amount of RAM on your computer would normally allow.

An estimated 125,000 people were active Linux users in 1994. (Because no licenses are issued to individual users, a more precise number can't be determined.) In 1997, just three years later, the estimated number of Linux users was 3 million and climbing rapidly. By the summer of 1999, the estimates were at more than 10 million. This compares to approximately 200 million Windows users.

Using Linux in Different Ways

Linux is a versatile operating system. Initially the sole domain of computer-science students, Linux is now used by businesses, individuals, and governments to cut costs, improve performance, and get work done. You can use Linux in a variety of ways: as a desktop workstation, a server system, an Internet gateway (a means by which you can connect your network to the Internet), a firewall, the basis of an embedded system (such as a smart VCR or a robot), or even as a supercomputer. Another prominent use of Linux is by Internet service providers (ISPs), who use it to provide information and services to the Internet and the World Wide Web. And thanks to the thousands of people working on different parts of Linux, the system becomes more flexible and capable with each passing day. Linux is a revolutionary system that would put Dilbert out of business.

Boosting your personal workstation

With the powerful Linux operating system, you can run many programs at the same time, handle the needs of more than one user at a time, and use high-quality graphics. Linux can handle files and programs of immense size. When used with the 64-bit Digital Alpha processor, for example, Linux can handle data *terabytes* (thousands of billions of characters in size). Linux uses a sophisticated windowing system called the X Window System (also known as X Windows, X11, or most commonly as X) and can share files not only with most UNIX systems but also with Windows, OS/2, and other operating systems.

Linux also includes the following:

- Compilers
- Database editors
- Freeware programs (such as mail readers, image editors, circuit design programs, and text formatters)
- HTML editors
- Slide/graphic presentation tools
- Spreadsheets
- TCP/IP
- Web browsers
- Word processors

Creating a free distribution

One of the most important decisions Linus Torvalds made in the early days of the Linux kernel was to freely distribute the code through a process known as *creating a distribution.* His genius was not only in developing the kernel but also in using the unrealized but huge resources of the young Internet. The volunteer process that he started created software that was developed very quickly and professionally.

This process also consisted of accumulating huge amounts of freely distributable software, available from the Free Software Foundation (FSF) and other places, adding the free software to the Linux kernel, and then creating a way to install the software on the computer. (Richard Stallman who believes that all software should be freely available to everyone formed the FSF. Linux would not have been possible without it.)

These free distributions were available in several forms: from the Internet, on CD-ROMs and floppy disks, from software publishers (who charged a distribution fee), or bundled with other programs (which organizations charged for). In every case, though, the base Linux kernel and other freely distributable code had to be identified and made available without charge.

The importance of the availability of the operating system source code can't be overstressed. Freely distributable source code has resulted in a Linux operating system that continues to improve rapidly. Each developer can build on the efforts of the one before, and these improvements benefit everyone — including you.

And if the number of freeware programs ported to Linux doesn't satisfy you, commercial applications such as databases, data manipulation programs, automated network backup systems, and office suites have been ported to Linux, too. With Linux, you can have the same environment on your notebook computer, desktop workstation, and large server system. Software such as Applixware, StarOffice, and WordPerfect allow you to use Linux as your personal workstation.

Sharing with file and print servers

Because of its multitasking capability, virtual memory, and powerful file system, Linux works well as a file and print server for Microsoft Windows systems. A software product called SAMBA allows Windows PCs to communicate with the file system and with printers attached to a Linux machine. AppleTalk allows Macintosh computers to use Linux as a file and printer server. And, of course, Linux can share files and printers with UNIX systems. By using Linux to do this work, you can save a lot of money because the operating system and the layered software that provide these services are freely available.

Connecting to an Internet gateway

Linux is a great tool for connecting your home or business network to the Internet. Software is available (such as diald, which is not on either of the accompanying CD-ROMs but can be downloaded from any Red Hat mirror) that automatically connects your Linux computer, and thus your private network, to the Internet whenever necessary. This gives your private network a permanent, virtual connection for the price of a single phone line.

Building a firewall

Linux can also provide protection from the bad guys on the Internet by acting as a *firewall.* A firewall is a system that controls access to your private network from any outside network (in this case, the Internet), and also is used to control access from your private network to the outside world. Linux is very flexible in this regard and several packages are available. One of the most popular and simple to use is the ipchain filtering software, which is included on the accompanying CD-ROM (CD1). Instructions on how to create firewalls is beyond the scope of this book, however.

For instructions on building a firewall, please check out *Linux Network Toolkit* or *Red Hat Linux for Small Business,* both by Paul Sery; and *The Linux Network,* by Butzen and Hilton (all published by IDG Books Worldwide, Inc.).

Providing Internet/intranet services

Many capabilities of the Internet (outside of a single business) and intranets (internal to a single business) are possible because of HTML and the World Wide Web. UNIX systems were at the forefront of these developments, and Linux shares many benefits of that heritage. Both the Internet and intranets require similar services, such as:

- **Firewalls** to keep the bad guys out
- **FTP** to help the good guys get files and software
- **Telnet** to support users in logging on and using their machines remotely
- **Web servers** to aid users in seeing Web pages
- **Samba and NFS** to share files over the network

Many ISPs use Linux to deliver these services to their customers, not just because Linux is free but also because the source code for the entire operating system is also available. When a problem arises, ISPs can correct it themselves quickly rather than wait for a commercial software vendor to correct the problem.

How critical is a timely correction? Well, in 1997, a problem with TCP/IP (resulting from a deliberate misuse of a program called ping) affected almost every UNIX system in the world. D'oh! This problem allowed bad guys to shut down other people's UNIX systems. The world needed a fix — and quickly! A fix for Linux was on the Internet four hours after the problem was identified, and people could easily get the fix and apply it to their systems. Various commercial UNIX vendors took weeks to develop the fix and send it to their customers.

Analyzing and solving problems by three-tier client/server

Whoa! What the heck is *three-tier client/server?* This large, standoffish term simply means that most computer problems can be broken down into three separate problems, or tiers, namely:

- Data storage and retrieval
- Data manipulation
- Data presentation

When you break down a problem into these three levels, the problem is typically easier to solve and change later as necessary. Until recently, the data presentation level consisted of Windows systems running on the desktop (perhaps using Visual Basic to develop the interface). The data manipulation level and the data storage and retrieval level consisted of UNIX or older systems communicating over the network.

Now, however, the data presentation level can be a Linux system running a freely distributed Web browser or Java system (a portable environment for applications). By using Linux, some firms can save thousands of dollars on operating system costs and yet still retain required security and operating system robustness.

Like most UNIX systems, Linux also has sophisticated data manipulation tools that make it a good second-tier system. Linux can extract data from several types of databases or reports kept in files from older systems, and then sort, search, combine, process, and otherwise manipulate the data, passing the newly created results to the presentation level on the desktop.

Finally, Linux has the facilities to act as a good data storage and retrieval level. Several commercial database packages work with Linux. If you can't afford a commercial database package, you can use one of the freely available ones, such as Postgres.

The three-tier concept is to divide work logically, but after you accomplish that, you can put all three pieces of functionality on one computer — a Linux system.

Linux all over

The Linux operating system has been ported from the 32-bit Intel architecture to a series of other architectures, including Alpha, MIPS, PowerPC, StrongARM, and SPARC, giving users a choice of machine manufacturer and keeping the Linux kernel flexible for new processors. The Linux operating system now handles *symmetric multiprocessing* (more than one CPU or mathematical and logical programming unit per system box). In addition, projects are in the works to provide sophisticated processing capabilities, such as:

✔ **Real-time programming:** Controlling machinery or testing equipment

✔ **High availability:** Running a reliable computer all the time

✔ **Scalability:** Boosting computer power by adding more system boxes rather than faster CPUs

This last capability — known as Extreme Linux systems — enables research organizations to create machines of supercomputer capabilities at a fraction of the price of supercomputers. In certain cases, Extreme Linux systems have been made from obsolete PCs, costing the organizations that make them nothing in material costs.

Protecting your turnkey system

A turnkey system is put together once and then duplicated in hundreds or thousands of places. Turnkey systems — not turkeys — are typically information kiosks, hotel reservation systems, doctor and lawyer office systems, and automotive diagnostic systems. Linux is perfect for this work because it provides the security, protection, and stability that turnkey systems need, without requiring payments for many copies of the operating system. For example, say that one application is needed on 4,000 systems. If the business had to pay, say, $500 for the operating system, the project would cost $2,000,000 extra, just to pay for the operating system.

Backing up your network server

Software is now available to automatically back up individual computers (Linux, UNIX, and Windows) over a network. Systems such as BRU2000 and Knox software's Arkeia provide you with the ability to program what, when and how often to backup any or all of your computers. Both Arkeia and BRU2000 offer free demo versions of their commercial packages at their Web sites:

```
www.arkeia.com
www.bru2000.com
```

Chapter 2

Accessorizing Linux

● ●

In This Chapter

▶ Discovering which Linux distribution is the one for you

▶ Getting Linux for free — or not

▶ Using Linux à la MS-DOS or Windows

▶ Examining text editors

▶ Making the most of mail interfaces

▶ Marveling at multimedia programs

▶ Cavorting with commercial programs

● ●

*T*he first accompanying CD-ROM (CD1) is based on Red Hat Linux, which is an excellent distribution. Some people, however, prefer other distributions. Several Linux distributions are available, and each one differs in certain ways, such as the manner in which you install and manage the distribution. We list some of these distributions in this chapter, in case you want to investigate them later. We also show you some text editors and mail interfaces, and demonstrate a few other programs, just to whet your appetite. (In other chapters, we cover these programs in greater detail.)

A distribution is the combination of the Linux kernel, supporting software, and the organization of all the files and directories. Companies like Red Hat add their own innovations and charge for the convenience of getting the total package on CD-ROM. Other non-profit organizations like Debian develop their own distribution and merely charge for the media. In many ways, distributions are like a favorite flavor of ice cream governed by personal preference. We say try them all!

Acquiring Distributions and Compendiums

Linus Torvalds and the Linux development team created the Linux operating system kernel. The *kernel* includes the software for managing memory, files, programs that are running, networking, and various hardware devices. Think of the kernel as a cop directing traffic.

The compilers and other programs that go into making up what most people think of as Linux come from a variety of people who distribute the programs over the Internet or on CD-ROM. Typically, these people add an installation technique, system management tools, a file system (the way that directories and files are organized), some applications (either freeware or commercial), and a distribution medium. The base Linux system must be able to be freely copied, even if value-added components are not.

In addition to a single distribution that may come on one or more CD-ROMS, you can find *compendiums* of distributions, which are like samples, that include several distributions as well as copies of Internet sites that hold Linux programs and documentation. Some information on compendiums is redundant and harder to use than if it came on a single-distribution CD; other information is useful and usually inexpensive. After you have Linux up and running, you may want to try out a compendium just to see what it holds for you.

The question you're probably asking now is "Which Linux distribution is best?" The answer is "It depends on what you want." Some people want a Linux distribution that works with an older kernel that has had time to mature; others want the latest and greatest distribution. Some people want small distributions with few programs other than the operating system; others want distributions overflowing with goodies. Most people, however, want a combination of those features as well as a stable name brand offering reliable customer support.

Linux distributions are so inexpensive that you can easily buy two or three versions to see what they're like. Many Linux distributions may be installed on multiple computers. And after you install Linux for the second or third time, think of the experience you'll have gained.

Different Linux systems are . . . well . . . different!

We don't have enough room to go into depth on all Linux distributions, but we can briefly describe a few major packages.

One of the first distributions Jon ever saw was the Yggdrasil distribution in 1993. After an easy installation, Yggdrasil started X Window System, displayed some MPEG videos, and croaked "Hello" through his computer's console speaker. It was the first time his computer had talked to him! He was hooked. Today, Yggdrasil Computing (www.yggdrasil.com) croaks out a variety of Linux products and compendiums of other people's freely distributable distributions. The company also provides support for Linux.

Another early distribution was Slackware. Distributed mainly by Patrick Volkerding and later by other slackers and resellers, such as Walnut Creek CDROM (www.cdrom.com), Slackware is divided into packages that are copied onto floppies from the Net or a CD-ROM.

The Debian (www.debian.org) distribution was put together by a group of volunteers who now distribute it over the Internet, on CD-ROM, and in many compendiums.

Red Hat Linux (www.redhat.com) is an early distribution from a collaboration of three Linux enthusiasts who were later joined by ACC, the company's largest distributor. The accompanying CD-ROM is a distribution of the freely distributable parts of Red Hat Linux. It is now regarded as the largest Linux distributor. When Red Hat went public in mid-1999, the company's stock shot into the Linux stratosphere.

SuSE GmbH (www.suse.com) is a German firm that puts out its own Linux distribution in German and English. The company also carries other distributions and products.

InfoMagic (www.infomagic.com) puts out a compendium of Linux distributions as well as various Linux products. One of its products is tailored as a workgroup server that ties together a small group of PCs or Apple machines and also acts as a Web server, FTP site, and more.

TurboLinux, Inc., (www.pht.com) is a company that provides translated copies of Linux, including Japanese and Chinese translations.

WorkGroup Solutions integrates a powerful business system called Flagship into its Linux PRO distribution. In its alter ego of the Linux Mall (www.linuxmall.com), WorkGroup Solutions carries a range of other vendors' products, which it publishes on the Web and in a catalog.

Caldera (www.caldera.com) puts out a commercial version of Linux aimed at the corporate desktop and intranet market. Caldera added licensed software including a graphical desktop, file and print software from Novell, and the Netscape Communicator browser for the Internet. Caldera also sells WABI, which allows most Windows 3.1 (16-bit) applications to run on top of Linux.

Corel (www.corel.com) now has a distribution called Corel LINUX, which is based on the Debian distribution and looks to make Linux easy to install and use. Corel LINUX is bundled — of course — with WordPerfect Office and is quickly becoming a major Linux player.

Comparing What's Free and What's Not

Linux applications differ widely in cost and appearance. This section checks out the different ways you can obtain applications, namely as:

- ✔ Freely available software
- ✔ Shareware
- ✔ Commercial applications

Freely available software is available for free use by the end user. Although software may be freely available, it is often not the same as *public domain software* (or software that you can do absolutely anything with). Freely available software is often owned and copyrighted by the author (or authors) who then allow people to use or make modifications to it.

Freely available software can be further divided into software that you can either *freely copy* or *freely distribute.* Some people make their software freely available only if you copy it directly from a particular site or from a noncommercial distribution. Other people let you copy their software from anywhere. Copying restrictions usually apply to people making a commercial distribution, not to the end user of that distribution. The distribution maker has the responsibility to be in compliance with the package's copying restrictions, which are usually outlined in the program's source code or About or Help section.

A lot of freely available software can be obtained from the Internet. Some can also be found in real, live stores. Most major electronic and computer and book chains carry commercial applications like Applixware and StarOffice. Comercial Internet sites like Amazon.com sell software, too.

Many freely available applications have been converted from UNIX to OS/2; Windows 3.1, 95, 98, and NT; and other operating systems. If you use an application that's been ported to many operating systems, such as the emacs(1) editor, you're more likely to be able to use the same application if you switch operating systems later.

When you see a word such as *emacs* followed by a number in parentheses, the name refers to a Linux command, and the number is the section of the Linux manual set that contains information on how to use that command. For example, emacs(1) is a text editor that you can use to manipulate text in files, and its documentation is located in section 1 of the manual pages. lpd(8) is a command found in the eighth section of the reference manual.

Nonfree applications consist of commercial applications and shareware applications. *Commercial applications* are sold outright. *Shareware applications* may be tried out or used for personal use. If you frequently use the shareware program or want to use the program commercially, you should pay the author; the amount is usually nominal.

After you install your Linux system and get your X Window System going, you can check out a list of nonfree applications by looking at the Commercial HOWTO file (which is like a help file but written in simple text), which you access by typing the following in a terminal emulator window:

```
netscape file:/usr/doc/HOWTO/other-formats/ html/ Commercial-
        HOWTO.html
```

The preceding file was pulled off the accompanying CD-ROM (CD1) when you installed the system. The file on the CD-ROM is probably an older version of what you can find on the Internet. For a more up-to-date list of nonfree applications, you can use a Web browser to look at the Linux Commercial HOWTO at the following URL:

```
www.cyrius.com/tbm/Commercial-HOWTO
```

More and more commercial software programs are available for Linux. A good way to find them is to look in magazines such as the *Linux Journal* (or in Germany or Poland, *Linux Magazin* or *LinuxPlus,* respectively). You can also look in Internet user groups such as `comp.os.linux.announce`.

Figure 2-1 is an example of a commercial package called Executor (by ARDI). This software program enables you to run many different Macintosh applications on an Intel-compatible Linux system.

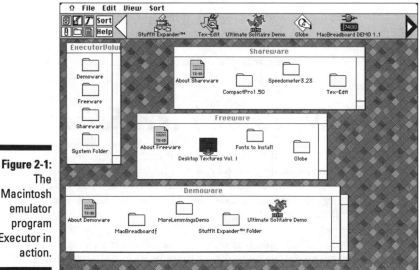

Figure 2-1:
The Macintosh emulator program Executor in action.

Considering Character-Cell or Graphical Applications

Linux applications are available not only as free and nonfree applications, but also as character-cell and graphical applications. *Character-cell applications* are textual types of applications in which you type a command and the system responds. MS-DOS is an example of a character-cell operating system. (Character-cell applications are sometimes referred to as text-based applications.) In a *graphical application,* you use the mouse as well as the keyboard to tell the computer what to do. Microsoft Windows is a ubiquitous example of a graphical operating system. The comparison is similar to the difference between an all-text book and a picture book — both are useful in different ways. The graphical portion of Linux is called *X Window System* or simply *X.* Unfortunately, there is no conspiracy with the X Files or even the X-Men.

If you use X and your system is running out of main memory or disk space, try switching Linux to character-cell mode.

UNIX started out as a character-cell operating system and had graphical window systems added to it. Linux inherited both character-cell and graphical features from UNIX.

You will probably spend most of your time using Linux in its graphical mode. Many Linux character-cell applications, however, were created before the age of X Window System or simply work better in character-cell mode. In Chapter 10, you can see a bunch of applications that work very well in character-cell mode.

If you're using a laptop for short periods of time (to take notes in a meeting, for example) and find that the startup time for X Window System and its associated programs is too long, you may want to opt for character-cell mode. You can get a lot of work done with simple text editors.

Manipulating Words with Text Editors

Linux systems often come with several different text editors. *Text editors* are programs that typically enable you to type and manipulate alphanumeric characters. Some text editors can do simple word processing tasks such as word wrap, but they can't perform most word processing functions, such as spell checking or italicizing text.

Text editors are good for simple text editing tasks and for writing simple or even complex programs. Most text editors have built-in help functions, and some have full-scale documentation built in or available online. In addition, you can find books about a few editors, such as vi(1) and emacs(1).

In this section, we describe character-cell text editors and graphical-based text editors that you can find as freely available software or as shareware. We also describe some commercial text editors.

Familiarizing yourself with character-cell editors

ed(1) is the oldest UNIX character-cell text editor and comes with every UNIX system. Because ed(1) doesn't normally show you the entire file and it doesn't show you the changes you've made until you ask it to do so, it may be difficult to use. Those who use ed(1) are usually long-time UNIX users with long, gray beards who wear suspenders with their shorts. Even with these downsides, knowing how to use ed(1) is useful because it usually comes with every Linux system.

Emerging soon after the introduction of ed(1) came an extended editor called ex(1) and a visual front end to it called vi(1). vi(1) was written in the mid-1970s and allowed people to see a whole screen of text at one time! Believe it or not, this was big news in those days. Many Linux systems ship with a new version of vi(1) called vim(1), for *vi improved.* Paul is old enough to actually remember using ed and being excited when the incredible vi came along. Many of his classmates grumbled, but he was very happy. Times, and word processing, sure have changed.

You can execute vim(1) by entering **vim at the prompt,** but most distributions also have made a link to it as vi and ex. A *link* is a way to give two names to the same program. Although the same program is being executed, the system is smart and looks at what the user types when starting the program. If the user types **vi,** the program acts like vi; if the user types **ex,** the program looks like ex. In this way, vi users can continue to type **vi** and see what they're used to seeing with vi(1), and vim(1) users can likewise type **vim.** If users type **ex,** they get vim, but it's made to look as if it was ex(1).

Another character-cell text editor is emacs(1), one of the shining stars of the Free Software Foundation. Devotees of emacs(1) claim that it is more than just a text editor; it's an interface to reading mail, debugging your programs, reading news from the Internet, and performing a variety of other text-oriented activities. The program can also emulate several character-cell editors. emacs(1) has also made the jump to a graphical mode. Downsides of emacs(1) are its size and its use of a fair amount of disk space.

Working with graphical text editors

xedit(1) is a mouse-based editing tool, with a file open and close window, an error message window, and a text window, as shown in Figure 2-2. xedit has limited functionality but is simple to use and fine for working on small files.

If X Window System is running, the emacs(1) editor, mentioned in the preceding section, appears in graphical mode, as shown in Figure 2-3.

And finally, you can run any character-cell editor under X Window System by invoking it with a terminal emulator (an emulator pretends, or simulates, the behavior of another device or system). The editor will run just as it does under the character-cell mode of Linux.

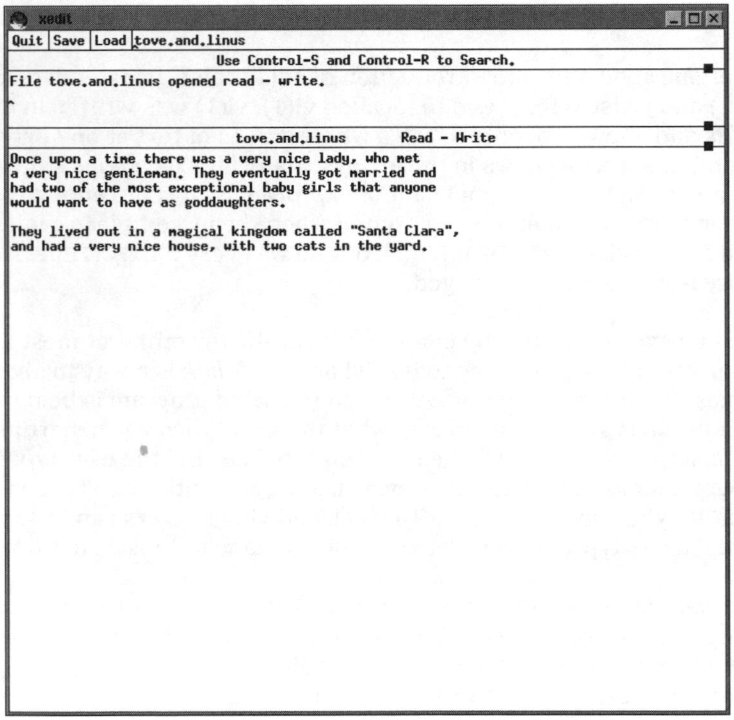

Figure 2-2:
The xedit(1)
text editor.

```
  xedit                                                        _ □ ✕
Quit  Save  Load  tove.and.linus
                  Use Control-S and Control-R to Search.          ■
File tove.and.linus opened read - write.
                                                                  ■
                  tove.and.linus        Read - Write             ■
Once upon a time there was a very nice lady, who met
a very nice gentleman. They eventually got married and
had two of the most exceptional baby girls that anyone
would want to have as goddaughters.

They lived out in a magical kingdom called "Santa Clara",
and had a very nice house, with two cats in the yard.
```

Figure 2-3:
emacs(1) in
graphical
mode.

Comparing commercial text editors

Several commercial text editors are available. Some have significant added value compared to simple text editors. In this section, we describe two of the most popular commercial text editors: Visual Slick Edit and Crisp by Vital.

Visual Slick Edit by MicroEdge is an X11-based editor that also runs on Windows 3.1, 95, 98, and NT platforms. The editor is language sensitive, so if you're programming in C, C++, Java, HTML, Perl, AWK, Pascal, FORTRAN, BASIC, dBASE, Modula-2, COBOL, Ada, or several other languages, Visual Slick Edit knows about these languages and tries to make the text more readable and searchable. Visual Slick Edit emulates several other editors (such as vi, emacs, and Brief) and integrates with other programs that help keep track of your program's code. Visual Slick Edit is definitely a programmer's editor, but nonprogrammers can use it, too.

Crisp by Vital is another language-sensitive, cross-platform editor. Cross-platform editors can run on many different UNIX and Linux systems as well as on Windows 3.1, 95, 98, and NT.

Several full-fledged commercial word processors are available for Linux. Applixware, StarOffice, and Corel WordPerfect provide Linux versions of their products. We describe them in more detail in Chapter 10.

Browsing Through Mail Interfaces

E-mail consists of two main parts: a *front end* (or interface) that you use to compose or read messages, and a *back end* that delivers your messages. In addition to the mail-specific programs described in this section, note that some Web browsers can read e-mail and Internet News (a series of information postings accessible over the Internet), handle FTP downloads of files, and perform other Internet-related tasks.

Examining character-cell interfaces

The first mail interfaces were available only in character-cell mode. In the following list, we discuss several character-cell interfaces; some are freeware and others are commercial packages. Some people prefer to use these systems for their simplicity.

- ✔ **mail(1),** one of the first e-mail interfaces, mail(1) is a character-cell interface for early versions of UNIX. mail(1) remains a powerful interface, and we sometimes use it when our systems are in character-cell mode and we want to send a quick e-mail or scan recent e-mail.

- ✔ **elm(1)** is an interactive screen-oriented mailer that you can use in place of mail(1) as a front end. elm is easy to use and presents a vim(1)-like editor for creating e-mail messages.

- ✔ **pine(1)** (which now means *program for Internet news and e-mail* but previously was known by the friendlier name *pine is not elm*) is another full-screen mail interface. Figure 2-4 shows the initial pine(1) screen.

  pine(1) has several of the features found in elm(1), plus a few additional ones. pine(1) uses a simple pico editor for composing mail and can handle MIME (Multipurpose Internet Mail Extensions), which enables you to send pictures, computer programs, and other nontext items through the mail. Figure 2-5 shows the screen for sending mail. Notice how pico formats all necessary headers for you and enables you to include MIME attachments.

  pine(1) runs on DOS and Windows systems as well as on many UNIX systems. It includes a built-in spell checker (always nice when writing messages to your boss). pine(1) can read NNTP, which is used to access Internet news. Finally, pine(1) can handle IMAP mail, which sends your mail to a holding place that you can access from anywhere on the Internet. This is especially nice when you're traveling with Linux on your notebook computer, because you can connect to your Internet service provider (ISP) and receive and answer your e-mail.

- ✔ **mh(1),** also known as the RAND Message Handling System, is a series of commands that enable you to manipulate mail at the command-line level. mh(1) Is a comprehensive mail interface, enabling you to create different folders for mail, scan mail in those folders in several ways, and reply, forward, and otherwise handle your mail. Because mh(1) consists of all these different commands, it was used to build two useful graphical mail interfaces — xmh(1) and exmh(1) — that we describe next.

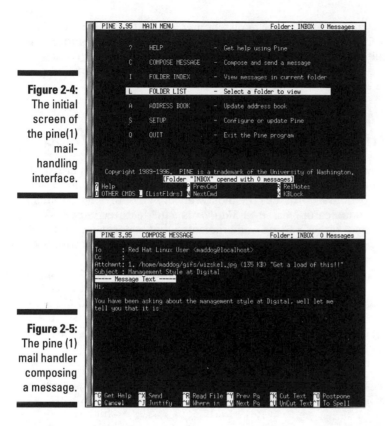

Figure 2-4:
The initial
screen of
the pine(1)
mail-
handling
interface.

Figure 2-5:
The pine (1)
mail handler
composing
a message.

Choosing the right graphical mail interface

Graphical mail programs offer a powerful and easy-to-use interface to read and manipulate mail. Graphical mail interfaces, like graphical text editors, require X.

xmh(1) is a graphical interface written for the character-cell-oriented mh(1) commands mentioned in the preceding section. As such, you can alternate between using mh(1) in the character-cell environment and xmh(1) in the graphical environment. xmh(1) is a simple interface written mostly to demonstrate early versions of X.

We prefer the exmh(1) graphical mailing program. exmh(1) is freely distributable, so you can use the same interface on systems at work, systems at home, and notebooks when you're traveling. This program is powerful — with MIME and POP (an earlier version of IMAP) capabilities, folder support, and easy ways to tailor printing, your editor, and a series of other parameters. The exmh(1) mailing program also highlights *URLs* (addresses of World

Wide Web pages) in the text of your mail; when you click the URL, exmh(1)
calls up your Web browser and displays the URL. exmh(1) has a comprehensive search facility for looking for mail messages sorted in folders. The
exmh(1) mail page is shown in Figure 2-7. The mail compose window is
shown in Figure 2-8.

Considering a commercial mail interface

As with the text editors, several commercial mail interface programs are available. Some are sold as individual programs; others are part of application
suites. Netscape, of course, provides the most well-known of these programs.
The Netscape Communicator *Messenger Mailbox* is a full-featured e-mail
system, which comes with Netscape Communicator that is packaged on the
companion CD-ROM (CD1). Figure 2-6 shows the Messenger Mailbox window.

Another commercial mail interface is found in Applixware, produced by Applix,
Inc. This product is an office suite consisting of a WYSIWYG (what-you-see-is-
what-you-get) text processor, an integrated spreadsheet, a presentation package, a graphical editor, and an e-mail front end. In Figure 2-7, you can see the
word processing package on the left, the presentation package (with a motif of
balloons) in the center, and the spreadsheet package in the lower right.

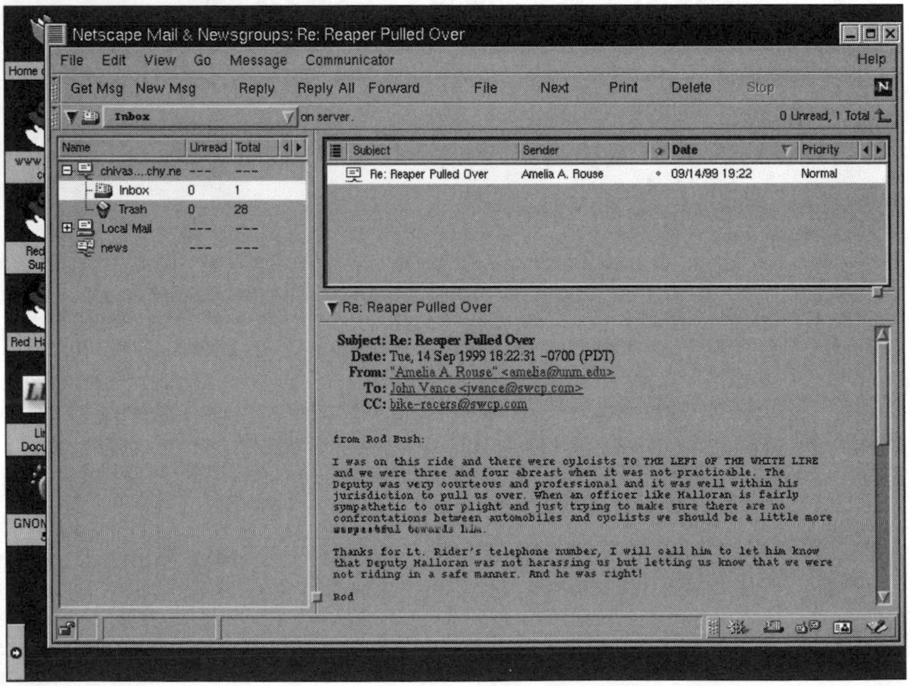

Figure 2-6:
The
Netscape
Messenger
Mailbox
interface.

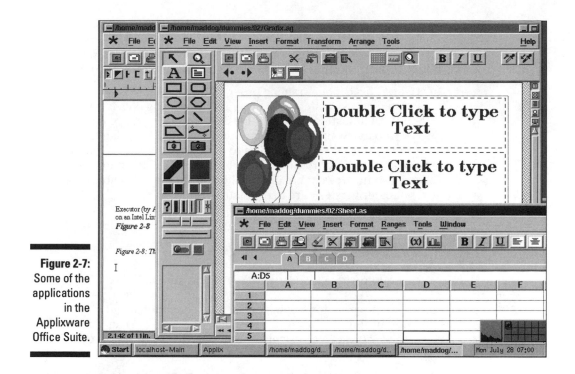

Figure 2-7:
Some of the
applications
in the
Applixware
Office Suite.

Sampling Multimedia Programs

Linux typically comes with a series of programs for simple drawing and painting as well as image viewing, conversion, and manipulation. Linux can display still and animated images, as well as record, manipulate, and play back audio (given that your hardware has a supported sound card).

Painting/artwork

If you actually do something cool with your computer, then here is a sampling of some multimedia freeware programs that you can use with Linux:

- **xpaint:** A simple drawing and paint program that you can use to read in an image and then perform simple manipulations to it. xfig is a somewhat more sophisticated drawing tool.

- **ImageMagick:** A freely distributed program for graphical image manipulation. This program can read many types of images, make them larger or smaller, cut portions of them, transform several still images into an animation, and store the images back to disk in a different format (if desired).

✔ **gimp:** A graphical image-manipulation program based on plug-ins, which extend a program's capabilities. A gimp feature that we like is the intelligent scissors feature, which enables you to cut out parts of a photo and paste them onto another photo (as in the movie *Forrest Gump*).

✔ **Ghostview:** This is not a training program that comes with a Ghostbusters video. Instead, it's program for viewing files from PostScript, an industry-standard page-description language for high-end printers. Ghostview uses a program called Ghostscript (Aladdin Enterprises) to print PostScript files to a dumb printer (one that does not have a PostScript program built into it) or to put PostScript files out to a fax machine. Newer versions of Ghostscript have distribution limitations, but older versions are freely distributable.

Audio/video

Here are some audio/video freeware programs that run on Linux:

✔ **xanim(1):** A program for playing back stills, animations, and video — including any audio — in various formats. The program can also attach audio streams of various formats to the video if it does not already have an audio track.

✔ **Applixware Presentation:** A program for creating slide shows and also simple graphics. It is similar to Microsoft's PowerPoint presentation program and can be used to accomplish all the same functions.

✔ **A series of programs that mix audio, play back audio, and even mail audio programs:** For instance, cdplay(1) is a character-cell rendition of a program to play audio CDs (assuming your system has a sound card). xplaycd(1), shown in Figure 2-8, is a graphical interface for playing a CD.

✔ **xmixer:** A program that controls the volume of your sound card. You can also mute the sound from the control panel, for those times when your parents — or your teenage children — come into the room complaining about the music you're playing.

Figure 2-8:
An example
of xplaycd
program.

Part II
Installing Linux

The 5th Wave   By Rich Tennant

"Whoa there, boy! You think you're gonna install Linux on that Windows 98 box?! Well you'd better hope to high heaven she's in a good mood today."

In this part . . .

You're about to embark on a journey through the Linux installation program. (If your Linux system is already installed, you can skip this part and peruse another one.) Perhaps you know nothing about setting up the operating system on your computer. That's okay. Linux is smart and reasonable. Plus, you have us to guide you.

In Chapter 3, you find out what the Linux traveler needs to know about your computer's hardware. Then, after backing up your system, you can move on to Chapter 4, where you do more all-important reconnaissance, such as creating a boot floppy disk. You also find out how to squeeze the existing files on your hard disk so you can fit Linux there, too.

Next, in Chapters 5 and 6, you get to do what you've been waiting for ever since you bought this book: install Linux. Like any good guide, we lead you along the various trails of the installation process, pointing out pitfalls and cautioning you about hazards. You get to enjoy the views, too, as you move screen-by-screen through your trek.

Your travels through the installation may not be over yet, however. Installing the X Window System can be tricky, which is why we provide an entire troubleshooting chapter on it. So, if you decide to include X Window System and have problems installing it, Chapter 7 is for you. If you installed X Window System without a hitch, break out the trail mix and enjoy a well-deserved rest.

Happy trails.

Chapter 3

Taking a Look at the Nuts and Bolts of Your System

In This Chapter

▶ Figuring out which resources Linux requires

▶ Identifying your hardware and its function

*T*he sole function of this chapter and the three that follow is to help you install your system. If your Linux system is already installed, count your lucky stars and skip this section. If you haven't installed your system, console yourself with the fact that you will find a lot of helpful information in this chapter and will be the better for it later. Your computer won't seem like such a stranger when you find out what's inside it. You'll also be able to impress your friends with your new-found knowledge.

We want to dispel the myth that Linux is more difficult to install than Microsoft's Windows. We believe that Linux is no harder to install than any other operating system. We've tried on several occasions to install Windows 95, and have met with frustration due to Plug and Play (often derisively called "Plug and Pray") or because the drivers were always on the *other* floppy disk. Windows *seems* easy to install because it's usually preinstalled, because most people only update it, and because people who do install it have all the hardware documentation.

You can buy Linux preinstalled if you want. Most companies that sell hardware and specialize in Linux sales will install it for you. The big boys, such as Dell Computer and Compaq, sell preinstalled Linux systems including Red Hat Linux. If you do purchase such a system, then all you need to do is turn it on — which makes the "installation" just as easy as Windows!

The next easiest way to install Linux is to buy it preinstalled on a hard disk. You put the disk in your system, boot the system, and Linux is installed.

If you're the rare reader who is buying a system just for Linux, find a hardware supplier on the World Wide Web or in a Linux magazine and ask the company to build a system for you.

If you're like most readers, however, you want to:

- ✔ Install Linux to your existing hardware.
- ✔ Use your existing hard disks.
- ✔ Keep MS-DOS, or Windows, or both on your system.

Installing Linux on your existing system is the most adventurous type of installation. Don't worry, though, because we're here to guide you through it.

Discovering What Hardware Linux Supports

Generally, Linux runs on any computer with an Intel processor that is a 386 or newer, as well as on various Digital Alpha, Sun SPARC, Motorola, MIPS, PowerPC, and HP/PA platforms. We concentrate on Intel PCs because they represent the bulk of systems. If you have one of these other systems, don't despair: They aren't that different, and you can probably adapt the instructions. However, you'll need a different CD-ROM than the one in the back of this book, because it supports only the Intel line of processors.

Linux supports *symmetric multiprocessing (SMP),* which means you can have more than one CPU (central processing unit) per computer. In fact, Linux supports several processors per system box. If your system has more than one CPU, Linux can also utilize those CPUs, either by speeding up a specific program written to take advantage of multiple CPUs or by allowing more programs to run at one time. (If you have an SMP system, would you care to trade with us?)

The Intel processor should have the following amount of RAM (main memory):

- ✔ Without graphics, Linux runs (er, walks) with 4MB.
- ✔ With graphics, Linux runs with a minimum with 8MB of memory; with 16MB, the graphics get much faster.
- ✔ With 32MB, Linux screams, and the speed of the application (particularly a graphics-oriented program) increases dramatically.
- ✔ Some Linux developers have 128MB in their systems because they tend to run many programs at a time, and each program takes up a certain amount of RAM when running.

Linux installs in 40MB of hard disk space, but for the graphical part of Linux, you need a total of about 150MB. And by the time you install all the goodies, you will probably have installed over 680MB of computer programs, data, games, and anything else you downloaded from the Internet. When considering whether your system needs more hard disk space or more RAM, remember that as a general rule, gluttony is a good thing, and you should get as much disk space and RAM as you can afford.

You usually install Linux from a CD-ROM. Some distributions, however, enable you to install from floppy disks or require you to make floppy disks and install from those. Installing from disk requires at least 150 floppies. Normal people, and even most nerds, would go insane after about the 10th floppy, so your sanity is well worth the cost of buying an inexpensive ($40 for instance) CD-ROM drive. Linux handles IDE/ATAPI and SCSI CD-ROM drives. Most PCs come with IDE/ATAPI interfaces, which is a standard type of disk drive controller. SCSI is a higher-speed interface that is typically used on high-end PC servers.

Some early CD-ROM drives are not IDE; they attach directly to sound cards and other devices. Most Linux distributions tell you how to detect and use these drives. If you don't have an IDE/ATAPI or SCSI CD-ROM drive, you need to know the make and model number of your CD-ROM drive and what type of controller (perhaps a specific sound card) the CD-ROM drive is attached to. To do this, you have to open up your system and look for the make and model number of the CD-ROM on the physical drive. CD-ROM drive manufacturers may not support Linux, so the Linux distributors like Red Hat are generally better sources of information about how to configure your drive.

You can install Linux — after making one or two disks — by copying files over a network. This is a viable way of installing Linux if you have access to the type of local area network used at colleges or businesses or if you have a friend who has a Linux system, a CD-ROM drive, and a networking card. However, if the network is not fast (that is, it can't transfer lots of data quickly), the easiest way to install Linux is by using a CD-ROM drive attached to your system. Trust us.

You can install Linux on a notebook by using the notebook's built-in CD-ROM drive (if it has one), or a CD-ROM drive attached to the notebook's docking station, or a SCSI CD-ROM drive attached to a PCMCIA (Personal Computer Memory Card Interface Adapter) SCSI controller. If you don't have any of these drives, you can try to get a PCMCIA Ethernet controller and do a network installation, given that another Linux system on the network has a CD-ROM drive installed.

Notebooks before PCMCIA support

Early notebooks had no built-in CD-ROMs, and until Linux had PCMCIA support, we were forced to install Linux by using floppies. Jon still remembers the day he got both his new notebook and the new release of Linux that had PCMCIA support. He ran out and bought a PCMCIA SCSI controller that night so he could use his SCSI CD-ROM to do the installation.

His life has been better ever since. Having used floppies to install Linux on various notebooks — not once or twice, but *seven* times — he would have paid ten times the amount for that PCMCIA card.

You also need a keyboard, a mouse, and a video card. Linux supports a wide range of video cards. Even if your card is not supported directly, Linux may support it as a generic VGA, XGA, SVGA or other graphical hardware standard video card. Most video cards that have been available for a while are supported.

 Linux supports a variety of sound cards, serial line cards (for attaching multiple serial printers or modems to a system), and other peripherals. The hardware components supported by the code on the accompanying CD-ROMs are listed in Appendix B.

Finding Out What You Have

One of the most important preliminary steps for a successful Linux installation is identifying the type of hardware you have. You can find most of this information in the manuals that came with your computer. The manuals won't be much help, however, if:

- ✔ You threw the manuals out.
- ✔ You lost the manuals.
- ✔ You bought your computer secondhand from someone who threw away or lost the documentation.
- ✔ Your dog ate the manuals.
- ✔ You become nauseous and pass out every time you look at them.
- ✔ You bought your PC with Windows already installed.

The last reason is the most insidious because it means that the company you bought the PC from did not bother to buy the documentation for each part of the PC when assembling it for you. (That would have cost the company more money.) Instead, it used OEM parts (read that "sans documentation and colorful box") and bought only one copy of the documentation for its use. With Windows already installed, the company reasons, "Why would an end user need any documentation about the system?"

Contact the place where you bought your system. Perhaps you can legally obtain a copy of the documentation from the dealer. Be careful not to copy copyrighted information.

If that doesn't work, open up your system and look at the components. For instance, one source of information about your hard disk is the label on top of the disk drive. If you don't feel comfortable opening up your system, you may want to take it back to where you bought it — assuming you didn't buy it by mail order — and perhaps the dealer can open it up and tell you what you have.

You can also look to the World Wide Web for information. Many vendors use their Web sites to provide technical data about their devices. To find the information about your device, you need to know your equipment's manufacturer, make, and model number.

Another source of information is MS-DOS, Windows 3.1, Windows 95, or Windows 98. Step-by-step instructions in the following sections show you exactly how to use these operating systems to get all the information you need. If you don't have any literature about your system, and you don't have Windows 3.1, Windows 95, or Windows 98 on your system (perhaps you like to run FAT free), and no dealer is within hundreds of miles, you're not out of luck. Linux is good at sniffing out and identifying hardware during the installation.

Knowing Your Hardware

Here are the questions you need to answer about your hardware:

- **Hard disk controllers.** How many do you have and what are their types (IDE, SCSI)? Which hard disk drives are connected to which controllers? If a SCSI controller is installed in your machine, what's its make and model number?

- **Hard disks.** How many hard disks do you have? For each disk, what is its size and order (which one is first, second, and so on)?

- **CD-ROM.** What is the interface type? Is it an IDE drive, a SCSI drive, or some other type? If you have a CD-ROM drive other than IDE (ATAPI) or SCSI, what is its make and model number?

- **RAM.** How much RAM is installed on the computer?

- ✔ **Mouse.** What type of mouse do you have — a bus mouse, a PS/2 mouse, or a serial mouse? How many buttons does it have? If you have a serial mouse, which COM port is it attached to and what software drivers does it use (such as Microsoft or Logitech)?

- ✔ **Monitor.** What is the make and model of the monitor? What are its vertical and horizontal refresh rates? You need this information only if you'll be using the graphical portion of Linux, called X Window System.

- ✔ **Video card.** What is the make and model number of the video card or video chip set and the amount of video RAM?

- ✔ **Network interface card (NIC).** If you have a network connection, what is the make and model number of the network interface card?

- ✔ **Network information**. If you have a network connection, what is your IP address, netmask, gateway IP address, name server IP addresses, and host and domain names? If you need help, contact your network administrator or Internet service provider (ISP).

To install most Linux distributions, you need to answer the questions in the preceding list. Now that you know what you should be looking for, the next section delves a bit more into how to locate and capture that information.

Comparing hard disk controllers

The two main types of hard disks are IDE and SCSI, and each type has its own controller. IDE is more common in PCs, and newer PCs usually have two IDE controllers rather than one. For each IDE controller, your system can have only two hard disks: a master and a slave. Therefore, a PC with two IDE controllers can have up to four hard disks. You should know which hard drive is which. Also, if you have a Windows system that you want to preserve, you should know which hard drive it resides on (a PC can use up to four). Normally, this is the configuration on a Windows system:

- ✔ The first controller's master disk is called C.
- ✔ The next hard disk is called D, and it's the slave disk on the first controller.
- ✔ The next hard disk is E, and it's the master disk on the second controller.
- ✔ The last hard disk is F, and it's the slave disk on the second controller.

Normally, Windows is located on your C disk, and data is on your other hard disks. This lettering scheme is just one possibility; your hard disks may be set up differently and even include CD-ROMs as drives on your IDE controllers.

Some high-end PCs have a SCSI controller on the motherboard or on a separate SCSI controller board, either in addition to or instead of the IDE controllers. Older SCSI controllers can have up to eight devices on them, numbered 0–7, including the controller. Newer SCSI controllers (known as *wide controllers*) can have up to 16 devices, including the controller itself.

If all you have is a SCSI hard disk, usually disk 0 or disk 1 is your C disk, and others follow in order.

If you have a mixture of IDE and SCSI controllers, your C disk could be on any of them. The sections later in this chapter — "Obtaining Information from Windows 95 or 98" and "Accessing Information from MS-DOS or Windows 3.1" — show you how to identify how many hard disks you have, what type they are, and the controllers to which they are attached.

Choosing a separate or shared hard disk

You need to decide if you want to put Linux on a separate hard disk from MS-DOS and Windows or have the two operating systems share one disk.

Most people think of Windows (either Windows 3.1, Windows 95/98, or Windows NT) as an operating system. Most Windows versions (not counting Windows NT or Windows CE), however, have an underlying system called MS-DOS, which manages the hard disk and many hardware components of your PC. From here on, unless we mention a particular operating system, when we refer to Windows, we're referring to the Windows/MS-DOS conflation.

Old systems and new hard disks

Hard disks are made up of cylinders of information, which in turn are made up of tracks of information, which in turn are made up of blocks of information. Because newer hard disks have more cylinders, older computer systems can't easily handle them. Therefore, a method called *logical block addressing,* or LBA, was created so that older computer systems can work with newer hard disks, which have more than 1,023 cylinders.

The BIOS setup under hard disks typically specifies whether your computer system is capable of LBA. (The BIOS is where your PC hardware — such as disk drives — is configured.) Your hard disk may already be accessed as an LBA disk. Some BIOS systems do this

automatically the first time a hard disk with a large number of cylinders is accessed. Note, however, that changing your disk to an LBA specification if it is not already LBA will make the data on the disk inaccessible. Therefore, before changing your hard disk to LBA, you should back it up if it contains any data. (You may decide that adding another hard disk is not such a bad idea as an expansion strategy.)

Different hardware systems have different ways to enter the BIOS setup. Usually, you can enter the BIOS setup when you turn on the power and start to boot; when you press the Reset button on the front of the system and start to reboot; or when you go through the normal shutdown of your Windows system and ask it to reboot.

We strongly recommend that you put Linux on a separate hard disk for two reasons. First, these days you can buy multiple gigabyte hard disks for less than $100 in U.S. currency. Second, the task of shrinking Windows small enough to allow Linux to reside in its full glory on an existing hard disk is difficult at best and impossible at worst. And although splitting the Linux distribution across hard disks is possible, doing so will make updating the distribution difficult.

If you do follow our recommendation and buy another hard disk, put it as the slave drive on the first IDE controller or as disk 1 on your SCSI controller, assuming that your existing Windows hard disk is either the first disk on your IDE controller or ID 0 on your SCSI controller. Adding hard disks is a hardware thing; the folks at the store where you buy the disk should be able to add it to your system for you. And while you're there, you can ask them to tell you the details about the other hardware in your system.

While installing Linux on your hard disks, you may be asked to supply the number of disk heads (or tracks), the number of cylinders, and the number of sectors per track. Most modern disk drives provide this information on a paper label on the outside of the drive. Some modern hard disks are set up for Windows, and Linux can access the number of disk heads, cylinders, and sectors.

If you have your computer apart looking for other information (shame on manufacturers who don't supply such useful information), you may as well write down all the hard disk information you can find. You should look for the number of heads, cylinders, and sectors. This information is used to tell the operating system where to put data with respect to the beginning of the disk. If you have trouble, check out the sections "Getting Information from Windows 95 or 98" and "Getting Information from MS-DOS or Windows 3.1." SCSI hard disk users don't have to supply this information because the SCSI controller and device drivers calculate it on-the-fly. SCSI hard disk owners should, however, know the size of their disks, which is printed on the disks or is available through the sections just mentioned.

Obtaining Information from Windows 95 or 98

If you have Windows 95 or Windows 98, you can use the msd program in MS-DOS mode, as described in the next section, to find out about the hardware in your system. Much more information is available, however, through the Control Panel in Windows 95/98. You can also find more information about this topic in *Windows 95 For Dummies* or *Windows 98 For Dummies,* both by Andy Rathbone (IDG Books Worldwide, Inc.).

With pencil and paper handy, it's time to access the Windows Control Panel and all that information. Follow along with these steps:

1. **Choose Start⇨Settings⇨Control Panel.**

   Note: We use a shorthand method for showing menu paths. When you see a line such as the following:

   choose Start⇨Settings⇨Control Panel

   it means, "Click the Start button, then click the Settings menu item, and then click the Control Panel item."

2. **Double-click the System icon.**

   The System Properties dialog box opens.

3. **Click the Device Manager tab.**

4. **At the top of the screen, select the View Devices by Connection option.**

   This view shows all the components and how they relate to each other. The screen looks similar to Figure 3-1.

If you have a printer attached to your system, at this point you can click Print in the Device Manager tab. Then, in the Print dialog box that appears, select the All Devices and System Summary option. Click OK. This procedure prints a full report about your system. You may not have all the information you need, such as which hard disk goes with which controller, but you won't get writer's cramp trying to list everything yourself. You should still continue on with your discovery process.

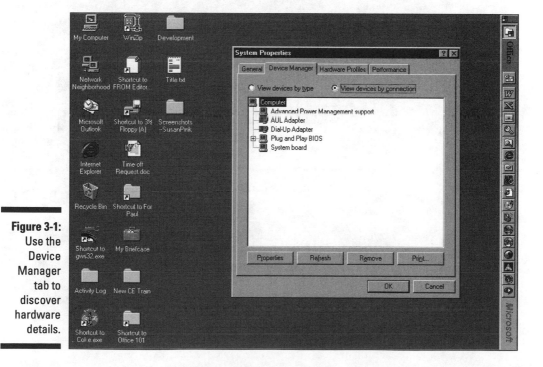

Figure 3-1:
Use the Device Manager tab to discover hardware details.

5. **In the list on the Device Manager tab, double-click Computer.**

The Computer Properties dialog box appears.

6. **Click the View Resources tab of the Computer Properties dialog box.**

The View Resources tab of the Computer Properties dialog box appears.

7. **At the top of the screen, select the Interrupt Request (IRQ) option and then write down the displayed information.**

The Setting column, at left, lists interrupt requests, as shown in Figure 3-2. The hardware that's using a particular IRQ is listed in the right column. Note that no two devices can use the same IRQ.

8. **Select the Direct Memory Access (DMA) option and then write down the displayed information.**

9. **Select the Input/Output (I/O) option and write down the pertinent information.**

Look for and write down entries regarding a sound card (if you have one) and a parallel port (LPT).

10. **Click Cancel.**

You return to the Device Manager tab of the System Properties dialog box.

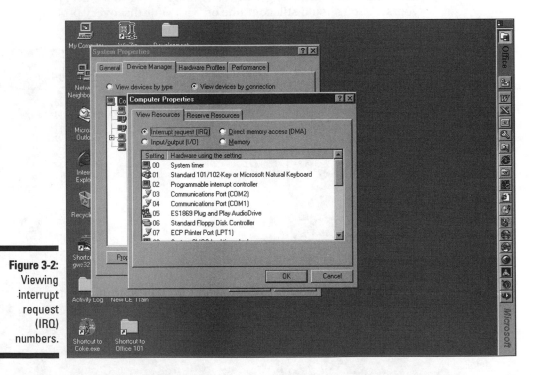

Figure 3-2:
Viewing
interrupt
request
(IRQ)
numbers.

Now you need to find out about the other devices in your system. This process takes some time, so you may want to pause here and grab something to drink, fix something to eat that's not going to give you heartburn, and put on some soothing tunes before following these steps:

1. **On the Device Manager tab of the System Properties dialog box, select the View Devices by Type option.**

   In the list, notice how a plus or minus sign precedes some icons. A plus sign indicates that the entry is collapsed. A minus sign indicates the entry is expanded to show all subentries.

2. **In the list, make sure that all items are expanded, as shown in Figure 3-3.**

   Expanded simply means that a minus sign precedes the icon. If a plus sign is there instead, click it, and it changes to a minus sign. As you expand some entries, you may see more plus signs. Click each plus sign to expand it. You may need to use the scroll bar to the right of the window to bring additional items into view.

3. **Look through the list for Hard Disk Controllers.**

   Write down the complete label, which tells you what type of hard disk controller you are currently investigating.

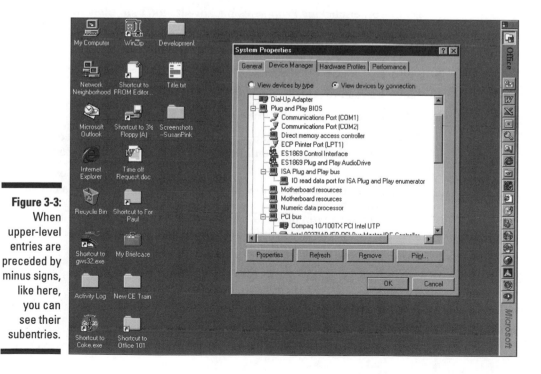

Figure 3-3: When upper-level entries are preceded by minus signs, like here, you can see their subentries.

4. **Look at the first subentry under that hard disk controller, if any. Write down the type of disk. Now double-click that disk entry.**

   The General tab of the Properties dialog box for that device appears.

   If the controller has no entries, there's still hope. Some systems have extra hard disk controllers (particularly if you're using SCSI hard disks) that are not connected to any hard disks. Also be aware that the first controller may have some other type of device connected to it, such as a tape drive or a CD-ROM. If no hard disks are attached to this controller, just go on to the next controller.

5. **Click the Settings tab, write down the drive type, and then click Cancel.**

   The screen returns to the Device Manager tab of the System Properties dialog box.

6. **Write down the highlighted information, which is the type of hard disk controller.**

7. **For each hard disk subentry for that controller, repeat Steps 4 through 6.**

8. **Follow the same general steps for any other hard disk controller entries.**

9. **For the Display Adapters entry, simply write down each subentry.**

   Don't bother clicking Properties because it won't supply you with any information that is useful for installing Linux.

10. **For the Keyboard entry, write down each subentry.**

11. **Likewise for the Monitor entry.**

12. **Like-likewise, for the Mouse entry.**

13. **Like-like-likewise, for the Ports (COM & LPT) entry.**

14. **Finally, for the Sound, Video, and Game Controllers entry, copy the information that appears on both the General tab and the Resources tab.**

    Double-click the first subentry, and the General tab appears (as usual). Write down the information. Then, instead of clicking Cancel, click Resources at the top of the screen to display the Resources tab, shown in Figure 3-4. Write down the information and then click Cancel.

15. **On the Device Manager tab, click Cancel.**

    The screen returns to the Control Panel.

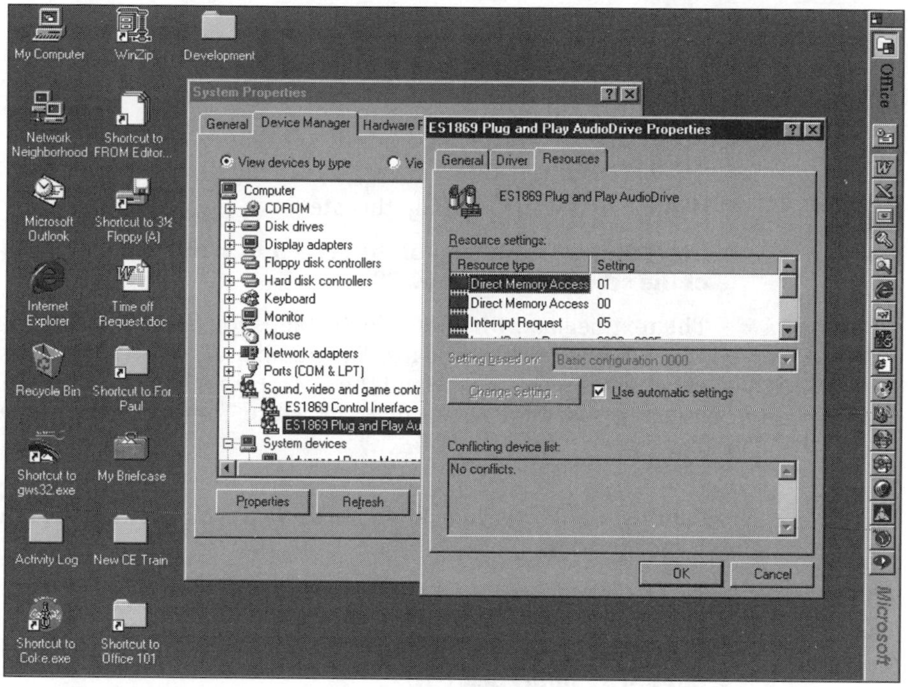

Figure 3-4:
The
Resources
tab of the
Sound,
Video, and
Game
Controllers
entry.

Whew. That was a lot of copying, but you aren't finished yet. Follow these steps for fascinating facts about your monitor:

1. **Make sure that the Control Panel is displayed.**

   If it isn't, choose Start⇨Settings⇨Control Panel.

2. **Double-click the Display icon.**

   The Display Properties dialog box appears.

3. **Click the Settings tab.**

   The screen displays your monitor's settings.

4. **Copy the information under Color Palette and Desktop Area in Windows 95 or under Colors and Screen Area in Windows 98.**

   The Color Palette information is 16 color, 256 color, High Color (16 bit), or True Color (24 bit or 32 bit). The Desktop Area information is 640 x 480 pixels, 800 x 600 pixels, 1,024 x 768 pixels, or some higher numbers.

5. **Click Cancel.**

   You return to the Control Panel.

And now, it's time to check the time:

1. **In the Control Panel, double-click the Date/Time icon.**

   The Date/Time Properties dialog box appears.

2. **Click the Time Zone tab.**

   Windows 98 users can skip this step.

3. **Copy the text at the top of the screen in Windows 95 or at the bottom of the screen in Windows 98.**

   The text begins with *GMT,* which stands for Greenwich Mean Time, which is the world standard. The number after GMT indicates the difference between your time and the GMT. Be sure to copy the words that indicate your time zone, such as Eastern Time (U.S. and Canada).

4. **Click Cancel.**

Tired of this yet? You're almost finished. Next, you discover delightful details about your printer:

1. **In the Control Panel, double-click the Printers icon.**

2. **Double-click to select the first non-networked Printer icon (one without a wire underneath it).**

   Another window appears. This new window has the same name as the printer you double-clicked. Don't click the icon labeled Add Printer.

3. **In the menu bar at the top of the window, choose Printer⇨Properties and then click the Details tab.**

4. **Copy the make and model and the communications port that the printer is attached to.**

   The make and model appears at the top of the screen, next to the printer icon. The communications port is listed after `Print to the Following Port`.

5. **Click Cancel.**

6. **Double-click another Printer icon and repeat Steps 3 through 5.**

   If you have only one printer, skip this step.

7. **Close any open windows by clicking the Close button.**

   The Close button is the one with the X, in the upper-right corner of a window.

The following, we promise, is the last set of steps. Here's how you get the hard facts about your hard drives:

1. **Double-click the My Computer icon on the Windows 95/98 desktop.**

2. **In Windows 95, select the first hard drive by right-clicking its icon and choosing Properties from the shortcut menu. In Windows 98, double-click the hard drive icon.**

   The Properties dialog box appears.

3. **Copy down the capacity and the free space left.**

   The total size and free space of the disk drive appears. Copy down this information.

4. **Repeat Steps 2 and 3 for all other hard drives.**

This information will be useful later as you make decisions about how much space to leave for Windows 95 or Windows 98 (if any) and how much space you have for Linux on each hard disk.

Accessing Information from MS-DOS or Windows 3.1

If you're running MS-DOS or Windows 3.1, you have a program on your system called Microsoft Diagnostics, or msd. This program tells you information about the hardware on your system, which you can then use to determine how to set up Linux.

If you have a printer attached to your system, you're in luck. You can avoid writing down all this information by following these steps:

1. **Make sure that your system is in DOS or MS-DOS mode.**

   If you have just booted, you may already be in MS-DOS mode. The screen will mostly be black with a prompt like this c:\>.

   If you have booted and are in Microsoft Windows 3.1, press Alt+F+X, which exits Windows and returns you to DOS. Then you see the c:\> prompt.

2. **Type** msd **to start the program.**

   The main screen appears, with categories such as computer and memory, as shown in Figure 3-5.

3. **Press Alt+F+P.**

4. **Press the spacebar and select Report All.**

5. **Press the Tab key until the cursor is in the Print To section.**

6. **Use the up- and down-arrow keys on the keyboard to select the port your printer is attached to or to create a file to hold the information.**

7. **Press Tab until the cursor is on the OK button.**

8. **Press the Enter key.**

9. **Fill in the Customer Information, if you want.**

10. **Press the Tab key until the cursor is on the OK button.**

11. **Press the Enter key to print the report or create the file.**

> If you're creating a file, you may want to press the Tab key to move to the text box that contains the name of the file that will be holding the report, and change the file extension to .txt so that the file will be easier to print later from Windows.

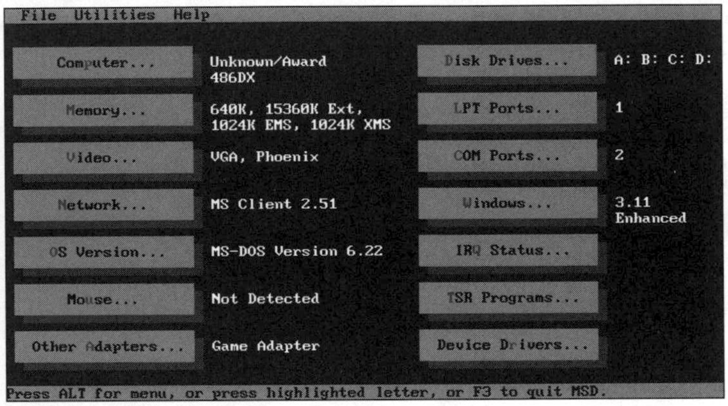

Figure 3-5:
The Microsoft Diagnostics program's initial screen.

Although you may not get all the information you need from this printout, you will get a great deal of it, and it will probably be more accurate than recording the information by hand.

If you don't have a printer, grab some paper and your favorite pen and prepare to copy some information:

1. **Make sure that your system is in DOS or MS-DOS mode.**

   See Step 1 in the preceding set of steps for more information.

2. **Type** msd **to start the program.**

   The main screen appears, with categories such as computer and memory (refer to Figure 3-5).

3. **Press P (for processor) and copy the information on the screen.**

   The screen displays the type of processor in your system (usually a 386, 486, or some other type of Intel, Cyrix, or AMD chip).

4. **Press Enter to return to the main screen.**

5. **Press V (for video screen) and copy the displayed information.**

You see your system's video adapter type (usually VGA, XGA, or SVGA). Also look for the display type (such as VGA Color or SVGA Color), manufacturer, and video BIOS version. Pay particular attention to the video BIOS version because it may also list the computer chip set used to make the video controller, which in turn is used to set up the graphical part of Linux.

6. **Press Enter to return to the main screen.**

7. **Press N (for network) and copy the displayed information.**

If your system has no networking capability or none that msd knows about, you may see a message that says `no network`.

8. **Press Enter.**

9. **Press U (for mouse) and copy the displayed information.**

Look for entries for mouse hardware, the driver manufacturer, the DOS driver type, and the number of mouse buttons. Well, you don't really need to refer to the screen to figure out that last one.

10. **Press Enter.**

11. **Press D (for disk drives) and copy the pertinent information.**

Now it gets interesting, as you can see in Figure 3-6. Copy your floppy drive's capacity and number of cylinders. (For a floppy drive, these values are usually 1.44MB and 80 cylinders, respectively.) Then look for your hard disk drives, usually designated as C, D, E, and so on. Each one should have a Total Size entry and a number such as 400M, which stands for 400 megabytes.

You should also see an entry such as CMOS Fixed Disk Parameters, followed by something like 731 Cylinders, 13 heads, 26 sectors/track. This information is useful in setting up your disks for Linux.

12. **Press Enter.**

13. **Press L (for parallel ports) and write down the pertinent information.**

The screen displays entries such as LPT1 and LPT2. Linux usually finds out about these ports all by itself. In case it doesn't, write down the port address, which is usually a number such as 0378H.

14. **Press Enter.**

15. **Press C (for the COM ports) and write down the pertinent information.**

The COM ports are your serial ports, which are typically used for a modem, a serial printer, and other interesting gadgets. Copy the port address, baud rate, parity, data bits, stop bits, and UART chip used. Usually, you don't need any of this information for Linux, but having a complete record of your system is useful.

16. **Press Enter.**

17. **Press Q (for IRQ list) and copy the information.**

    The different hardware pieces use IRQ, which stands for *interrupt request,* to signal to the main CPU that they have some data that has to be processed.

    No two devices can have the same IRQ. Copying the information in these columns for all 16 IRQs (0–15) is important for later sanity.

18. **Press Enter to go back to the main screen and then press F3 to end the msd program.**

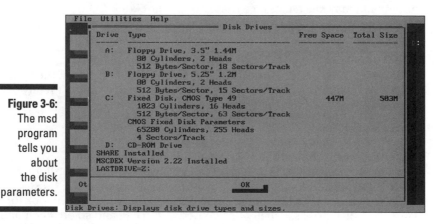

Figure 3-6: The msd program tells you about the disk parameters.

Leaving a Trail of Bread Crumbs

This next step is very important: Back up your system! Follow your system's directions for making a backup disk that includes your master boot record, or MBR. See Chapter 4 for more information on backing up your system.

Chapter 4

Move Over Windows:
Finding Space for Linux

● ●

In This Chapter

▶ Finding out what you need to install from the accompanying CD-ROM (CD1)

▶ Creating a boot disk

▶ Squeezing Linux onto your hard disk

● ●

*A*fter you're familiar with the hardware in your system, you're finally ready to open your distribution. (Unless you're the impatient type like us and have already ripped it from its packaging like a child the night before Christmas.) If you haven't identified your hardware yet, take a look at Chapter 3. This chapter describes how to install Red Hat Linux, which you can find on the first accompanying CD-ROM (CD1).

Installing Linux from a CD-ROM

The easiest way to install Linux is on a system with a CD-ROM drive (especially an ATAPI/IDE or SCSI CD-ROM). First, you must create a boot floppy from files on CD1 that comes with this book. The boot floppy is necessary to get the Red Hat installation process started. If you need to use a PCMCIA card for a CD-ROM controller to install Linux, you have to make the PCMCIA version of the boot floppy, which is also on CD1.

The follow sections delve into the exciting details of creating boot floppy.

Creating a boot disk in Windows

If you have a Windows 3.1, 95, 98, or NT system, then you can use your system to read CD1 as well as create your boot floppy. CD1 includes a program called RAWRITE.EXE, which you can use to make the floppies while you're running Windows.

In the following instructions, we assume that your CD-ROM is drive D and your floppy drive is A. If your drive letters are different, substitute the appropriate letters for *D* and *A*.

Follow these steps to create a boot floppy:

1. **Make sure that you have a formatted, high-density (1.44MB) 3½-inch floppy.**

2. **Insert CD1 into your CD-ROM drive.**

3. **Change to the directory on the CD-ROM drive or other hard drive where RAWRITE.EXE is stored, and follow along by entering the following code after each prompt:**

```
C:\> D:
D:\> cd \dosutils
D:\DOSUTILS\> rawrite
Enter disk image source file name: d:\images\boot.img
Enter target diskette drive: a:
Please insert a formatted diskette into drive A: and
        press -ENTER- : <Enter>
D:\DOSUTILS>
```

RAWRITE copies the boot image to the floppy. That floppy can *boot* (start up) your computer and also begin the Red Hat Linux installation process.

If you need to install Red Hat Linux over a network — if, for instance, your PC or notebook does not have a CD-ROM drive but another computer on the network does — then you need to create a different boot disk. Instead of using the BOOT.IMG file, you should use either the BOOTNET.IMG or PCMCIA.IMG disk. The former is when you have a computer with an Ethernet connection, whereas the latter is typically used for notebooks with PCMCIA-type Ethernets. Installing via a network is an advanced process and is not within the scope of this book. However, knowing that such methods exist is useful.

4. **Remove the boot floppy and then label it** *Boot Floppy* **so you know what it is.**

   Now you can use the RAWRITE program again to copy the rescue image to the other blank disk to create the *rescue disk*. You can use the rescue disk to boot your computer in case something gets misconfigured or fails.

The floppy disk that you created (the boot disk) is a normal MS-DOS file system containing boot images and messages. You can list the directory of the floppy disk that you made with MS-DOS.

While you're in this directory, copy FIPS.EXE onto your C disk. You use FIPS in "Choosing nondestructive repartitioning," later in this chapter, to partition your disk in a nondestructive partitioning. Type the following:

```
D:\DOSUTILS> copy fips.exe c:\fips.exe
```

If you're using a FAT32 system, then copy the FIPS.EXE program from the FIPS20 directory. FAT32 is a enhanced version of the traditional FAT file system that is used with Windows 98 and NT, and newer versions of Windows 95. FAT32 allows long file names, for instance. The FIPS.EXE program will not work with the NTFS file system.

Making boot disks in Linux

If you don't have access to MS-DOS or Windows but you do have access to another Linux system, this section is for you. To make the boot disk in Linux, you must be logged in as a user with permissions to write to the 3½-inch drive, which Linux refers to as /dev/fd0.

To create the boot disk and supplemental disk, follow these steps:

1. **Insert a blank, formatted floppy in the floppy drive.**
2. **Place CD1 into your CD-ROM drive and then mount the Linux CD (make it visible to the rest of the file system) by typing the following:**
   ```
   mount /dev/cdrom /mnt
   ```
3. **Change to the images directory by typing this command:**
   ```
   cd /mnt/images
   ```
4. **Finally, type the following command:**
   ```
   dd if=boot.img of=/dev/fd0
   ```
5. **You may dismount the CD-ROM (remove it from the rest of the file system) by typing these commands:**
   ```
   cd /
   umount /mnt
   ```

   Wait until the floppy drive light is out before removing the floppy disk.

Newer PCs can boot directly from the CD-ROM drive. If you have such a computer, then you don't need to create a boot floppy. You can start the Red Hat Linux installation process, described in Chapter 5, directly from CD1. But you do need to modify your BIOS configuration so that you computer looks to the CD-ROM to start from.

Making Room for Linux

Before you can install Linux on your system, you need to make room for it. Some people find space by getting rid of MS-DOS and Windows. Others don't want to make such drastic changes and prefer to have Linux and their other operating system peacefully coexist. If this latter setup fits the bill for you, the easiest way to go is to add a new hard disk — either IDE or SCSI — to your system and install Linux on that.

If you don't want to get rid of your current operating system and can't add another hard disk to your system, your only remedy is to *defragment* your other operating system — make its disk space smaller — and then install Linux in the freed-up space.

MS-DOS systems usually have one big DOS partition. A *partition* is simply a method for organizing the space on a disk. If a disk — like most Windows installations — has one partition, then the entire disk is used in one big chunk, the famous C: drive. If there are two partitions, then the disk is divided into two chunks. For instance, if you have two partitions on a Windows disk, then you will see two drives — C: and D: for instance.

That's the spot you want to make smaller so you can install Linux in the left-over space. You can shrink the DOS partition by using *destructive repartitioning,* which wipes out all the data on the hard disk, or *nondestructive repartitioning,* which is not supposed to wipe out all the data on the hard drive. Yep, this process is an adventure, but as your tour guides, we'll steer you clear of the pitfalls. Please keep your hands inside the car.

Note: If you decide to keep space on your hard drive for DOS, try to keep DOS in the first partition because it makes managing DOS and Linux together much easier.

Before performing any major work on restructuring your hard disk, as you are about to do, backing up your disk is wise in case something goes wrong. You don't want to lose any data or programs that you worked hard to install. Please refer to your system's owners' manual to find out how to back up your system and how to restore the data if necessary. We can't stress this strongly enough. Backing up is like buckling up: It saves lives. Okay, maybe it's not that important, but it certainly saves your sanity if you lose your valuable data.

Choosing nondestructive repartitioning

If you can't add another hard disk to your system, and your only choices are destructive and nondestructive repartitioning, nondestructive repartitioning is definitely the better choice of the two. You still need to back up your system, just in case you have to restore it afterward.

You use an MS-DOS utility called FIPS (which is a clone of FDISK) to nondestructively resize your DOS partitions. FIPS is included on the accompanying CD-ROM (CD1) and on most Linux distributions. We suggest that you read the documentation in the fipsdocs subdirectory on CD1 before you use the FIPS utility.

Although FIPS is supposed to be nondestructive, make sure that you always back up your system before using it.

Newer versions of Windows 95/98 have a 32-bit file allocation table (FAT) and drive management that provide for single-disk configurations larger than 2GB. Older versions of Windows 95 had a 16-bit FAT; to use the space above 2GB, the drive had to be partitioned into logical drives of 2GB or less. Newer computers often have drives larger than the old 2GB limit. If the drive is repartitioned, the large drive management system is disabled, and DOS and Windows partitions are once again limited to 2GB.

The FIPS utility works by dividing the drive into two partitions. The first one is the DOS partition. The second one, beginning at the end of the space used by DOS and Windows software and encompassing the rest of the drive space, is the non-DOS partition where Linux loads. If you want to use the FIPS utility to partition your drive, keep in mind that your new DOS partition can hold only 2GB or less. If the amount of used space on your C partition is greater than 2GB, you won't be able to nondestructively repartition unless you either delete some files or move them to another disk.

The problem with older computers is that the BIOS doesn't recognize computers over a certain size (such as 400MB), and hard disk makers have used software overlays to trick the BIOS into recognizing the entire disk. You may be risking the loss of all your data by using a utility like FIPS (or even a commercial package like PartitionMagic) on an existing hard drive with these software overlays, so be careful!

The following two sections on nondestructive partitioning consist of steps to defragment the disk and to use FIPS to carve the disk into segments.

Defragmenting your disk

The process of *defragmenting* a disk simply moves all the data to the front of the disk segment, leaving the empty space behind for Linux. Follow the steps that apply to your system to defragment your C partition by running the defragmentation program.

In Windows 3.1 and MS-DOS:

1. **Close all programs and windows on your system.**

2. **If you're running Windows 3.1, exit from Windows into MS-DOS.**

   To do so, go to the Program Manager window, choose File➪Exit Windows, and allow Windows 3.1 to exit as gracefully as it can.

3. **Now that you're in MS-DOS, change to your C disk and go to the C:\DOS directory by typing the following:**

```
c:\> cd \dos
```

4. **Initiate defragmentation under MS-DOS by typing this command:**

```
c:\dos> defrag
```

The DEFRAG program asks you which disk to defragment.

5. **Select the drive that you want to defragment.**

The defragmentation program looks at the disk to determine whether it needs defragmentation.

6. **Defragment the disk — even if the program says the disk doesn't need defragmenting.**

After what may seem like a long time, defragmentation finishes, and all useful blocks of information are now at the beginning of the disk, making it ready for the FIPS program in the next section.

In Windows 95 and Windows 98:

1. **Close all programs and windows on your system, leaving just the desktop and icon bar.**

2. **Double-click the My Computer icon on the desktop.**

3. **Select your C disk by clicking it. (Right-click with Windows 98 systems.)**

4. **Choose File⇨Properties⇨Tools.**

5. **Click Defragment Now.**

You may get a message telling you that it's not necessary to defragment because your disk is not very fragmented. Under normal circumstances this may be true, but in this case, defragmenting your disk is necessary because you're going to move the end of the file system and make it smaller. Any data outside that barrier is lost, so you have to move the barrier closer to the front.

6. **Click Start.**

The defragmentation window appears.

7. **Click Show Details.**

Depending on the size of your hard drive, defragmentation can take some time to finish, so grab a cup of coffee and a snack while you're waiting. As the defragmentation continues, you can scroll up and down the large window to watch the progress, which is represented by different colored blocks (see

Figure 4-1). You can expect to see white space appear toward the bottom of the window, which represents the end of your disk. The movement of the blocks around the screen shows that the data is being moved forward on the disk. At the end of the defrag process, no colored blocks should be at the bottom of the window, and all the blocks should be compressed toward the top of the window. The colored blocks represent programs and data, and the white space is free space in your MS-DOS file system that you may now allocate to the Linux file system.

Resizing with FIPS

After moving the data in your C partition as far to the front of the partition as possible, you can now use the FIPS program to shrink the C partition. The fips.exe program for the FAT file system that comes with Windows 95 can be found in the DOSUTILS directory on the companion CD-ROM. For FAT32 on Windows 98 systems please use the fips.exe program that comes in the DOSUTILS\FIPS20 directory. Make sure that you back up your system before continuing.

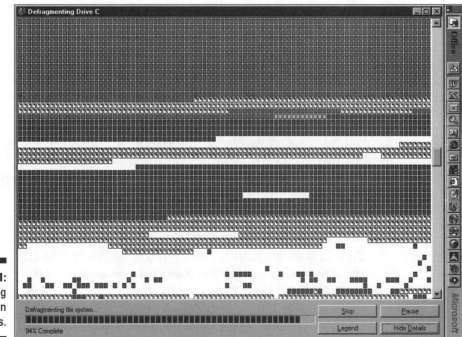

Figure 4-1:
The defrag
program in
progress.

If you haven't copied the FIPS program from the accompanying CD-ROM to your C disk yet, see the end of the "Creating boot and rescue disks in MS-DOS" section for details.

First you must shut down your Windows system until you're at the MS-DOS prompt. The easiest way to do this is as follows:

1. **Click the Start button.**

2. **Click the Shut Down button.**

3. **Select the Restart the Computer in MS-DOS Mode option.**

4. **Click the Yes button.**

When the computer restarts, your system is in MS-DOS mode.

Next, you begin the process of starting the FIPS program and shrinking the C partition. This process involves quite a few steps, but each step is simple:

1. **Type** cd \ **and press Enter.**

2. **Type** FIPS **and press Enter.**

   Some messages appear, but you can ignore them — well, ignore all but the following one.

3. **When you see the message** Press any key, **do so.**

   You see all the existing partitions on the disk.

4. **When you see a message to** Press any key, **do so.**

   You're getting pretty good at this. A description of the disk and a series of messages appear. Then FIPS finds the free space in the first partition.

5. **When asked whether you want to make a backup copy of sectors, type** y **for yes.**

   The screen asks whether a floppy disk is in drive A.

6. **Place a formatted floppy disk into drive A and then press** y.

   A message similar to Writing file a:\rootboot.000 appears, followed by other messages and then the message Use cursor key to choose the cylinder, enter to continue.

   Three columns appear on the screen: Old Partition, Cylinder, and New Partition. The Old Partition number is the number of megabytes in the main partition of your disk. The New Partition number is the number of megabytes in the new partition you're making for the Linux operating system.

7. **Use the left- and right-arrow keys to change the numbers in the Old Partition and New Partition fields to give you the space you need for both the Windows operating system and Linux. (See Figure 4-2.)**

A minimum Linux system, without X Window System (the graphical environment), requires 40MB of disk space. (See Chapter 2 for the details.) A minimal graphical environment requires about 150MB of disk space. The full distribution, along with all the programs and compilers on the disk, requires about 680MB of disk space. Then you have the amount of data space you need for your own files. The amount of data space that you leave for the Linux and Microsoft operating systems is up to you.

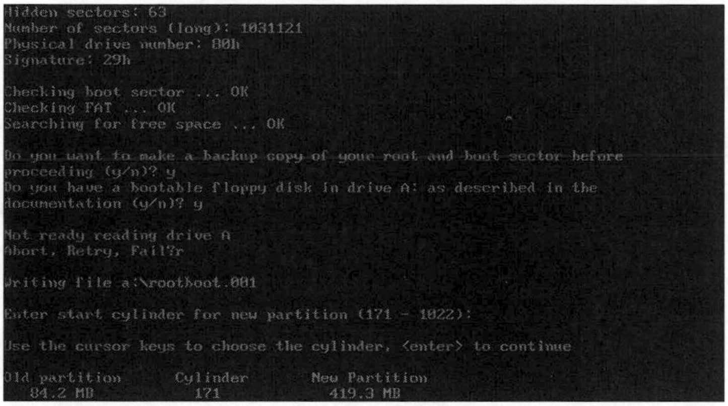

Figure 4-2:
The FIPS program, carving up a disk.

8. **When you have the correct amount of disk space in each field, press the Enter key.**

   FIPS displays the partition table again, showing you the new partition that has been created for the Linux operating system. This new partition will probably be partition 2; your C drive is probably partition 1.

   You also see a message at the bottom of the screen asking whether you want to continue or reedit.

9. **If you are *not* satisfied with the size of your Linux and Microsoft OS partitions, type r, which takes you back to Step 7. Otherwise, type c to continue.**

   You see many more messages about your disk. Then a message appears, stating that the system is ready to write the new partition scheme to disk and asking whether you want to proceed.

10. **If you type n, FIPS exits without changing anything on your disk. If you type y, FIPS writes the new partition information to the disk.**

    By typing **n**, your disk will be exactly the way it was after you defragmented it.

11. **To test that nondestructive partitioning worked properly, reboot your system by pressing Ctrl+Alt+Delete.**

12. **Allow Windows to start and then run ScanDisk by choosing Start⇨Programs⇨Accessories⇨System Tools⇨ScanDisk.**

   ScanDisk then checks all of your folders and files. It indicates whether you have all the files and folders you started with and whether anything was lost.

   To be on the safe side, keep those backup files around for a while.

Now you're ready to install the Linux operating system.

Using destructive repartitioning as a last resort

If you're keeping your current operating system, *and* you can't add another hard disk to your system, *and* nondestructive repartitioning doesn't work (you tried it and found that you couldn't use your other operating system afterward), you need to use destructive repartitioning.

You use an MS-DOS utility called FDISK to wreak your destruction, as follows:

1. **Make a full backup of your system.**

   If you want to reinstall DOS and Windows data, follow the instructions for your Windows backup utility. At a minimum, copy anything you can't rein-stall from original program disks. This data includes your files from a word processor, a spreadsheet, and a database, as well as e-mail you want to save. Most people customize settings for the programs themselves, so to save those settings, too, you really need to back up everything.

2. **Exit Windows 3.1 and enter MS-DOS.**

   From the Program Manager window, choose File⇨Exit Windows.

3. **Place a blank, formatted floppy disk in the floppy drive (which we assume is drive A) and type the following:**

   ```
   FORMAT /s A:
   ```

   This disk will be the MS-DOS bootable backup disk.

4. **Copy FDISK.EXE and FORMAT.COM to the disk by typing the following:**

   ```
   cd \
   cd dos
   copy format.com a:
   copy fdisk.exe a:
   ```

   Please check the manual for your backup program to see whether any other utilities are needed to restore files. Copy those utilities at this time as well.

5. **Boot your PC with the disk you just created.**

   Place the disk in the floppy drive and restart your computer.

6. **Run FDISK (the MS-DOS one).**

   At the A: prompt, type the following:

   ```
   FDISK
   ```

7. **Use the FDISK menu options to delete the partitions you want to change and to make new ones for DOS and Linux. Do not choose the large disk support in the first message (just press Enter).**

8. **When FDISK asks you to** Choose one of the following, **shown in Figure 4-3, select 4 and then press Enter.**

   You see a partition table showing all the partitions and their types.

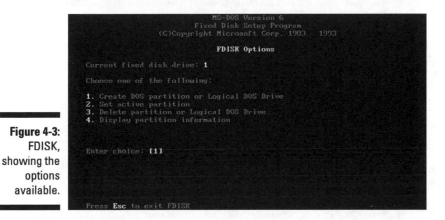

Figure 4-3:
FDISK, showing the options available.

9. **Delete enough partitions to allow space for Linux. Delete all of them, if you want.**

   The FDISK Options dialog box appears.

10. **Select 1 to create a DOS partition.**

    The Create DOS Partition or Logical DOS Drive dialog box appears.

11. **Select 1 to create a primary DOS partition.**

12. **Enter the partition size in megabytes, shown in Figure 4-4, and then press Enter.**

    The current DOS partitions appear.

13. **Press Esc to continue.**

    The FDISK Options dialog box appears.

Figure 4-4:
Using FDISK
to set the
partition
size.

14. **Select 2 to set the active partition (also known as the bootable partition), as shown in Figure 4-5.**

    Choose the first (and only) partition as your active one.

15. **Press Esc to return to the FDISK Options dialog box.**

16. **Press Esc to exit FDISK.**

17. **Use the DOS FORMAT utility to format the new DOS partition by typing the following:**

    ```
    format /s C:
    ```

18. **Restore your backup files according to the manual for your backup program.**

Wasn't that an exciting adventure? The ride is just beginning. Now you're ready for the Red Hat installation to create partitions for your Linux system, as described in the Chapter 5.

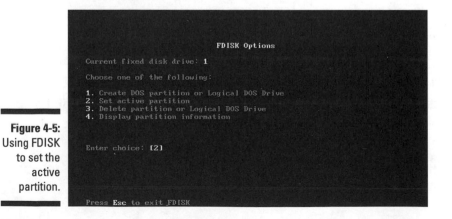

Figure 4-5:
Using FDISK
to set the
active
partition.

Chapter 5

Installation: The Home Stretch

● ●

In This Chapter

▶ Starting the actual installation

▶ Start configuring your new Linux installation

▶ Partitioning and formatting your disk

▶ Installing the Red Hat Linux software

▶ Configuring networking

● ●

*S*it down, grab your favorite drink, and contemplate the excitement about to unfold. Okay, okay, sit down and contemplate that you won't have to work that hard to install Linux. And after you're done, you'll have a powerful computer capable of performing most, if not all, of your daily chores. The exciting thing is that you'll have all that for the cost of this book! That's pretty amazing when you think about it. For a few bucks, you get the power that it took a million dollars to get just a few years ago.

This chapter describes the first half of the Red Hat installation process. The process is divided into the installation of the software and its configuration. We describe the installation here and the configuration in Chapter 6.

Beginning the Installation

Red Hat gives you two installation interface choices: a graphical and a menu-based one. The graphical system simplifies the process by grouping similar configurations choices together. The menu-based one takes you step by step through the entire installation.

The menu-based installation system works on more computers than the graphical one. The graphical system doesn't recognize all video cards. Therefore, we describe the menu-based one here. If you want to use the graphical system, you can use these instructions as a reference — they describe all the information that you need to supply to install Red Hat.

Tiptoeing through the dialog boxes

During the installation, you and Red Hat talk to each other by using — what else — dialog boxes. An example is shown here:

```
┌──────┤ Components to Install ├──────┐
│ Choose components to install:        │
│  ┌─────────────────────────────┐#    │
│  │[ ] Printer Support          │     │
│  │[*] X Window System          │     │
│  │[*] Mail/WWW/News Tools      │     │
│  │[ ] DOS/Windows Connectivity │     │
│  │[*] File Managers            │     │
│  │[ ] Graphics Manipulation    │     │
│  │[ ] X Games                  │     │
│  │[ ] Console Games            │     │
│  │[*] X multimedia support     │     │
│  └─────────────────────────────┘     │
│    [ ] Select individual packages    │
│                                      │
│    ┌────┐          ┌──────┐          │
│    │ Ok │          │Cancel│          │
│    └────┘          └──────┘          │
└──────────────────────────────────────┘
```

To maneuver between highlighted options in a dialog box and make your choices, use the following keys (note that *cursor* means the cursor or the highlight):

Tab	Moves the cursor to the next section in the screen
Alt+Tab	Moves the cursor to the previous section in the screen
Left arrow	Moves the cursor backward through a list of options
Right arrow	Moves the cursor forward through a list of options
Up arrow	Moves the cursor up through a list of options
Down arrow	Moves the cursor down through a list of options
Spacebar	Selects an item from a list of options
Enter	Selects the highlighted item
F12	Accepts the values you chose and displays the next screen

Now is the time to refill your drink and begin these detailed installation steps:

1. **Place the boot floppy that you made with** RAWRITE **or** dd **in the first floppy drive, which is usually drive A. Then place CD1 in the CD-ROM drive.**

   For details on creating a boot floppy, see Chapter 4.

   Alternatively, you can skip using the floppy disk and instead boot directly from CD1. Your computer must be capable of booting from CD-ROM, of course. If this is the case, then while your computer is powering up, press the Delete key when prompted (note that some computers use one of the function keys that appears at the top of the keyboard). You then go to a setup utility that controls the basic configuration of your computer. Use the cursor keys to select the Advanced CMOS Setup option. From there — if your computer is of a recent vintage — you can change the first Boot Device to use the CD-ROM. Save your changes when exiting. Detailed instructions for completing this process are beyond the scope of this book, but usually the CMOS configuration system provides a simple dialog box describing what keys are used to do what. Please note that the names and terms used here may vary among computers.

2. **Start your computer.**

   If you're using the boot floppy method, then your PC BIOS should be set
   to boot from the floppy drive — please don't kick your floppy disk.
   Alternatively, if your computer is capable of booting from the CD-ROM,
   then set your BIOS accordingly and insert CD1. You can modify your
   BIOS settings by pressing the F8 or Delete keys when prompted, soon
   after you turn on the power to your computer. Describing how to modify
   the BIOS is beyond the scope of this book; however, when you press
   the F8 or Delete key, you're placed into a menu system that has a simple
   help system.

   The `boot:` prompt appears, and then an informational screen is displayed.

3. **Press Enter to continue the installation process.**

   The Linux kernel is loaded and gives you a couple of pages of hardware
   and system information.

4. **When you arrive at the Welcome to Red Hat Linux dialog box, enter
   the following:**

   ```
   boot: text
   ```

   The process should continue without problems.

5. **In the Language Selection dialog box, select the language that you
   speak.**

   You can choose from several languages. If you're adventurous, select
   one you don't speak.

6. **In the Keyboard Selection dialog box, select the keyboard that you
   want to use, as shown in Figure 5-1.**

   For an explanation of the types of keyboards, see the "What's your
   keyboard's nationality?" sidebar later in this chapter.

   After completing this step, Red Hat introduces itself. You're now finished
   with the preliminary configuration process.

Figure 5-1:
The
Keyboard
Selection
dialog box.

Red Hat Linux detects your hardware

A series of messages scrolls by, indicating whether your hardware is being detected by the Linux kernel. If the hardware is not being detected, you may have to reboot and add some options at the `boot:` prompt. For example, if the system doesn't detect your CD-ROM drive, you may have to enter the following:

```
boot: linux hdc=cdrom
```

If you continue to have problems, you can get more installation information from Red Hat's online installation manual — in HTML format — located on the CD1 in the /mnt/cdrom/doc/rhmanual/manual directory. You can mount the CD-ROM on another Linux or Windows system and view the document with Netscape Communicator.

Most of the time — particularly with newer systems — Linux detects all the basic hardware. Then a welcome message, `Red Hat Linux/ Welcome to Red Hat Linux!`, appears, and the installation program begins.

If you want to stop the installation process, simply eject the boot disk, remove the CD from the drive, and reboot your machine.

7. **Select the Ok button to continue.**

Red Hat produces a complete and detailed installation guide, which is included on the Red Hat Linux Publisher's Edition CD-ROM (CD1) that comes with this book. You obviously can't use the computer that you're installing Red Hat on until you install Red Hat. But after you install Red Hat, then you probably don't need the installation guide. If you have access to another computer — Linux or Windows — you can mount CD1 on that computer and look at the manual with Netscape Communicator or another browser. If you have another Linux computer, then open the /mnt/cdrom/doc/rhmanual/manual/index.htm file. On a Windows computer, look at D:\doc\rhmanu\manual\index.htm file, assuming that your CD-ROM drive is the D drive.

8. **In the Installation Type dialog box, select an installation method.**

Red Hat provides several installation methods, two standard workstation classes and one server class. You can also use a custom method as well as upgrade an existing Red Hat installation. For our purposes here, select the Install Custom System option.

This book uses the custom method for two reasons. First, it is the most flexible of the installation methods — you can choose every aspect of your installation. Second, seeing how the partitions are created and being able to choose your own packages is handy — as well as more interesting. However, if you feel lucky, then give the other methods a try. (Their advantage is that they make some decisions for you. For instance, they choose the software packages to install for you.)

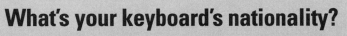

What's your keyboard's nationality?

Different countries have different keyboards. Linux, like many UNIX systems, has a keyboard mapping feature that enables you to use it with different keyboards.

Figure 5-1 lists some of the keyboard maps for your system. If you're in the United States, you will probably select the us option. Even then, however, you may have a different keyboard than the us keyboard, so browsing through the list to see what else it offers is worthwhile.

If you're not in the United States, you will probably choose something other than the us keyboard, unless you bought your system in the United States. If you don't see an obvious choice, choose something that looks close. If it seems to work, finish the installation. After the installation, you can change the keyboard mapping if necessary with the /usr/sbin/kbdconfig command.

If you choose one of the workstation or server installation types, then be careful that you don't accidentally erase your existing partitions. Red Hat gives you the option to manually create the partitions or let Red Hat choose them automatically. The manual method works exactly as described in the section "Partitioning your Hard Disk," which uses the Disk Druid utility.

Partitioning Your Hard Disk

The steps in this section describe the most crucial configuration decisions that you need to make. You need to decide how to partition your hard disk. Partitions are where the software that comprises Linux are stored.

Red Hat uses the Disk Druid program to partition your disk. No, some hooded guy from 'ol England isn't behind the screen. Disk Druid is a Red Hat program that simplifies the job of partitioning your hard disk.

If you chose to test for bad blocks during the formatting of the swap partition(s), testing the surface of the disk may take a while. Don't panic if nothing seems to be happening for a few minutes.

The Disk Druid window, similar to the one shown in Figure 5-2, shows all the existing partitions on your hard drive. Note that if you're using a SCSI hard drive, then your drives show up as *sda, sdb*, and so on. If you, like most people, have a typical PC, then you use an IDE hard drive. In that case, your drives show up as *had, hdb*, and so on, as shown in Figure 5-2. Whatever type of drive you have doesn't affect how Disk Druid works, so don't worry that our example figures differ from yours.

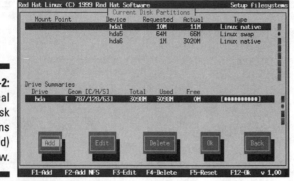

Figure 5-2:
A typical
Current Disk
Partitions
(Disk Druid)
window.

The Disk Druid screen has five columns of information about your hard disk partitions: Mount Point, Device, Requested, Actual Partition Size, and Type. Disk Druid also has a row of command buttons labeled Add, Edit, Delete, Ok, and Back. Read on for a whirlwind tour of these areas:

✔ The first column is a listing of the mount point for each partition. A mount point is a directory where a partition is attached to your Linux computer. Your Linux kernel keeps track of all the resources on your computer and must know where to find each partition. Please refer to the "Introducing the Linux file system tree" sidebar for more information.

✔ The device is shown in the second column. It starts with the letters *hd* for IDE hard disks or *sd* for SCSI hard disks. In Figure 5-3, you can see disks sda and sdb, which are two SCSI disks. For all the details on how disk drives are bestowed names, see the "Finding out all about files" sidebar later in this chapter.

✔ The third and forth columns are Requested and Actual. You need to specify the size of each partition as you create them — this is the Requested size. If you choose to allow a partition to grow, then it will take up part or all of the remaining free disk space, and the Actual size may be different than the Requested size. If you don't select the grow option, the Actual is the same as the Requested. (Note that *M* means megabytes.)

✔ The last column shows the type of the partition. Generally, you choose either Linux native or Linux swap. However, you can also select either DOS 16-bit <32M or DOS 16-bit >= 32M types.

The buttons that appear at the bottom of the screen enable you to create, modify, and remove new or existing disk partitions. The back key takes you to the previous Installation Type dialog box.

When you format a partition, you erase all the data on that partition. All newly created partitions are empty, so you should format those. If you have data that you want to keep in any partition, *do not* format that partition. For example, many people have data in /home or /usr/local, so these partitions shouldn't be formatted.

Follow these steps to partition your hard drive:

1. **(Optional) Remove one or all of the existing partitions, if you want.**

   This book assumes that you will be using your entire hard disk for Linux, and the examples and figures reflect that assumption. However, recall that you can install Linux along side another operating system, such as Windows, if you want. Linux is a good and friendly neighbor. Chapter 4 describes how to shrink an existing operating system installation to free up space for Linux if you need to. If you choose this method, then Disk Druid shows the existing partition(s). Leave the existing partition(s) in place while you add Linux partitions.

   If you have existing partitions that you want to remove to free up all or part of your hard disk, then first highlight the partition by using the up- and down-arrow keys. Next, use the Tab key to select the Delete button at the bottom of the screen. Press the Enter key, and you're asked if you really want to remove the partition. If — after checking, double-checking and triple-checking — you want to delete it, select Yes. Otherwise, select No. You return to the Disk Druid dialog box after either choice.

2. **To create one or more Linux partitions, press the Tab key to highlight the Add button at the lower left of the Disk Druid dialog box. Then press Enter.**

   With Disk Druid, you see all the existing partitions — if any — that you have. If you don't have any partitions, then no mount points are displayed. The caveat is that if you have already attempted to install Linux and have restarted the process, you see the disk partitions without their mount points. You can reuse those settings if you edit each one and add the mount point.

   After completing this step, the Edit New Partition dialog box appears. (See Figure 5-3.) You can do the following things in this dialog box:

     • Specify a mount point.

     • Enter a size.

     • Choose a file system type. (Linux Swap, Linux Native, DOS 16-bit <32M, or DOS 16-bit >=32M).

     • Choose the option to allow the partition to grow and take up the remaining disk space.

3. **The first partition to add is root (/). Start by adding the / in the Mount Point field, as shown in Figure 5-3.**

   Use the Tab key to select each item in the window.

4. **Enter** 80 **in the Size (Megs) field. Tab to the Type field and leave it as Linux native. Tab again to the Grow to Fill Disk field and leave it blank.**

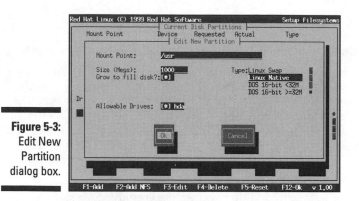

Figure 5-3:
Edit New
Partition
dialog box.

5. Use the Tab key to select the Ok button and then press Enter.

Congratulations, you have just created your first Linux partition!

6. Repeat Steps 2 through 5 to create additional partitions.

This book uses /, /usr, /usr/local, /var, /home, and swap partitions. See the "Choosing your disk partitions" sidebar for more information.

Go ahead and create all of these partitions. If you have a relatively small hard drive, such as a 1GB, then consider using the partition sizes shown in Table 5-1. Keep in mind that partitions, such as root, should not be much larger than the suggested values, because they should not vary much after you create your system. Partitions such as swap cannot be larger than 128MB. Your mileage may vary, so use your best judgment if these numbers don't work for you.

If you have a larger drive, for instance a 4GB drive, then check out Table 5-2. In other words, you can let your belt out a little and relax.

After you create the partitions, Disk Druid shows you those partitions.

Table 5-1	Suggested 1GB Partition Sizes	
Mount Point	*Min Suggested Size (MB)*	*Max Suggested Size (MB)*
/	30	80
/usr	400	500
/usr/local	100	200
/var	100	100
/home	100	100
swap	2.5 times your RAM	2.5 times your RAM

Table 5-2	Suggested 4GB Partition Sizes	
Mount Point	*Min Suggested Size (MB)*	*Max Suggested Size (MB)*
/	30	80
/usr	400	1,000
/usr/local	200	800
/var	100	200
/home	100	1,000
swap	2.5 times your RAM	2.5 times your RAM

7. **Check each partition, in order, and make sure that it matches what you intended to enter. When you're satisfied, use the Tab key to select the Ok button and then press Enter.**

   The Save Changes dialog box appears.

8. **If you're satisfied with the partitions that you have created, select Yes.**

   Until you select the Yes button, you have not actually written any partitions to disk. You do have the option to select the No button, which takes you to Step 9. If you select Cancel, you return to the Disk Druid dialog box with all of your partitions still in place.

   If you have an older system with less than 32MB of memory, then you see the Low Memory dialog box. This dialog box tells you that the Red Hat installation process will format and activate the swap partition immediately. Select Yes to continue.

9. **In the Choose Partitions to Format dialog box, choose either to format or not to format each of your partitions.**

   The default is to format. If this is your first installation or you want to start with a completely fresh one, then tab down to the Ok button and press Enter.

   If you're reinstalling Linux and you want to save the information stored on such partitions such as /home or /usr/local, then tab down to those menu items and press the Space bar to deselect the asterisk. From there, tab to Ok and press Enter.

Introducing the Linux file system tree

The Linux file system is like a tree turned upside down, as shown in the following figure. The top of the upside-down tree is represented by a / (slash) and is called the root. A series of limbs, branches, and leaves are below the root. The limbs are called mount points, the smaller branches are your directories, and the leaves are your files. Each *mount point* is a disk partition, and that disk partition is *mounted* on a directory of the limb above it. When the disk partition is mounted on the directory branch, it turns that branch into another limb, allowing for even more branches to be positioned and attached below the mount point.

Normally, you need at least a root partition in your directory structure (the upside-down tree) and a swap space (particularly if you have a system with under 16MB of RAM). Therefore, at a minimum, you should set up two types of disk space: a Linux file system starting at the root

and a swap space. Theoretically, you don't have to set up swap space, and some people choose not to. If you do, however, you can run more programs than you have real memory for and use data of sizes greater than the real memory you have on your system.

As mentioned, at a minimum, setting up a separate partition for your user files (usually called the home directory) is better and setting up multiple disk partitions for your Linux files is even better still. This setup makes backing up your files and updating your system to new versions of Linux much easier. The downside is that you have to leave empty space in each partition for new files, and these empty spaces add up. A reasonable analogy is using a filing cabinet to store your personal files versus a single box. The box is easier to obtain and takes up less space, but in the long run, a filing cabinet is much more useful and efficient.

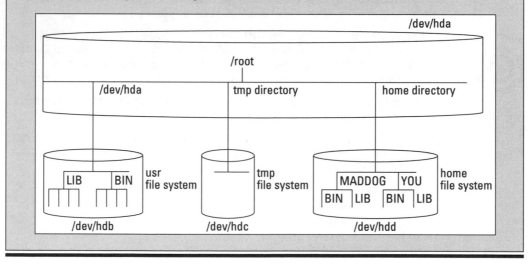

Choosing your disk partitions

You can install Linux several different ways. You can install it, and your personal files, all in one large partition. When you want to reinstall Linux (such as when you get an updated version or a different distribution), however, you have to back up and restore all your data files.

The other extreme of installing Linux is to create a partition for each of the following areas:

✓ A **root** partition mounted as / (the root directory), where the kernel that's necessary to boot the system and the system configuration files reside. This partition needs to be only 30MB to 50MB.

✓ A **swap** partition, which enables Linux to take advantage of virtual memory. If you have 16MB of RAM or less in your machine, you should have a swap partition. Actually, you should have a swap partition even if your system has more than 16MB. The swap partition should be the same size as the memory installed in your computer. If you have 32MB of RAM installed on your computer, for example, your swap file should be 32MB. In that way, Linux can run in 64MB of virtual memory. On the other hand, having more swap space allows more programs to run simultaneously or larger programs to run with more data. Linux allows each swap partition to be up to 127MB, with up to 16 swap partitions for Intel systems.

✓ A **/home** partition, where the users' home directories go. Its size is influenced by how many users you have planned for the system.

✓ A **/usr/local** partition, for storing programs you want to separate from the rest of the Red Hat Linux software. It is a good idea to keep such software separate because when you re-install the operating system you can leave this partition untouched.

Therefore, you don't have to re-install the applications.

✓ A **/usr** partition, where most of the software on the Linux system resides. It should be about 150MB to 350MB, depending on what packages you're installing.

The following partitions are optional:

✓ The **/opt** partition. This is for optional applications and other software. Many software vendors automatically install to this directory. It is a good idea to keep such software separate because when re-install the operating system you can leave this partition untouched. Therefore, you don't have to re-install the applications.

✓ A **/tmp** partition, an additional partition for temporary files in larger multi-user systems and network file servers.

✓ A **/usr/src** partition, which contains much of the Linux source code.

The problem with this type of setup is that you have a lot of separate partitions that can't share their space. If you need a little more space in your /tmp partition, for example, and your /home partition is almost empty, Linux can't easily utilize the space in /home for /tmp usage. This limitation is particularly true of smaller systems that have fewer disks and less disk space.

A happy medium that we often use is to create a root partition that includes /usr, /tmp, /usr/src, and /usr/local, another partition for swap space, and another partition for /home. On larger systems with more disks, we usually create more separate partitions. The preceding list shows the order that we sometimes use when creating separate partitions, in priority from top to bottom, stopping when we feel that the disk space is becoming too fragmented.

(continued)

(continued)

Some PC BIOSs have rules about where you can install the root partition. You must consider the following if you'll be installing the root partition on your hard drive:

- ✔ **If you have two IDE (EIDE) drives:** The root partition must be on one of them. If the hard drive and the CD-ROM drive are on the primary controller, the root partition must be on that hard drive.

- ✔ **If you have one IDE drive and any SCSI drives:** The root partition must be either on the IDE drive or on the SCSI drive that is ID 0. Other SCSI IDs won't work.

- ✔ **If you have no IDE drives but do have SCSI drives:** The root partition must be on either ID 0 or ID 1; no other SCSI ID will work.

- ✔ **If your Linux kernel must live below cylinder 1023:** This requirement is because the BIOS can't see things far out on the disk, beyond the 1023rd cylinder. The major

booting process for Linux, called LILO, depends on the BIOS for some of its functions; if the Linux kernel is beyond cylinder 1023, LILO can't find it and start the booting process.

On IDE drives, cylinder number 1023 is generally below the 512MB mark; for SCSI drives, it's usually below the 1GB level. If you're using smaller disks, you're probably okay. Otherwise, you probably need to take this issue into account when you install the system. The easiest way to ensure that the kernel is located on cylinders 0 through 1022 is to make your entire root partition below the 1023rd cylinder level; you can specify this with the fdisk program when you get to disk partitioning. Newer versions of BIOS support Logical Block Addressing (LBA), so they may not have this limitation. By using LBA, you can fool the BIOS into seeing the disk as having less than 1023 cylinders.

Finding out all about files

Linux, like UNIX, refers to everything as a *file*. In other words, the name for a device such as a hard drive is the *file address* of its driver. For example, /dev/hda is the name of the first IDE hard drive, and /dev/sdb is the name of the second SCSI hard drive.

Linux refers to disks and disk partitions by using a system of letters and numbers, which may seem confusing to the DOS or Windows user. Following is a short description of the naming conventions for hard drives and partitions.

Letters refer to the devices on which the partitions are located. IDE hard drives, for example, are named *hda, hdb, hdc,* and so on. SCSI drives

are referred to as *sda, sdb, sdc,* and so on. (The *hd* stands for hard drive, and the *sd* stands for SCSI drive.)

Numbers designate the partitions. Linux supports only four partitions, but one may be an extended partition, that is, subdivided into more *logical* partitions. The numbers 1, 2, 3, and 4 denote primary partitions; the logical partitions start at 5. For example, /dev/hdb3 is the name for the third primary partition on the second IDE hard drive. In a SCSI world, /dev/sdc6 is the name for the second logical partition on the third SCSI hard drive.

Living La Vida LILO

When you reboot your new Linux computer in Chapter 6, it needs to know where to find Linux on the hard disk. If you are using the multiple boot method and want to also have an operating system like Windows on the same disk with Linux, then your computer needs to know where both systems are. The system that performs that function is called Linux Loader, or LILO, which is detailed in the following steps:

1. **In the LILO Configuration dialog box, tab down to the Ok button and press Enter.**

   This dialog box is important only if you're using SCSI drives. It is beyond the scope of this book to describe such installations. If you need to do so, please consult the documentation from your SCSI manufacturer and enter any appropriate parameters.

2. **In the LILO Bootable Partitions dialog box, tab down to the Ok button and press Enter.**

   You can edit the label that LILO uses for each bootable partition. The default label for a Linux partition is, you guessed it, *linux*. The default for a Windows or DOS partition is *dos*. Figure 5-4 shows a typical Linux computer with multiple partitions; Linux is selected as the default.

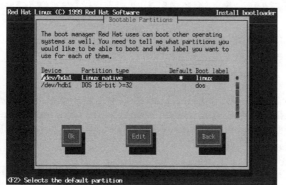

Figure 5-4:
The LILO
Bootable
Partitions
dialog box.

Getting loaded

Linux has a bootstrap loader called *LILO* (for Linux loader) that enables you to boot your Linux system. The installation program configures and installs LILO for you.

You can configure LILO to boot most operating systems on your disks. LILO can also be configured to wait a specified time and then boot a default operating system, if a specific operating system is not specified.

When you start to boot your system, the LILO prompt appears as follows:

```
LILO boot:
```

When you see the preceding prompt at boot time, do the following:

1. **Press the Tab key.**

   The system displays all the names for booting various operating systems or versions of operating systems. For instance, if you have installed only Linux, then you see:

   ```
   LILO boot: linux
   ```

   If you have installed Linux along with Windows, you see something like:

   ```
   LILO boot: linux dos
   ```

2. **Type the name you want and then press Enter.**

   The chosen operating system boots. Whenever you boot, LILO prompts for the operating system name again.

Configuring Your System for Networking

The Network Configuration dialog box appears next. If you want your machine to be a stand-alone workstation, select No, press the Enter key, and go on to the next section.

Otherwise, if your system is connected to a network, select Yes and press the Enter key. The next two dialog boxes help you configure your system for a network. This is where you use some of the information that we ask you to gather in Chapter 3.

As you fill in the dialog boxes, you may find that Linux guesses what information is needed and fills in some sections automatically. If Linux has guessed incorrectly, simply change the information.

Follow these steps to configure your system for a network:

1. **In the Hostname Configuration dialog box, enter the name of your Linux computer.**

   For instance, enter the name **shamet** at the prompt, select the Ok button, and press Enter. If things go wrong, you can always say "oh SHAMET!"

   Tab to the Ok button and press Enter.

2. **In the Load Module dialog box, select the type of Ethernet adapter that you have.**

   You are given a list of Ethernet adapters to choose from. You must select the manufacturer and model of your adapter. Note that Ethernet adapters are often referred to as network interface connectors (NIC).

3. **Configure your Ethernet adapter.**

   Red Hat can attempt to find the configuration information about your adapter. If you select the Autoprobe option and your Ethernet adapter is less than a few years old, then Red Hat most likely will detect the information. Otherwise, use the Specify Options and enter the information yourself.

4. **Choose whether to enter your IP address manually or to have a BOOTP or a DHCP server hand you a dynamic IP.**

   The latter two options — BOOTP and DHCP — are not frequently used in home or small networks. This book uses, and you should select, the Static IP address option.

5. **Enter your IP Address, Netmask, Default Gateway (IP), and Primary Nameserver.**

   The following list gives a brief description of the four parameters. But describing the Internet Protocol (IP) is beyond the scope of this book. Please consult the various networking HOWTOs on the accompanying CD-ROM.

   - **IP address.** This is the numeric network address of your Linux computer and is what your computer is known as on your local network and — in many cases — the Internet. If you haven't registered your private network's (also known as local networks or LANs) address space with the InterNIC (the organization that is in charge of distributing IP addresses), then you can use the public address space that goes from 192.168.1.1 to 192.168.254.254.

   - **Netmask.** Private networks based on the Internet Protocol (IP) are divided into subnetworks. The netmask determines how the network is divided. For addresses such as the one in the preceding bullet (192.168.1.1, and so on), the most common netmask is 255.255.255.0.

   - **Default gateway (IP).** This is the numeric IP address of the computer that connects your private network to the Internet (or another private network). Red Hat guesses the address of 192.168.1.254, for example, if you choose an address of 192.168.1.{1-254} for the IP address. You can accept this address, but leaving it blank is a better option, unless that address is your actual gateway. Chapter 15 describes how to configure your Linux computer to connect to the Internet via a telephone connection. If you do that, then setting a default route now can interfere with your connection.

- **Primary namesever.** The Internet Protocol uses a system called Domain Name Service (DNS) to convert names such as www.redhat.com into numeric IPs. A computer that acts as a DNS is called a namesever. Red Hat again makes a guess based on the IP address and netmask that you use. However, we suggest leaving this box blank, unless you are on a private network with a nameserver or will be connected to the Internet (your ISP will supply a DNS). When you designate a nonexistent nameserver, then many networking programs work very slowly as they wait in vain for the absent server.

Figure 5-5 shows the first networking box filled in with typical values for a simple private network.

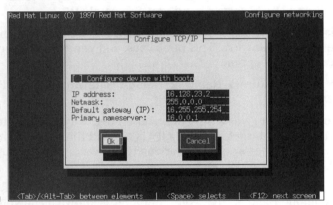

Figure 5-5:
The first networking dialog box completed.

6. **When you finish with this dialog box, select the Ok button and press Enter.**

The Configure Network dialog box appears.

7. **Enter the information for your computer. A completed screen is shown in Figure 5-6.**

The Configure Network dialog box wants information about the following items:

- **Domain name.** A domain name is, as you may guess, the name that your network is known as. It's like a nickname. For instance, redhat.com is the domain name of the Red Hat people.

- **Host name.** This is the name of your computer with the domain name added. For instance, if your domain name is shamet.com, then your host name can be paunchy.shamet.com.

- **Secondary and Tertiary nameservers (IPs).** These are the IP addresses of the second and third DNS servers that your computer will use. They are generally the addresses of your ISP nameservers.

8. **When you finish filling in this dialog box, select the Ok button and press Enter.**

Figure 5-6:
The second
networking
dialog box is
filled in.

Taking a Break

It's time to take a break now. Get another cup of java and put your feet up. You've just completed the hardest part of the installation. The next chapter describes how to finish up the process.

Chapter 6

Installation: Crossing the Finish Line

*A*fter you've finished installing the Red Hat Linux software components (see Chapter 5 if you haven't done this yet), you're ready to finish the installation process. This chapter describes how to complete the configuration process. So fill up your glass again and fortify yourself for the final sprint. You're in the home stretch, about to cross the finish line.

Completing Configuration

It's back to the drawing board. Now you're at the point where you need to select your mouse type, choose your time zone, establish a password, and add a friend or two to view your valuable information. Follow these steps to finish configuring your system:

1. **In the Mouse Selection dialog box, select your mouse type. Then select Ok and press Enter.**

   If you have a two-button mouse, then you can select the Emulate 3 Buttons option. With this option, you can press both mouse buttons to simulate the third — middle — button.

If the Red Hat installation process does not find a PS/2 mouse, the Device dialog box appears.

2. If the Device dialog box appears, select the serial port that your mouse is attached to.

PCs can have up to four serial ports. The port names — ttyS0, ttyS1, ttyS2, and ttyS3 — correspond to DOS/Windows COM1, COM2, COM3, and COM4. If you don't know which port your mouse is connected to, make your best guess (a mouse is usually connected to ttyS0 or ttyS1) and use the mouseconfig program to reconfigure after the installation is complete. At that time, you simply eliminate each port until you zero in on the correct one.

If you do not know which port it is attached to, you can also refer to Chapter 3 for more information.

3. In the Time Zone Selection dialog box (shown in Figure 6-1), select your time zone, tab to the Ok button, and press Enter.

Need to change the time after your setup is complete? You can change your system's clock setting any time by using the `/usr/sbin/timeconfig` command.

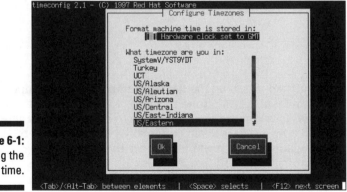

Figure 6-1:
Setting the
system time.

4. In the Root Password dialog box (shown in Figure 6-2), enter a password to use for logging into your Linux system for the first time. Type your password again and then select Ok.

The password is for the *root user,* also known as the *superuser,* who has access to the entire system.

We suggest that you log in as the root user only to do system maintenance or administrative tasks. The root user is the only user with access to critical system files. To avoid making unwanted changes or deletions, add another user for yourself.

Your password must be at least six characters long, but using eight is better. We recommend that you use a combination of uppercase and lowercase letters as well as numbers to make the password as difficult to compromise as possible. In addition, do not choose names or items that are easy to associate with you. In other words, your name, your dog's name, qwerty, 123456, passwd, and the like are poor choices. Beer, for example, is a poor selection for Jon's password, even though it has both uppercase and lowercase letters, if people easily associate him with that word. Enter a password and then be sure to write it down where it won't get lost. Don't write it on a sticky note attached to your monitor, please.

You have to enter the password two times to make sure that you typed it correctly. The password doesn't appear on the screen as you type it. Holy breach of security, Batman! You wouldn't want someone to be able to look over your shoulder and get your password, now would you?

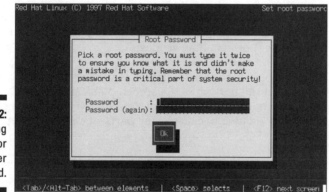

Figure 6-2:
Inputting
your root, or
superuser
password.

5. **In the Add User dialog box, enter the account name and password that you want to use for yourself.**

   For instance, if you're Joe Sixpack, then you can enter a Linux user name like *j6pack* in the User ID box. You can optionally enter your full name in the (guess what?) Full Name box. Finally, you must enter your password twice, just like for root. Using a good password as you did for root is just as important. You don't want Joe Blow to be able to look at your valuable information.

6. **In the User Account Setup dialog box, enter any or all of the people you want to be able to log in to your Linux computer.**

   Your new user name is displayed. This screen allows you to add, delete, and edit new or old users. Don't worry about getting everyone added at this point because you can do so at any time after you've installed Linux.

7. **In the Authentication Configuration dialog box, leave the defaults as they are and select Ok.**

Red Hat gives you the option of using systems like the Network Information System (NIS) and shadow passwords. NIS provides such systems for sharing a single password file among multiple computers. *Shadow passwords* extract the encrypted passwords out of the /etc/passwd file and place them in a separate /etc/shadow file. Shadow passwords increase the security of Linux systems, and NIS makes working and managing networks easier.

The discussion of NIS is beyond the scope of this book. Using shadow passwords is a good idea and doesn't cost you anything.

Installing Red Hat Linux Software

The programs and files of Linux are installed as *RPM packages,* which are described in Chapter 13. Several of these individual packages may be lumped together into functional *groups.* For instance, many of the networking oriented packages make up the Networked Workstation group. The installation program gives you two choices: installing individual packages (perhaps saving some disk space) or installing groups.

Unless you'll be using Linux for a specific job, leave the Select Individual Packages check box at the bottom of the screen blank (that is, with no asterisk in it). Unless you know exactly what you're doing, trying to select individual packages isn't a good idea because some parts of a package depend on others being there.

Red Hat Software, which created the distribution, preselects certain components. Leaving them selected is usually a good idea, unless you specifically know you won't be using them.

Follow these steps to install the Red Hat Linux software:

1. **In the Package Group Selection dialog box, select all the groups and components to install. Then select the Ok button and press Enter.**

   The menu in this dialog box allows you to select or deselect individual groups and/or packages. You can safely tab down to the Ok button and press Enter to continue with the installation.

   If you feel lucky, use the arrow keys to maneuver through the list of groups to install. A group is selected when an asterisk appears next to it. To make the asterisk appear or disappear, press the spacebar while the selection is highlighted. (The spacebar acts as a *toggle,* adding or deleting the asterisk.)

   If you have plenty of room on your drive, you may want to scroll to the bottom of the list and select the Everything option; this option installs all the packages included on CD1.

2. **In the Install Log dialog box, select Ok.**

   The installation process begins for real.

   If you selected a component that needs another component that was not selected for installation, the system displays the Package Dependencies dialog box, which shows the *dependency* and allows you to go back and select the necessary component.

3. **If the Package Dependencies dialog box opens, go back and select the necessary component to install.**

   After you resolve any dependency problems, the installation program begins installing the packages and lists them in /tmp/install.log on your system. The Install Status dialog box appears, listing each package being installed, along with a brief description of the contents and the estimated time to complete the installation. The installation time varies from minutes to hours. On Paul's system, loading all the packages took just under 16 minutes. Your mileage may vary, so remember to fill up your glass with your favorite beverage.

   Eventually, depending on your computer hardware, either the Probing Result or Configure Mouse dialog box appears. This means that all your components were installed, and the configuration phase of the Red Hat installation process has begun. Congratulations!

4. **Select a video card. Then select the Ok button and press Enter.**

   Red Hat provides a long list of video cards, as shown in Figure 6-3. Use the arrow keys to move through the list. If you don't see your video card but you see a previous model by the same manufacturer, then select that. After you select the video card, Red Hat installs the RPM video driver package from the CD-ROM (CD1).

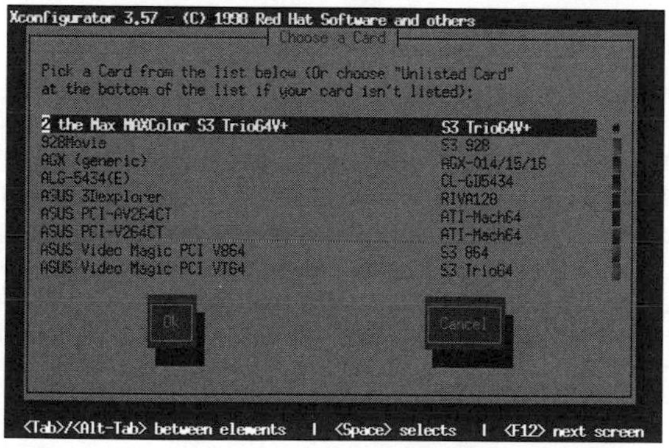

Figure 6-3:
Choosing
your video
card.

If you don't see a video card that matches your equipment, then you have two choices. You can choose (1) the Unlisted Card, which is the very last option in the menu, or (2) the Generic VGA option. Both options are described in Appendix B.

The Monitor Setup dialog box appears with a list of monitors to select from.

5. **In the Bootdisk dialog box, create a boot disk.**

Creating a boot disk is a good idea, just in case something happens to the boot partition on your disk. Microsoft products, for instance, have a bad habit of overwriting the Master Boot Record (MBR) — and therefore your Linux booting system — when they are installed or even updated.

We recommend that you get a blank, formatted, labeled floppy disk ready to become a boot disk, select Yes, and then press the Enter key — you will be prompted at the end of the installation process to insert the floppy. If you think that nothing will ever happen to your MBR, select No, press Enter, and then listen while we tell you about a bridge we have for sale in New York City. . . .

The Red Hat installation process is ready to start writing software to your hard disk.

6. **In the Installation to Begin dialog box, select Ok to start the Red Hat Installation process or select Back to redo part or all of the previous steps.**

After you select Ok, your partitions are formatted, and then the Red Hat packages are written to those partitions. This process can take several minutes.

Configuring X

Phew. You're almost to the finish line. Really.

One of the last things that you need to do is install X Server so that you can use the X graphical user interface (GUI) to interact with Linux. Configuring an X Server means that you specify the video card and monitor for your system, including how much video memory it has, what speed it runs at, and a series of other options. Sometimes — particularly with newer systems and newer graphics cards — most of this information is provided automatically by the system.

In the Choose a Card dialog box, follow these steps to install the X Server:

1. Select a monitor that fits your own.

Figure 6-4 shows the beginning of the list. If your monitor is not included in the list, then you can select Custom, Generic Monitor, or Generic Multisync. In that case, see Chapter 7 for more instructions.

Older monitors can't handle resolution rates and scan frequencies higher than what they were designed for. A monitor designed for a 640 x 480 resolution (and a low scan frequency) can't display a 2,048 x 1,024 resolution (and a high scan frequency). More importantly, if you try to make the monitor display that high of a frequency, it may burst into flames. (Jon didn't believe this either until he saw a monitor smoking.) Modern monitors, called multisync, can automatically match themselves to a series of scan frequencies and resolutions. Some of these monitors are even smart enough to turn themselves off if the frequencies become too high, instead of bursting into flames. Finding the documentation and matching your vertical and horizontal frequencies properly is the best way to go (particularly with older monitors). Lacking this information, try a lower resolution (VGA or SVGA) first, just to get X running.

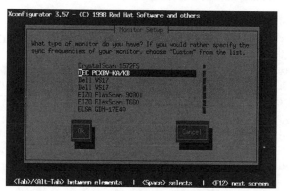

Figure 6-4:
Choosing
your monitor
type.

2. In the Screen Configuration dialog box, specify whether you want to probe to find out the configuration of your video card.

To probe or not to probe? Probing tries to determine the configuration of your video card. If the probe is successful, then you don't have to make any guesses about your hardware.

Some computers can *hang up* — that is, stop responding to your keyboard — as the result of probing. If that happens, you must restart the installation process.

If you decide not to probe, then the next screen asks you to specify the amount of video memory that you have.

3. **Specify the amount of memory on your video card. After you select the memory amount, select Ok and then press Enter.**

   Note that this memory is different than the amount of main memory. Most modern cards have 1, 2, 4, or 8MB of video memory. Use your arrow keys to move down the list.

   If you don't know how much video memory your card has, try 1MB (the 1 Meg option). Although this setting limits the resolution of your screen, you will probably be able to get X going. Later, you can experiment with the Xconfigurator program (described in Chapter 7) to figure out the best values for how much video memory you have, if the probe did not work properly.

4. **Specify your video clockchip.**

   This specification is a vestige of older systems and older video boards. We recommend that you select the No Clockchip Setting option. After you make your selection, use the Tab key to select the Ok button and then press Enter.

   Note that this dialog box doesn't appear if the probe was successful.

5. **Select the video mode that you want to use.**

   You are asked to select the combination of screen resolution and the number of colors, as shown in Figure 6-5. You need to make the choice because the memory in your video card must be used for both purposes. The fewer color bits that you use mean the fewer shades of color that your display will use. The higher resolutions pack more detail onto your screen.

   Make a reasonable choice. If you're already running Windows on your system, you can look at the Display dialog box in the Control Panel to see how it's set up and then use that configuration as your starting point for Linux.

Figure 6-5:
Selecting
the
resolutions
and color
depths.

6. **In the Starting X dialog box, select Ok.**

   Red Hat now tests your new X configuration.

If you configured X correctly, this message appears: Can you see this message?. You have 10 seconds to either select Yes button or press the Enter key.

7. **If you want to start X automatically at boot time, choose Yes. Otherwise, choose No.**

   You have the option of starting X every time you boot or reboot your computer. This book assumes that you choose that option, and X is the default environment used in all further discussions.

   If you choose No, then your system will start up in character-cell or text mode. You can always manually start X with the startx command or modify the /etc/inittab to automatically start X. The line id:3:initdefault should be changed to id:5:initdefault in the inittab file to do that.

   After you make your choice, an informational screen appears, telling you where the configuration file can be found. It also points you to the X README.Config file for more information.

   If you have a problem with your X configuration, then you are regretfully informed about the situation. You have the option of quitting or going back and starting over. If you're game, go back and try, try again.

If, for some reason, you can't get X working at this point, you can always try finishing the configuration of X later by running the Xconfigurator program (see Chapter 7).

Setting Up Services for Linux

Now you're ready to set up services that should be started automatically for Linux when it starts to boot. At this point, the Services dialog box appears, similar to the one shown in Figure 6-6. This dialog box enables you to specify whether things such as the automounter daemon or the bootparam daemon should be started.

Figure 6-6:
Setting up the boot-time services for Linux.

Don't know what these things are? That's okay for now, because the creators of the distribution have put their best feet forward and given you a good set of defaults. Accept the defaults for now by selecting the Ok button. You can figure out what you really want after you become more familiar with Linux.

Installing a Printer

The next dialog box, Select Printer Connection, asks whether you want to install a printer, as shown in Figure 6-7. You can install a *local printer* (one attached to your machine), a *remote printer* (one attached to another machine), or a printer managed by LAN Manager software. The steps for connecting a *local* printer are as follows:

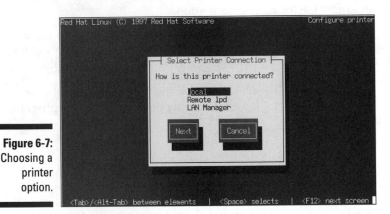

Figure 6-7:
Choosing a
printer
option.

1. **Select the type of printer connection and then select Next.**

   For example, select the Local option. The Standard Printer Options dialog box appears, as shown in Figure 6-8.

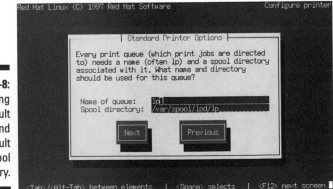

Figure 6-8:
Choosing
the default
queue and
default
spool
directory.

2. Enter the name of the print queue and the spooling directory.

If you have only one printer, you can choose the default name and default directory offered, as shown in Figure 6-8. The name of the printer's print queue would then be lp, and the print command will use the /var/spool/lpd/lp print queue directory by default. See the "Getting in the print queue" sidebar for all the exciting details.

If this is a second or third printer, you can name the printer's print queue lp2 or lp3, respectively, and then (for consistency) name the print queue /var/spool/lpd/lp2 or /var/spool/lpd/lp3. Note that the designations lp2 and lp3 are arbitrary; you can call them anything else you want, as long as the names are unique.

3. Select the Next button and then press Enter.

The Local Printer Device dialog box appears.

4. Enter information about your printer port, if necessary. Press the Tab key to select the Next button and press Enter.

If your printer is connected to the system and turned on, Linux may be able to detect which port the printer is connected to — especially if the printer is connected to the parallel port, as shown in Figure 6-9. If Linux doesn't detect the port, you have to enter the correct information. If your printer is connected to LPT1:, type **/dev/lp0** as the printer device. For a printer connected to LPT2:, enter **/dev/lp1** as the printer device.

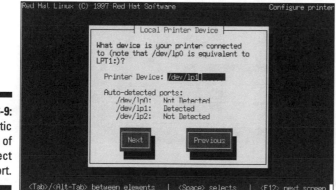

Figure 6-9:
Automatic detection of the correct printer port.

5. In the Configure Printer dialog box, select the printer type and then select the Next button.

If you don't find your printer in the list shown in Figure 6-10, consult your printer documentation to see whether your printer is compatible with one of the printers in the list. If so, choose that printer instead.

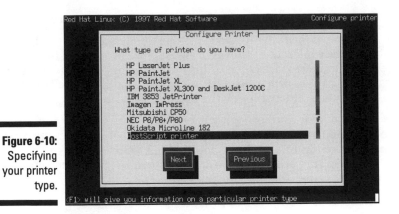

Figure 6-10:
Specifying
your printer
type.

6. **If you're asked to provide more information, do so and then select Next.**

   Like a good user, always do what your system asks. You may be asked for some specific information about the printer. If so, a dialog box like the one shown in Figure 6-11 pops up.

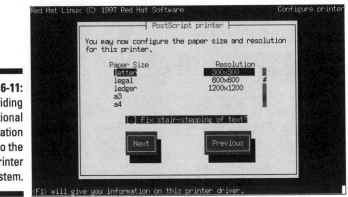

Figure 6-11:
Providing
additional
information
to the
printer
subsystem.

7. **Check the information about your printer and make any necessary changes.**

   The installation program displays the information for your printer, as shown in Figure 6-12. Now is your chance to change anything (by using the Edit button).

8. **When you're finished, select the Done button.**

   Linux asks whether you have any additional printers to add.

9. **If you have additional printers to add, go back to Step 1 and follow the steps again. Otherwise, move on to the next section.**

Getting in the print queue

When you print a file, it doesn't go directly to the printer. Instead, it goes to an area called a *print queue.* The printer then prints the files waiting in the queue, in the order in which they arrived at the queue. In this way, one program doesn't have to wait for the printer to stop printing before giving the command to print a file. In addition, the queue allows multiple programs to print to the same printer at the same time, without having to wait for the physical printer to become idle.

Each printer in your system needs a queue name and a place to put the queue. This place is called the *spool directory.* You enter this information in the dialog box shown in Figure 6-9.

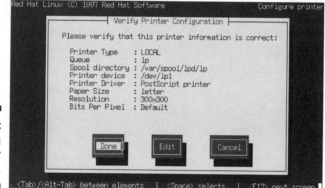

Figure 6-12:
Verifying
your printer
information.

You're Done!

Tada! You're finished with the installation. Not surpassingly, the Done dialog box appears.

Follow these steps to start your system:

1. **All that's left to do is select Ok.**

   Before the system reboots, remove the CD and the floppy disk. Otherwise, you'll be faced with going through the entire installation process again. There's no need to groan — you can always re-reboot and then remove the pesky critters.

   Your system reboots, and you can start Linux.

2. **When you see the** LILO boot: **prompt, press the Tab key.**

You see a list of operating system names that you chose to represent your different systems to LILO. Type the name that represents Linux and then press Enter. Watch the next glorious event: Your Linux system boots! Pass out the champagne!

3. **After the startup messages stop and the X** login: **prompt appears, type** root **and then press Enter. Then enter the root password.**

You are now logged in as superuser, also known as root.

If you did not give your a computer a name and domain name during the network configuration process, then it is referred to as localhost.localdomain. Otherwise, the welcome screen refers to whatever name you gave it, for instance, Welcome to shamet.paunchy.net.

This installation may or may not have seemed like the most odious task since digging the Panama Canal, but you have finished it. Congratulations! You've done more at this point than most people have with their computer systems, and now you're ready to move forward with Linux by using it as a tool.

Chapter 7

Configuring and Fixing X

. . . .

In This Chapter

▶ Uncovering details about your video controller, monitor, and mouse

▶ Sleuthing with SuperProbe

▶ Configuring X

▶ Finding some help if X still doesn't work

▶ Paying attention to shutting-down etiquette

. . . .

Did you receive an error message during the installation, informing you that X was not installed properly and that you had to install it later? Or was your video card or monitor not included in the supported hardware (see Chapter 6)? If so, this chapter is for you. Take solace in the fact that X is one of the trickiest parts of the Linux system to get working properly.

Discovering Your Hardware's True Identity

Before you start X, you need to find out information about your video controller card, monitor, mouse, and keyboard.

For your video controller card, you need to find out:

✔ The model number (and perhaps the video chip used)

✔ The amount of video RAM it has

You should be able to find this information in your system's documentation or by using MS-DOS or Windows, as described in Chapter 3. But now that you have Linux up and running, the next best method for finding that missing information is to run the SuperProbe program, which comes with most versions of Linux. We describe how to run SuperProbe in the next section.

Then, you need to know the following about your mouse:

- The model number and manufacturer
- Whether it is a PS/2 bus mouse or a serial mouse

Again, your system's documentation should tell you, and often the bottom of the mouse offers some basic information.

A PS/2 mouse usually has a round connector on the end of its wire, or tail. A serial mouse has an oblong connector with nine holes. All varieties of PS/2 bus mice look the same to Linux. Different serial mice, however, have different characteristics. If you have a serial mouse, you need to know its model number and manufacturer, or whether it emulates some other well-known mouse.

Three-button mice work best with Linux, but you can get by with a two-button mouse. To X, holding down both buttons at the same time on a two-button mouse is equivalent to holding down the middle button of a three-button mouse, but only if the system is configured correctly. You can find out how to configure the mouse in Chapter 6.

Finally, you need to know about your monitor. Most monitor manuals have a table at the back with such information as:

- Horizontal sync range
- Vertical sync range
- Resolution
- Whether it is *multisync,* which means your monitor can run at several resolution rates

Older monitors, particularly VGA monitors that came with older systems, often aren't multisync. These monitors can be damaged if you try to use them at a higher resolution than VGA, which is 640 x 480.

Horizontal and vertical sync range numbers help X determine how to place the dots on the screen. The resolution number tells X how many dots can be on the screen horizontally and vertically. The 640 x 480 resolution is usually considered to be the worst, and 1,280 x 1,024 is usually considered to be the best for normal use. Strive for 800 x 600 resolution as a minimum and 1,024 x 768 as an ideal for most systems.

Higher video resolution uses more video memory (which is on the video card and therefore separate from the system memory), allows fewer simultaneous colors on the screen (for a given amount of video memory), and typically shrinks text on the screen, making it harder to see. On the other hand, using a higher resolution means that more information can be visible on the screen at one time for the same size monitor (even though the writing may be so small that you can't read it without getting new glasses). Some video cards can be upgraded to add more video memory, and some cannot.

Most newer monitors have built-in protection mechanisms to keep them from burning up in what is known as *overdriving*, but older monitors do not. Older monitors can literally catch on fire. Try to find the specifications for your monitor from the manual, from a dealer, or from the manufacturer's Web page.

If you hear noise from your monitor or smell burning components, turn off your computer immediately. If you think that the screen doesn't look right, press Ctrl+Alt+Backspace right away to stop X Server and then try a lower resolution. Otherwise, you can easily damage the monitor.

Running SuperProbe

In this section, we assume that you've booted your system and that it's in command-line mode (not a bad assumption if you're having problems running X). You may or may not have all the information needed to configure X. A final chance to gather information is to run the SuperProbe program, which is included on the accompanying CD-ROM (CD1).

You may be asking yourself, why didn't you have me run SuperProbe right off the bat? Well, SuperProbe is a great program, but it's not perfect. It may *hang* your system (make it unresponsive), forcing you to reboot. It may not give you all the information you need. It can even be fooled from time to time. Despite its drawbacks, SuperProbe is a good tool.

To run SuperProbe, follow these steps:

1. **Log in as** root.

2. **Change the directory to /usr/bin/X11 by typing** cd /usr/bin/X11.

3. **Execute the SuperProbe program in that directory by typing the following:**

```
[root@shamet X11]# ./SuperProbe
```

A lot of information spews from the program, followed by this rather frightening message:

```
WARNING - THIS SOFTWARE COULD HANG YOUR MACHINE.
    READ THE SuperProbe.1 MANUAL PAGE BEFORE
    RUNNING THIS PROGRAM.
    INTERRUPT WITHIN FIVE SECONDS TO ABORT!
```

Although SuperProbe can hang your machine, most of the time it doesn't. And even if it does, simply press the reset button on your machine or turn the power off and reboot.

If SuperProbe does its job and does not hang your machine, it may come back with information like the following:

```
First video: Super-VGA
Chipset: S3 86C928PCI (PCI Probed)
Memory: 2048 Kbytes
RAMDAC: AT&T 20C491 15/16/24-bit DAC with gamma correction
      (with 6-bit wide lookup tables (or in 6-bit mode))
      (programmable for 6/8-bit wide lookup tables)
```

Awesome. This information tells you that your video board is made up of an S3 chip set (a lot of them are), is model number 86C928, and fits into the PCI bus. It has 2048K (2MB) of video memory and uses a RAMDAC made by AT&T. This last piece of information is not that helpful when used with the rest of the configuration programs, but write it down anyway. As you use this information about chips, be aware that sometimes the chips are known by nicknames. For example, the S3 86C928 may show up in the configuration programs as S3 928.

Running Xconfiguration

After you find out all about your video hardware, you're ready to start configuring X. We assume that you don't have X up and running. If it is up and running, you can skip the rest of this chapter.

The next step is to use a program called Xconfigurator. This program asks you a series of questions, such as the type of mouse, the type of graphics card, and the amount of video memory in your system. As you supply the answers, Xconfigurator builds a file that X Server uses later to communicate with your mouse, the video card, and the rest of the system. (Xconfigurator is the same program that the Red Hat installation system uses.)

Xconfigurator also tries to obtain information by probing the hardware. Sometimes the program is accurate, but it can make a mistake, particularly in older PCs, or with older video cards, or with serial mice. Therefore, you may have to supply information to the program. As Linux becomes more sophisticated in the methods that it uses to probe hardware, and as hardware becomes more sophisticated in the information it can return to the operating system, fewer questions need to be asked. For now, though, you have Xconfigurator.

To run the Xconfigurator program, follow these steps:

1. **Log in as** root **and type the following:**

   ```
   [root@shamet /root]# Xconfigurator
   ```

2. **After an information screen appears, select the Ok button to continue.**

3. **In the Choose a Card dialog box, select your graphics controller and then select Ok.**

   The list in this dialog box contains all the video cards that Red Hat knows about. The beginning of the list is shown in Figure 7-1.

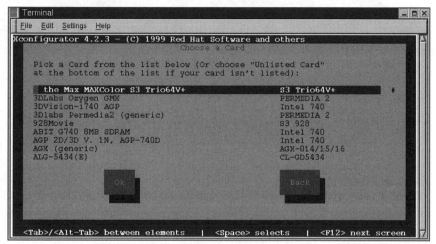

Figure 7-1:
Selecting
your
graphics
controller.

Use the arrow keys to maneuver through the list. If you can't find a match, try the Unlisted Card option, which is the last item in the list.

If you select the Unlisted Card option, VGA16 or SVGA is a good guess for most cards. Using these options won't run your video adapter at its maximum capacity, but at least it'll work.

You may not see the dialog box shown in Figure 7-1. If you have a PCI-based video card, it's intelligent enough to give a lot of information to the program, so you'll be told that your video card was found. All you need to do is select Ok to accept the information.

After you make your video card selection, the Monitor Setup dialog box, shown in Figure 7-2, appears.

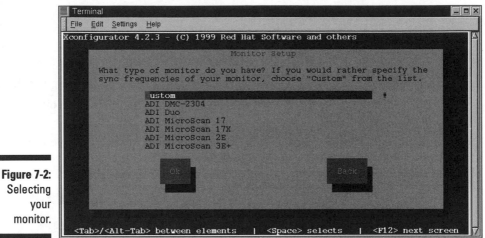

Figure 7-2:
Selecting
your
monitor.

4. **Select your monitor from the list and then select Ok.**

   After you select your monitor, the Monitor Setup dialog box appears. (The following instructions describe how to manually configure a Custom monitor).

   If your monitor model isn't listed, select Custom, or Generic Monitor, or Generic Multisync. Steps 4 through 6 describe how to configure a Custom monitor. The setups for the Generic and Multisync options are very similar to the Custom option, so use Steps 5 through 7 as a general guideline if you want to select those options.

   After completing this step, an informational screen appears.

5. **In the informational screen, select the Ok button.**

   Don't worry, you don't have to call any 1-800 numbers.

6. **In the Custom Monitor Setup dialog box, select a monitor setting.**

   The Custom Monitor Setup dialog box, shown in Figure 7-3, gives you four generic monitor options. The screen resolution and horizontal sync range are shown for each selection. Following are descriptions of each setting:

   • **Standard VGA.** This is the most basic resolution that you can use. It works in more circumstances than any other resolution. However, it is pretty lame for getting work done. If you have trouble with the higher resolutions, then try this one — if only to find a starting point for getting to a higher one. It's your safest bet.

   • **Super VGA.** This is an intermediate resolution. It has a high enough density to get a reasonable-looking screen that you can get work done on. It's also low enough to work on a large number of systems.

- **8514 Compatible.** This one is a leftover from ancient times. We don't ever run into these monitors, but they may still exist in some numbers. If you have one, then try it. Otherwise, don't bother with it.

- **Super VGA, 1024 x 768.** This is the highest resolution that you can get from the Custom setup. If your video card can handle it, then you'll pack a lot of information onto your screen. Otherwise, try a lower resolution. Standard VGA works in more situations than any of the others.

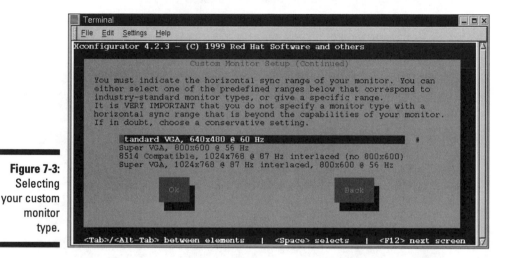

Figure 7-3:
Selecting
your custom
monitor
type.

7. **Enter the vertical sync rate.**

   This setting works in more situations than any of the others.

   If you want to use another setting, please look in the documentation for your monitor to get the correct number. You may also be able to find the number on the back of your monitor. If in doubt, select the lowest rating of 50–70.

8. **If any of the following bulleted statements are true, skip the probing and head to Step 10. Otherwise, select the Probe button and press Enter.**

   If you have a PCI-based video card, this probing has probably been completed. If you don't have a PCI-based video card and have supplied all the information correctly up to this point, the Xconfigurator program has enough information to try probing. You may not want to probe for several reasons:

   - You are unsure of the information you provided to Xconfigurator.
   - You know all the information and want to supply it yourself.
   - SuperProbe (which does the probing) hangs your system.

Use your best judgment and remember that you can always re-run the Xconfiguration program as many times as you want.

9. **In the Probing to Begin dialog box, press Enter.**

   If the probe works, the Probing Finished dialog box appears.

10. **If the probing is successful, then you can select the Use Default option to go with the values that the probing found.**

    If you select the Let Me Choose button, control then passes to the Video Memory dialog box, as described in Step 11.

11. **If you decide not to probe, or if probing fails, then enter the amount of video memory your adapter has and then select Ok (see Figure 7-4).**

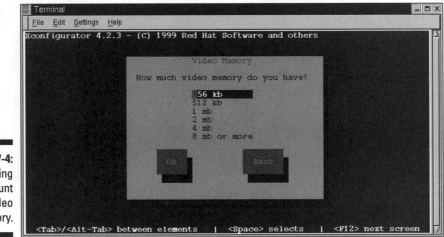

Figure 7-4: Entering the amount of video memory.

If you don't know the amount of video memory in your video card, enter less rather than more just to get X working. The less memory you tell X you have, however, the fewer colors you have available for any given screen resolution.

12. **If asked, tell the system which RAMDAC to use.**

    Most of the time, you don't need to specify any RAMDAC. Select the `No RAMDAC` setting.

13. **If the Clockchip Configuration dialog box appears, as shown in Figure 7-5, tell the system the clockchip setting.**

    This is another leftover from the early days of video cards. In most cases, selecting the No Clockchip Setting (recommended) option is best.

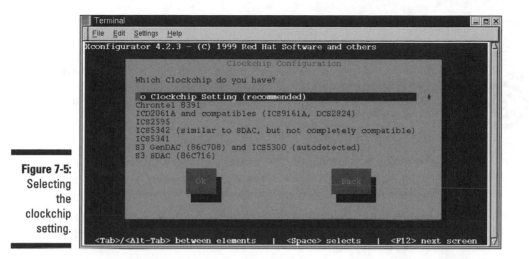

Figure 7-5:
Selecting
the
clockchip
setting.

14. In the Select Video Modes dialog box, select a screen resolution.

You have the choice of one or more screen resolutions with 8, 16, or 24 bits of color, as shown in Figure 7-6. The more bits you select, the more colors you can see. However, the number of colors takes up the memory on your video card. More memory is used as you go up in resolution, too.

The lowest (8 bit) allows only 256 colors on the screen at one time. The 16-bit *(high color)* option allows for 32,767 colors, and 24 bit *(true color)* allows for more than 16 million.

Figure 7-6:
Choosing
your monitor
resolution.

To select the different resolutions, use the Tab and arrow keys to move among the choices, and use the spacebar to select and deselect entries.

Select a reasonably high resolution/colors setting, and if it doesn't work, then back off to a lower setting until you find your maximum setting. (Alternatively, start low and work your way up.)

If you select more than one resolution at any one mode, you can switch between them after starting X Server by pressing Ctrl+Alt+Plus and Ctrl+Alt+Minus. If you have only one resolution at any one mode, pressing Ctrl+Alt+Plus does nothing.

15. In the Starting X dialog box, select Ok and then press Enter.

Xconfiguration needs to test its new configuration.

If your X Server has been configured correctly, then a graphical - X - window appears with a small dialog box that asks you if you can see it.

16. If you can see the graphical - X - window, then everything is cool, and you should select the Yes button. If you can't see it then you should select the No button.

You don't have to select a button that you can't see. If you don't respond to the question within 10 seconds, Xconfiguration assumes that you can't see it and answers no for you. In that case, you see a dialog box that indicates an error has occurred. You then have the chance to go back and reconfigure.

After completing this step, a dialog box without a title displays.

17. Select Yes if you want X to start automatically every time you start your computer.

Otherwise, your computer starts in text mode.

18. In the next dialog box that appears, press Enter.

That's it! You've just successfully configured X. You can press Ctrl+Alt+Backspace to stop X. If, during installation, you configured X to start at boot time, it will restart automatically. Otherwise, you can restart X manually by entering the following command:

```
[root@shamet /root]# startx
```

If you still have problems, then start the entire Xconfiguration system again. You should also consult the HOWTO documents in the /usr/doc/HOWTO/XFree86-HOWTO documents for more help.

Starting Your Engine

Now you're ready to try out X. If you're running in text mode, simply type the following:

```
[root@shamet X11]# startx
```

The screen goes black, flashes, displays a tweed pattern (probably with an *X* in the middle of the screen), and — if all goes well — displays some nice color or pattern and perhaps a small toolbar at the bottom of the screen.

Or maybe not. (Sigh.) If the screen reverts to a character-cell interface, you see all sorts of messages about what may have gone wrong. It may be that you specified the video card incorrectly or that you answered some other question incorrectly. If you run into trouble, you can do several things:

- ✔ Find out more detailed information about your video card by using DOS, Windows 95, or Windows 98, as described in Chapter 3.

- ✔ Find a newer version of XFree86 code at `www.xfree86.org`.

- ✔ Find a seasoned Linux guru to help you.

- ✔ Buy a solution.

- ✔ Take a cruise to Fiji, where at the University of the South Pacific they have a really good computer science department in which everyone uses Linux. (Hi folks!)

If you try these solutions and still don't have X running, look around for a Linux users' group at a local college or high school. Or perhaps a group of computer professionals in your area may help. If you call the local university's computer science department, the folks there can probably help you find a student or staff member who uses Linux, has installed it on several types of machines, and can help you either figure out why your graphics system is not working or get a newer version of XFree86 that may support your video card.

If you feel strange going to these people to ask them for help, remember that they were once new to Linux, too, and probably had to struggle through an even more difficult installation. When you do go, remember to take *all* the accumulated information about your system that you have detected. This preparation will save both you and them time and energy.

Finally, if your hardware is too new or proprietary, or if you have a notebook computer, you may want to buy a commercial X Server from Metrolink (`www.metrolink.com`) or Xi Graphics (`www.xigraphics.com`). Sometimes their codes work when XFree86 does not. Plus, if you buy an X Server, you can call the company's technical support line if you can't get it installed.

If you knew all the issues involved in working with PC video hardware, you'd think it's fantastic that the XFree86 developers can get it working at all (for more on XFree86, see the "Introducing the gods of X" sidebar. Even though XFree86 is freely distributable, you may want to make a donation to its development fund, at `www.XFree86.org`.

If your X Server is working and you want it to stop, press Ctrl+Alt+Backspace. You can then log off the root account. If you want to start X working again, log in to an account and type **startx**. X Server starts in a few moments.

Introducing the gods of X

Your X programs come from code that was contributed to the X Window System project, which was first connected with Project Athena at the Massachusetts Institute of Technology. Later, the project became the main focus of the X Window System Consortium, a nonprofit group established to develop the X Window System technology.

Because the source code was freely distributable, a group of programmers from all over the world formed to give support to X Window code on low-end PC systems. They called themselves XFree86 based on the fact that their code was free and directed toward PCs, which were largely based on Intel x86 compatible processors.

Over time, they ported their code to freely distributable operating systems on other architectures. They did this — and continue to do this —

for the love of programming. The XFree86 team of programmers tries to give support to new video controllers as they come out. Unfortunately, giving this support is often difficult for several reasons:

🖛 They have no relationship with the video controller manufacturer.

🖛 The video controller manufacturer thinks that keeping the programming interface secret gives it an edge against its competitors.

🖛 The video board is built into a larger system board.

🖛 The video controller is simply too new.

Until support is available, most people rely on SVGA compatibility mode to get the card to work.

Shutting Down the System

If you're accustomed to MS-DOS or Windows 3.1, having a section on shutting down the system may seem strange. After all, shouldn't you just turn off the power switch? No! Linux systems require a systematic process to shut down the operating system, after which you can turn off the power switch.

If you have just finished installing the system, you are logged in as a systems administrator called root. Follow these steps to shut down the system:

1. **If X is running, press Ctrl+Alt+Backspace to stop X.**

   The system returns to character-cell mode, and the # prompt appears. The # prompt tells you that you have the powers of the systems administrator (don't let it go to your head) and that you can shut down the operating system.

2. **Type** shutdown -h now **at the prompt.**

   This command tells Linux to halt the operating system now rather than later.

shutdown is a Linux command. Some commands have options, or flags, that provide additional information about what the command should do. -h means to halt the system after it shuts down, rather than reboot. -r means to start rebooting after shutdown. now means to start the process of shutting down immediately. Without the now, the shutdown command would hesitate and send warning messages to people still working on the system, telling them that the system is about to be turned off.

One other method of rebooting the system is the infamous three-finger salute that all Microsoft users know: Ctrl+Alt+Delete. The three-finger salute simply sends a shutdown -r now command to Linux, and the result is the same as if you had typed this command.

As a Linux user, rebooting the system should be an infrequent occurrence. Because the login procedure provides a Linux system with the necessary security, you don't need to shut it down between sessions. Linux is stable, so it does not freeze often, as do some other PC-based operating systems. If you have multiple operating systems on the same machine, however, rebooting takes you back to the LILO prompt (or the System Commander, or some other booting program) to allow you to boot another operating system.

Delving deep into color depth

Color depth — the number of colors your system can have active on the screen at any one time — is loosely a function of both the amount of video memory your system has and the screen resolution.

If your system has a small amount of memory (such as 1MB), your screen can have a resolution of 1,024 x 768 pixels (dots) with 256 colors (8 bits) on the screen at one time. If your system has 2MB, you can have 64K colors (16 bits) on the screen at the same time at the same resolution. If you have an older video board with a small amount of video memory but some additional video memory sockets, you may be able to upgrade the amount of video memory on the video card.

If you have only 1MB and want to see 64K colors on the screen at one time, you can reduce your resolution from 1,024 x 768 to 800 x 600 pixels. If you want true color (24 bits), you can set your resolution to 640 x 480 pixels. The picture that

you're viewing will take up more of the screen, but color depth versus resolution is a trade-off that you can make by choosing the right options.

When you want to display an image and the color depth is not correct, nothing drastic happens. The picture may look a little lackluster or not quite normal. X has an interesting capability to have virtual color maps, which allow the active window to utilize all the colors of the bits of color depth, even if other windows are using different colors. When this option is turned on (as it is with the Red Hat distribution on CD1), the various windows turn odd colors as your mouse moves from window to window, but the window that your mouse activates is shown in the best color available. With newer video cards and larger video memories, which allow for true color at high resolutions in every window, this option is less useful.

Part III
Just the Basics

The 5th Wave   By Rich Tennant

Brad was beginning to feel pressured to find a way his Linux users could talk over a peer-to-peer network.

In this part . . .

*H*ere you find out about the basics of running a Linux computer. This section starts your travels by describing Linux files. You then jet to the wonderful world of shells and shell scripts. You touch down briefly into the land of disk drives and upon returning home, you discover that Red Hat's RPM has changed the Linux world.

Chapter 8 starts you on your journey by describing the basic tasks that you must do to use Linux. You find yourself starting up the computer that Linux runs on; discovering the ins-and-outs of the "login" process; and finally, how to create Linux user accounts.

In Chapter 9, you take a journey through the Linux system, and meet file types, subdirectories, and the root user along the way. Then you use commands to navigate through the Linux file system, changing, moving, creating, and deleting files as you go.

Any far-flung traveler knows the necessity of a good interpreter. In Linux, you use a command interpreter, or shell. The shell is similar to the DOS prompt — with many differences of course. Chapter 10 introduces you to this foreign — to Windows/DOS users — world.

If you travel enough, you might want to learn a new language or two. Chapter 11 helps you stumble through the foreign tongue of shell — not sans — script. It's really an easy language and you'll recognize much of it with a little effort.

Finally, on your return home you'll be introduced to Red Hat's RPM. RPM has made life much easier when it comes to installing software. RPM is like a jet airliner versus an old propeller one. It makes life so much easier.

Chapter 8

Using Linux for the First Time

Congratulations! Linux is now on your system and eager to go, and we're sure you're anxious to start using it. But before you find out how to use Linux for work — or play — you have to make an *account* for yourself, which will be the place for you to log in and do whatever your heart desires.

Linux is a multiuser system (unlike Microsoft Windows 3.1, 95, 98, or NT), so you — and every other user — need an individual name and password to protect your information and keep your tasks separate from other people's tasks. You find out how to create user accounts in this chapter, too.

Names and passwords in Linux have one other advantage over those in Windows 3.1, 95, and 98 systems: Linux has a rich file permissions strategy that keeps either you and/or others from erasing and replacing system files. This feature is important in a network environment or just when a system is sitting idle at a desk.

Giving Linux the Boot

Are you ready to boot Linux? Follow these steps to start it up:

1. **Make sure that your computer is off.**

2. **Turn on all peripheral devices, such as printers and scanners.**

3. **Turn on the power to the monitor (if it's separate from the main system box).**

4. **Turn on the computer's main power switch.**

After a short time, `LILO boot:` appears on your screen.

5. **Press the Tab key to see all the operating systems that are available to boot.**

You may see something like the following, depending on what options you chose during installation:

```
LILO boot:
dos linux
boot:
```

6. **Type the name of one of the operating systems listed and then press Enter.**

That operating system boots.

If you do nothing — that is, you ignore our wonderful instructions — then the first operating system listed, which is known as the *default system,* boots after a short time.

In order for Linux to boot, one of the following must be true:

✔ Linux is the only operating system installed.

✔ Linux is the first operating system listed so that it boots as the default system.

✔ You're fast enough to type **linux** after the boot prompt. (You have five seconds to start typing in the name.)

Otherwise, you may have to wait for the other operating system to finish booting, shut it down, reboot, and make sure you're fast enough to type **linux** after the prompt.

As the Linux operating system boots, you see all sorts of messages scrolling by on the screen. After the scrolling stops, the last line should be

```
login:
```

Now you're ready to log in to the system and set up an account to use for your day-to-day work. See the following section for logging on and setting up an account.

If you choose to have X start automatically when you boot your system, then you see the graphical equivalent to the `login:` prompt.

Logging into Linux

When you use Linux, you must log in as a particular user with a distinct login name. Why? Linux is a multiuser system, and as such, it uses different accounts to keep people from looking at other people's secret files, erasing necessary files from the system, and otherwise doing bad things. The unique identity also helps to keep the actions of one person from affecting the actions of another, because many people may be using the same computer system.

For now, log in as root, which in Linux terms is a superuser. The *superuser* is a privileged account that enables a person to go anywhere and do anything on the system. Superusers can add drives, do backups, restore damaged files, and turn the system off and on. They can also damage the system if they make a mistake. Because superusers are all-powerful, their mistakes can be disastrous.

This is a good time to create another account for yourself that's non-privileged. That way, if you make a mistake while getting familiar with Linux — and who doesn't — the mishap is limited to the power of your account. You can accidentally erase your own files and data but not someone else's files or the system's files. Comforting, isn't it?

Before you can create that safe, new account for yourself, though, you need to log in as root. To do that, you need to enter the superuser password you typed during installation (refer to Chapter 5):

```
login: root
Password:
```

You don't see the password as you type it on the screen. This secrecy ensures that anyone watching over your shoulder won't see the password and try to log in later as root.

If you make a mistake while typing the password (or while typing the word **root**), the system responds with

```
Login incorrect
```

and gives you another chance by redisplaying the login: prompt. Type **root** and then type your password.

After logging in as `root`, the following appears on the screen:

```
[root@shamet /root]#
```

The # at the end of the line indicates that you're a superuser with extraordinary powers, so be careful.

We strongly recommend that you do most of your experimentation with Linux as a non-privileged user and switch to superuser only when you absolutely need to. You run the risk of corrupting your system and reinstalling over again or losing data if you operate as root.

Now you're ready to create that safe, non-privileged user account. If you have installed X, you can use the Red Hat graphical tools on CD1 to add a user account. If you haven't installed X, you can still add a user account by going to the "Creating a General Account without X" section later in this chapter.

Creating an Account with LinuxConf

Different Linux distributions give you various system administration tools in graphical format. Red Hat offers you the LinuxConf, as shown in Figure 8-1. To use this control panel to create an account for your general use, follow these steps:

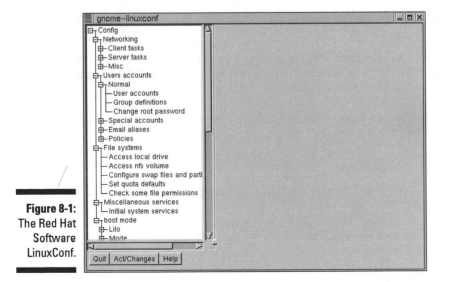

Figure 8-1:
The Red Hat
Software
LinuxConf.

1. **log in as root.**

   The following instructions assume that you're using the Enlightenment/ Gnome window manager, which is the Red Hat default.

2. **If X is not started, enter the following command:**

   ```
   [root@shamet /root]# startx
   ```

3. **Click the Gnome Main Menu button. (It looks like a footprint on the toolbar in the lower-left desktop corner.)**

   This button works in a similar fashion to the Windows Start button.

4. **Choose System⇨LinuxConf Menus.**

   The LinuxConf help window appears, as shown in figure 8-1. The first time that you start it, it shows a welcome.help dialog box. This is an informational screen. Select the Enter key to continue.

5. **Select the User accounts option by clicking the plus sign (+)⇨Normal menu items⇨Users accounts sub menu.**

   The User account program starts, as shown in Figure 8-2. You use this program to add, delete, and modify user accounts on the system.

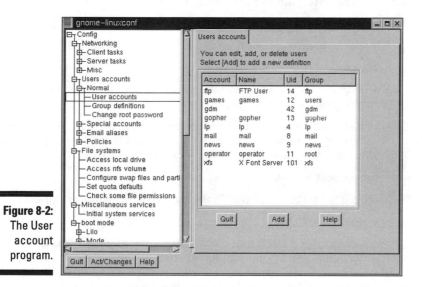

Figure 8-2:
The User account program.

6. **Click the Add button.**

   The User account creation form appears, as shown in Figure 8-3.

```
gnome-linuxconf                                              _ □ ×
□  Config                    │ User account creation
 ├┬ Networking              ▲ │
 │ ├─ Client tasks          │ │ You must specify at least the name
 │ ├─ Server tasks          │ │ and the full name
 │ ├─ Misc                  │ │
 ├┬ Users accounts          │ │ ┌Base info │ Params │ Mail aliases │ Privileges │
 │ ├┬ Normal                │ │
 │ │ ├─ User accounts       │ │             □ The account is enabled
 │ │ ├─ Group definitions   │ │  Login name        [                ]
 │ │ └─ Change root password│ │  Full name         [                ]
 │ ├─ Special accounts      │ │  group (opt)        [              ]√│
 │ ├─ Email aliases         │ │  Supplementary groups [            ]
 │ └─ Policies              │ │  Home directory(opt)  [            ]
 ├┬ File systems            │ │  Command interpreter(opt) /bin/bash  │√│
 │ ├─ Access local drive    │ │  User ID(opt)       [            ]
 │ ├─ Access nfs volume     │ │
 │ ├─ Configure swap files and parti │
 │ ├─ Set quota defaults    │ │
 │ └─ Check some file permissions │
 ├┬ Miscellaneous services  │ │
 │ └─ Initial system services │
 ├┬ boot mode               │ │
 │ ├─ Lilo                  │ │  ┌Accept┐ ┌Cancel┐ ┌Del┐  ┌Tasks┐  ┌Help┐
 │ └─ Mode                 ▼ │
 ├─────────────────────────  │
 ┌Quit│Act/Changes│Help┐
```

Figure 8-3:
The User
account
creation
form.

7. **Fill in information about yourself, because you are the user you're adding. Everything but the username is optional.**

   Most of this information is self-explanatory. Here are a few hints:

   - Make the username short and use all lowercase letters.

   - You can enter your full name.

   - Among your many choices for a default shell, /bin/bash is a good choice. For more on shells, check out Chapter 10.

   - You are assigned two numbers called UID and GID. These numbers help the system determine who you are. Use the ones the program offers, unless you have a reason for changing them.

8. **Click the Accept button.**

   The account is created, and the Changing Password window appears.

9. **Enter a good password.**

   A good password is a word that can't be found in any dictionary. Information such as birthdays and anniversaries aren't good choices. Good passwords are short phrases, with non-alphabetic characters, that make sense to you and you alone. Something like what$upd0c is reasonable.

   Red Hat Linux uses the Pluggable Authentication Module — PAM for short — to prevent you from entering a trivial or otherwise dangerous password.

10. **Retype the password.**

The new password should be different from the one you use for root. As you type the password, little asterisks, rather than the actual password, appear on-screen. Linux is showing its paranoid side again.

11. Type the password again and then press Enter.

The program makes you retype the password to ensure that the password you typed is the one you thought you typed. If you don't retype the password exactly as you did the first time (which is easy to do because it doesn't appear on the screen), you have to repeat the process starting at Step 9.

12. Click the Quit button.

If everything is all right, the LinuxConf window has an entry for your new account.

13. Click the LinuxConf Quit button to leave the application.

By doing so, the control panel remains on the screen.

Did you make a mistake? If so, you can simply retrace the preceding steps.

Good job. You've created a new account by using Red Hat's graphical interface. Other distributions may have similar graphical interfaces for adding users, and they typically ask for and supply the same type of information. If X isn't working, or if you can't find the graphical interface that your distribution supplies, follow the steps in the next section to create a user account.

Creating an Account without X

If X isn't working, or if you want to work from a terminal emulator, you can still add the non-privileged user account that we advise you to add. To do so, you use the useradd command:

```
[root@shamet /root]# useradd <name>
```

where *<name>* is the login name for the non-privileged login account.

Next, you use the passwd command to change the password of the new account, which had a default password assigned to it by the useradd command. What good is a password if you use the default one? In the following lines, remember to replace *<name>* with your login name:

```
[root@shamet /root]# passwd <name>
New Unix password:
Retype new UNIX password:
passwd: all authentication tokens updated successfully
[root@shamet /root]#
```

In the preceding example, we typed the password correctly twice. You can't tell that, however, because the program doesn't let you — or anyone — see the passwords as they're typed. Marker dots don't even appear on the screen.

Ending Your First Session

Logging off the system and restarting the login process is simplicity itself.

If you're running X, press Ctrl+Alt+Delete to shut down the graphics and return to character-cell mode. Then type the word **logout** or **exit**. In a few seconds the `login:` prompt appears, ready for you (or someone else) to log in again.

Choosing meaningful login names

Your login name is also the name you will use to send and receive e-mail, so choose the name carefully. Names that seem cute or appropriate now may not be later. And avoid choosing a name that is too long, because you may have to type it several times a day. You may also have to give your e-mail address over the telephone, so a login name such as *phool* will result in missent messages, leaving you feeling very phoolish, indeed.

Years ago, Tom Chmielewski, a former student of Jon's, came to work at Jon's company location. The corporate standards stated that login names had to be employee's last names. When setting up Tom's account, Jon realized that people would have trouble spelling his name correctly, so he created Tom's account as TomC. Tom Chmielewski became known as TomC throughout the group, the department, and the entire company of 130,000 people. When Tom left the company recently, his new company had the same policy as his former company. But before his first day was over, he was TomC again.

Chapter 9

Filing Your Life Away

● ●

In This Chapter

▶ Discovering the ins and outs of files and directories

▶ Finding your way through the Linux file system

▶ Changing where you are in the Linux file system

▶ Creating, moving, copying, and destroying directories and files

▶ Giving permissions and taking them away

● ●

*I*n this chapter, you take your first steps through the Linux directory structure. We introduce you to file types, subdirectories, and the root directory,
as well as show you the way home — to your home directory, that is.

Next, you discover that you don't need a map to find your way through the
Linux file system; a few commands do the trick. Then, after you're oriented
with the file system, you're ready to make some changes. You find out how
to copy and move files and directories, as well as how to create and destroy
them. We also detail the process of changing a file's ownership and permissions.

Getting Linux File Facts Straight

Linux files are similar to DOS, Windows, and Macintosh files — and a lot like
UNIX files. Follow the bouncing prompt as we make short work of long files.

Storing files

A *file* is a collection of information with a distinct identification made up of a
filename and a location (called a *directory path*) where the file is kept. Linux
can store many files in the same directory — as long as the files have different
names. Linux can also store files with the same name in different directories.

Confused? An example may help. Suppose you get a grand idea and decide to keep it in a file named *idea* in your directory called /wonderful. Now suppose you're having a very fertile day and come up with another idea. If you want to keep your second idea file in the /wonderful directory, you use a different name, such as /wonderful/idea2. (We hope your ideas are more original than our filenames.) You can also, however, keep the file in another location — called the /bizarre directory. If you decide to keep your second idea in /bizarre, you can call it *idea,* and the filename becomes /bizarre/idea. Linux sees this file and the /wonderful/idea file as different files. Remember, though, that each directory may contain only one file with the same name.

Linux filenames can be as long as 256 characters. They can contain uppercase and lowercase letters (also known as mixed case), numbers, and special characters, such as the underscore (_), the dot (.), and the hyphen (-). Because filenames can be made up of mixed case names, and each name is distinct, we call these names *case sensitive.* For example, the names *FILENAME, filename,* and *FiLeNaMe* are unique filenames of different files on some systems (such as Compaq's OpenVMS), however, to Linux they are the same filename.

Although filenames technically can contain wildcard characters, such as the asterisk (*) and the question mark (?), using them is not a good idea. Various command interpreters, or *shells,* use wildcards to match several filenames at one time. If your filenames contain wildcard characters, you'll have trouble specifying only those files. We recommend that you create filenames that don't contain spaces or other characters that have meaning to shells. In this way, Linux filenames are different than DOS and Windows filenames.

Sorting through file types

Linux files can contain all sorts of information. Five categories of files will become the most familiar to you: user data files, system data files, directory files, special files, and executable files.

- ✔ **User data files** contain information you create. User data files, sometimes known as *flat files,* usually contain the simplest data, consisting of plain text and numbers. More complex user data files, such as graphics or spreadsheet files, must be interpreted and used by a special program. These files are mostly illegible if you look at them with a text editor, because the contents of these files are not always ASCII text. Changing these files generally affects only the user who owns the files.

- ✔ **System data files** are used by the system to keep track of users on the system, logins, passwords, and so on. As system administrator, you may be required to view or edit these files. As a regular user, you don't need to be concerned with system data files except, perhaps, the ones that you use as examples for your own private startup files.

✔ **Directory files** hold the names of files — and other directories — that belong to them. These files and directories are called *children*. Directories in Linux (and UNIX) are just another type of file. If you are in a directory, the directory above you is called the *parent*. Isn't that homey?

When you list files with the ls -l command, lines containing directory files begin with the letter *d*. For example:

```
[maddog@shamet maddog]$ ls -ld plot
drwxr-xr-x 2 maddog maddog 1024 Jul 111997 plot
[maddog@shamet maddog]$
```

In this example, we used the d option of the ls command to tell the command that we wanted to see the directory as if it were the only file in the directory. If we had not used the d option, we would have seen every file in the plot directory, along with the directory itself.

✔ **Special files** represent either hardware devices (such as a disk drive, a tape drive, or a keyboard) or some type of placeholder that the operating system uses. The /dev directory holds many of these special files. You can see this directory by typing the following:

```
ls -l /dev
```

✔ **Executable files** contain instructions (usually called *programs,* or *shell scripts*) for your computer. When you type the name of one of these files, you're telling the operating system to *execute* the instructions. Some executable files look like gibberish, and others look like long lists of computer commands. A lot of these executable files are located in /bin, /usr/bin, /sbin, and /usr/sbin.

Understanding files and directories

You can think of the Linux file system as one huge file folder that contains files and other file folders, which in turn contain files and other file folders, which in turn contain files and . . . well, you get the point. In fact, the Linux file system is generally organized this way. One big directory contains files and other directories, and all the other directories in turn contain files and directories, and so on.

Directories and subdirectories

A directory contained, or *nested,* in another directory is called a *subdirectory*. For example, the directory called /mother may contain a subdirectory called /child. The relationship between the two is referred to as parent and child. The full name of the subdirectory is /mother/child, which would make a good place to keep a file containing information about a family reunion. It could be called /mother/child/reunion.

The root directory

In the tree directory structure of Linux, DOS, and UNIX, the big directory at the bottom of the tree, which is the parent for all the other directories, is called the *root* directory and is represented by a single / (pronounced "slash"). From the root directory, the whole directory structure grows like a tree, with directories and subdirectories branching off like limbs.

If you could turn the tree over so that the trunk is in the air and the branches are toward the ground, you would have an *inverted tree* — which is the way the Linux file system is normally drawn and represented (with the root at the top). If we were talking about Mother Nature, you'd soon have a dead tree. Because this is computer technology, however, you have something that looks like an ever-growing, upside-down tree.

What's in a name?

You name directories in the same way that you name files, following the same rules. Almost the only way that you can tell whether a name is a filename or a directory name is the way that the slash character (/) is used to show directories nested in other directories. For example, usr/local means that local is found in the usr directory. You know that usr is a directory because the trailing slash character tells you so; however, you don't know whether local is a file or a directory.

If you issue the ls command with the -F option, Linux lists directories with a slash character at the end, as in local/, so you would know that local is a directory.

The simplest way to tell whether the slash character indicates the root directory or separates directories, or directories and files, is to see whether anything appears before the slash character in the directory path specification. If nothing appears before the slash, you have the root directory. For example, you know that /usr is a subdirectory or a file in the root directory because it has only a single slash character before it.

Home again

Linux systems have a directory called /home, which contains the user's home directory, where he or she can:

- Store files
- Create more subdirectories
- Move, delete, and modify subdirectories and files

Linux system files as well as files belonging to other users are never in a user's /home directory. Linux decides where the /home directory is placed, and that location can be changed only by a superuser, not by general users. Linux is dictatorial because it has to maintain order and keep a handle on security.

Your /home directory is not safe from prying eyes. To be sure that your privacy is maintained, you need to lock your directory. (We tell you how in the "Granting Permissions" section.) However, anyone logging on to your system as root (superuser) can see what's in your /home directory, even if you do lock it up.

Moving Around the File System with pwd and cd

You can navigate the Linux file system without a map or a GPS. All you need to know are two commands: pwd and cd. (These commands are run from the command line.)

Figuring out where you are

To find out where you are in the Linux file system, simply type pwd at the command prompt as follows:

```
[maddog@shamet maddog]$pwd
/home/maddog
[maddog@shamet maddog]$
```

This command indicates that we're logged in as maddog and in the /home/ maddog directory. Unless your alter ego is out there, you should be logged on as *yourself* and be in the /home/*yourself* directory, where *yourself* is your login name.

The pwd command stands for *print working directory*. Your *working directory* is the default directory where Linux commands perform their actions. When you type the ls(1) command, for example, Linux shows you the files in your working directory. Any file actions on your part occur in your working directory unless you are root. For security reasons that we won't go into here, the root user is not configured by default to be able to work on the current working directory. You can change this, but in general, the root user must explicitly specify the current working directory. For instance, it you are root and are in the /etc directory, and you want to indicate the hosts file, then you must enter cat ./hosts instead of just cat hosts.

Type this command:

```
ls -la
```

Brushing up on Linux syntax

You'll be seeing a lot of Linux commands, so you may find benefit from a quick review of the syntax of Linux commands:

✔ Text *not* surrounded by [ ], { }, or < > must be typed exactly as shown.

✔ Text inside brackets [ ] is optional.

✔ Text inside angle brackets < > must be replaced with appropriate text.

✔ Text inside braces { } indicates that you must choose one of the values that are inside the braces separated by the | sign.

✔ An ellipsis (. . .) means *and so on* or to repeat the preceding command line as needed.

You see only the files that are in your working directory. If you want to specify a file that isn't in your working directory, you have to specify the name of the directory that contains the file, as well as the name of the file. For example, the following command lists the passwd file in the /etc directory:

```
ls -la /etc/passwd
```

Specifying the directory path

If the file you want to read is in a subdirectory of the directory that you are in, you can reach the file by typing a relative filename. *Relative filenames* specify the location of files relative to where you are.

In addition to what we tell earlier in this chapter about specifying directory paths, you need to know these three additional rules:

✔ One dot (.) always stands for your current directory.

✔ Two dots (..) specify the parent directory of the directory you are currently in.

✔ All directory paths that include (.) or (..) are relative directory paths.

You can see these files by using the -a option of the ls(1) command. Without the -a option, the ls(1) command does not bother to list the . or .. files, or any filename beginning with a period. This may seem strange, but the creators of UNIX thought that having some files that were normally hidden kept the directory structure cleaner. Therefore, filenames that are always there (. and ..) and special-purpose files are hidden. The types of files that should be hidden are those that the user normally does not need to see in every listing of the directory structure (files used to tailor applications to the user's preferences, for example).

Now specify a pathname relative to where you are. For example:

```
[maddog@shamet maddog]$pwd
/home/maddog
[maddog@shamet maddog]$ ls -la ../../etc/passwd
```

The last line indicates that to find the passwd file, you go up two directory levels (../../) and then down to /etc.

If you want to see the login accounts on your system, you can issue the following command from your home directory:

```
[maddog@shamet maddog]$ ls -la ..
```

This command lists the parent directory. Because the parent directory (/home) has all the login directories of the people on your system, this command shows you the names of their login directories.

You have been looking at relative pathnames, which are relative to where you are in the file system. Filenames that are valid from anywhere in the file system are called *absolute filenames*. These filenames always begin with the slash character (/), which signifies root.

```
ls -la /etc/passwd
```

Changing your working directory

Sometimes, you may want to change your working directory because doing so allows you to work with shorter relative pathnames. To do so, you simply use the cd (for *change directory*) command.

To change from your current working directory to the /usr directory, for example, type the following:

```
cd /usr
```

Going home

If you type cd by itself, without any directory name, you return to your home directory. Just knowing that you can easily get back to familiar territory is comforting. There's no place like home.

You can also use cd with a *relative* specification. For example:

```
cd ..
```

If you are in the directory /usr/bin and type the preceding command, Linux takes you to the parent directory called /usr, as follows:

```
[maddog@shamet maddog]$ cd /usr/bin
[maddog@shamet bin]$ cd ..
[maddog@shamet usr]$
```

Here are a couple of tricks: If you type cd ~, then you go to your home directory (the tilde ~ is synonymous with /home/username). If you type cd ~<username>, then you can go to that user's home directory. On very large systems, this command is useful because it eliminates the need for you to remember — and type — large directory specifications.

Using cat to Create and Add to Files

Unlike cats, the cat command is simple, easy to use, and one of the most useful Linux commands (sorry, Paul likes dogs and is allergic to cats). The name cat stands for *concatenate,* meaning *to add to the end of.* The cat command does exactly what you tell it to and takes your input (mostly from the keyboard) and outputs it to the screen. Real cats like to do what they want to do and will not help display the contents of Linux files.

Make sure that you are *not* logged in as root when you go through this section and the sections that follow. Wait until you are thoroughly familiar with this chapter before you log in as root and try the examples. Linux (for the most part) doesn't have an *undo* function, although a change is in the works.

To find out what the cat command is all about, follow these steps:

1. **Make sure that you are in the /home directory.**

   To go home, click your heels . . . no, that's another book. Type cd at the prompt and then type pwd.

2. **Type cat at the command line:**

   ```
   [maddog@shamet maddog]$cat
   ```

   The cursor moves to the next line, but nothing else happens because cat is waiting for you to input something.

3. **Type Hi and then press Enter. Then type a few more lines.**

   Here's what we typed and what appeared on the screen:

   ```
   Hi
   Hi
   What?
   What?
   Hey! How do I get out of this?
   Hey! How do I get out of this?
   ```

Everything you type is repeated on the screen after you press Enter. Big deal, you say? We explain why this is useful in a moment.

4. **To get out of the** `cat` **command, press Ctrl+D. If you're not at the beginning of a line, press Ctrl+D twice.**

Most UNIX and Linux people write Ctrl+D as ^D, which means *end of file* (EOF) to Linux. When the `cat` command sees ^D, it assumes that it's finished with that line and moves to the next one. If ^D is on an empty line by itself, the `cat` command has no other input to move to and thus exits.

We promised that we'd explain the usefulness of the `cat` command. We always try to keep our promises, so here goes. You can use the first two symbols in the following list to save the output of the `cat` command to a file and use the third symbol to read the content of a file and send it to the cat command:

✔ > is known as *redirection of standard output.* When you use it, you tell the computer, "Capture the information that normally goes to the screen, create a file, and put the information into it."

✔ >> is known as *appending standard output.* When you use this symbol, you tell the computer, "Capture the information that would normally go to the screen and append the information to an existing file. If the file doesn't exist, create it."

✔ < is used to tell the computer, "Take the information from the specified file and feed it to *standard in* (also known as *standard input*), acting as though the information is coming from the keyboard."

In this example, you use the `cat` command to create a file by redirecting the output of the `cat` command from the screen to the filename you want:

1. **At the command line, type** `cat` > **followed by the name of your file. Then type your heart out.**

Here's what we typed:

```
[maddog@shamet maddog]$ cat > dogfile
Hi again
Dogfish. Dogleg. Dog days.
Shamet. Dogfight. Doggone.
```

Everything is repeated to the file called dogfile rather than to the screen. Linux created dogfile for us because the filename didn't already exist.

2. **When you finish typing, just press ^D on an empty line.**

You're right back at the Linux prompt.

Are you wondering whether the `cat` command did what you wanted? You can check by using the `cat` command and the filename again:

```
[maddog@shamet maddog]$ cat dogfile
Hi again
Dogfish. Dogleg. Dog days.
Shamet. Dogfight. Doggone.
[maddog@shamet maddog]$
```

This time the `cat` command took the file off the disk and put the output to *standard out* (also known as *standard output*), which in this case is your computer screen.

If you think of something else you want to add to the file, you can use the append symbol (>) with the filename. Linux adds whatever you type to the end of the filename. Returning to dogfile:

```
[maddog@shamet maddog]$ cat >> dogfile
Dog-eared. Doggerel.
```

Are we confusing you? You use the `cat` command to concatenate files or concatenate input to either the beginning or the end of the file. It is the only command created to do this.

You can use the >> symbol with many Linux commands. For example:

```
cat file1 file2 file3 file4 >fileout
```

joins file1, file2, file3, and file4, putting the results in fileout. In the following:

```
sort file1 >>file2
```

the `sort` command sorts the contents of file1 and appends it to a (perhaps already existing) file2. If file2 doesn't exist, the system creates file2 and then puts the sorted output into it.

When you finish, be sure to end the session with ^D.

Manipulating Files and Directories

Linux has many ways to create, move, copy, and delete files and directories. Some of these features are so easy to use that you need to be careful: Unlike other operating systems, Linux doesn't tell you that you are about to over-write a file — it just follows your orders and overwrites!

We said it once, but we'll say it again: Make sure that you are *not* logged in as root when you go through these sections.

Creating directories

To create a new directory in Linux, you use the mkdir command (just like in DOS). The command looks like this:

```
[maddog@shamet maddog]$mkdir newdirectory
```

This command creates a subdirectory under your current or working directory. If you want the subdirectory under another directory, change to that directory first and then create the new subdirectory.

Create a new directory called santa_cruz. Go ahead, do it:

```
mkdir santa_cruz
```

(Can you tell where we would rather be right now?)

Now create another directory called work:

```
mkdir work
```

And then change the directory to put yourself in the santa_cruz directory:

```
cd santa_cruz
```

Now create a file under santa_cruz called radman, by using the cat command (see the "Using cat to Create and Add to Files" section earlier in this chapter):

```
cat >radman
Once upon a time there lived a handsome prince.
^D
```

Now create another file:

```
cat >jewels
Once upon a time there lived a beautiful princess.
^D
```

And one more:

```
cat >moody
The handsome prince and beautiful princess had a dog named
Moody.
^D
```

Now you have some files to work with.

Moving and copying files and directories

The commands for moving and copying directories and files are mv for move and cp for copy. If you want to rename a file, you can use the move command. No, you're not really moving the file, but in Linux (and UNIX), the developers realized that renaming something was a lot like moving it. The format of the move command is as follows:

```
mv <source> <destination>
```

With your example files from the preceding section, you can move the file named radman to a file named bryant by executing the following command:

```
mv radman bryant
```

This command leaves the file in the santa_cruz directory but changes its name to bryant. So you see the file was not really moved, but just renamed.

Now try moving the bryant file to the work directory. To do that, you have to first move the file up and then move it into the work directory. You can do it with one command:

```
mv bryant ../work
```

Note that the destination file uses the .. (or parent directory) designation. This command tells Linux to go up one directory level and look for a directory called work, and then put the file into that directory with the name bryant, because you did not specify any other name. If you instead did this:

```
mv bryant ../work/supersalesman
```

the bryant file would move to the work directory named supersalesman. Note that in both cases (with the file maintaining its name of bryant or taking the new name supersalesman), your current directory is still santa_cruz, and all your filenames are relative to that directory.

Strictly speaking, the file still has not really moved. The data bits are still on the same part of the disk where they were originally. The *file specification* (the directory path plus the filename) that you use to talk about the file is different, so it appears to have moved.

In early versions of UNIX, you were not allowed to use mv to move a file from one disk partition to another; you could only copy it by using the cp(1) command. Linux allows you to use the mv command to move a file anywhere. Normally, mv leaves the data in place and just changes the file's name or the directory where the name is placed. But when the file is moved across disk partitions (for example, from /usr to /home in a lot of Linux systems), the data is copied to the new disk partition, the new name is put in place in that partition's directory structure, and the name and file's data are removed from the old disk partition.

Copying a file does move some data. The syntax is like so:

```
cp <source> <destination>
```

Look familiar? It's the same syntax you use for the move command.

Now make two copies of the jewels file. Because you can't have two files of the same name in the same directory, you have to think of a new name, such as jewels2. (Hey, we're writing this early in the morning. How creative can we be?)

```
cp jewels jewels2
```

If you want a copy of a file but in a different directory, you can use the same filename. For example, suppose you want to copy a file called moody to the ../work directory. You can keep the name moody because its full pathname has work in it instead of santa_cruz:

```
cp moody ../work
```

As you can see, the pathname specifications for files are similar from command to command, even though the file contents and commands are different.

Removing files

The command for removing, or deleting, a file is rm. If you've been following along in our little story, the handsome prince now has two beautiful princesses (jewels and jewels2) in the santa_cruz directory. As most people know, this is probably one too many princesses, so get rid of the second one:

```
rm jewels2
```

You have removed the extra file from the current directory. To remove a file from another directory, you need to provide a relative filename or an absolute filename. For example, if you want to expunge moody from the work directory while in the aforementioned santa_cruz directory, you would type the following:

```
rm ../work/moody
```

You are allowed to use wildcards with rm, but please be careful if you do so! When files are removed in Linux, they are gone forever — kaput, vanished — and can't be recovered.

The following command removes *everything* in the current directory and all of the directories under it that you have permission to remove:

```
[maddog@shamet maddog]$rm -r *
```

To lessen the danger of removing a lot of files inadvertently when using wild-cards, be sure to use the -i option with rm, cp, mv, and various other commands. The -i option means *interactive,* and it lists each filename to be removed (with the rm command) or overwritten (with the mv or cp command). If you answer either **y** or **Y** to the question, the file is removed or overwritten, respectively. If you answer anything else, Linux leaves the file alone.

Removing directories

You can remove not only files but also directories. If you are still following along with the story about the handsome prince and his princess, you now have two directories in your home directory that are taking up a small amount of space. Because you are finished with them, you can delete them and recover that space for other tasks.

First, return to your home directory:

```
[maddog@shamet maddog]$ cd
```

Now remove the santa_cruz directory:

```
[maddog@shamet maddog]$rm -rf santa_cruz
```

This command removes the santa_cruz directory and all files and directories under it. Note that this is just the rm command with options for recursively and forcefully. (*Recursively* means to keep going down in the directory struc-ture and remove files and directories as you find them. *Forcefully* means that the file should be removed if at all possible; ignore cases where rm may prompt the user for further information.)

Another command specifically for removing empty directories is called rmdir. With rmdir, the directory must be empty to be removed. If you attempt to remove the work directory without first deleting its files, the system displays the following message:

```
[maddog@shamet maddog]$ rmdir work
rmdir: work: Directory not empty
[maddog@shamet maddog]$ rm -rf work
```

Granting Permissions

Files and directories in Linux have owners and are assigned a list of permissions. This system of ownership and permissions forms the basis for restricting and allowing access to files. File permissions can also be used to specify whether a file is executable as a command and to determine who can use the file or command. Ownership and permissions are important to know because even if you are the only one who uses your system, some commands and databases are owned by other users, including root (the superuser). Permissions on these files either allow or disallow you, the general user, to update these files.

Using the `ls` command with the `-l` option allows you to see the file's permissions, along with other relevant information, such as who owns the file, what group of people have permission to access or modify the file, the size of the file or directory, the last time the file was modified, and the name of the file.

First, create a file with the `touch` command. The UNIX and Linux communities use the `touch` command for many things, one of which is to create a little zero-length file:

```
[maddog@shamet maddog]$ touch partytime
[maddog@shamet maddog]$ ls -l partytime
-rw-rw-r-- owner group 0 Oct 31 16:00 partytime
```

The `-rw-rw-r--` are the permissions for the partytime file: The owner is you, and the group is probably you but may be someone or something else, depending on how your system is set up and administered.

You may be wondering how you can become an owner of a file. Well, you are automatically the owner of any file you create, which makes sense. As the owner, you can change the default file permissions — and even the ownership. If you change the file ownership, however, *you* lose ownership privileges.

To change the ownership of a file or a directory, use the `chown` command. (Get it? Chown — change ownership.) In general, you have to be root to do this.

Suppose you've decided to settle down and lead a more contemplative life, one more in line with a new profession of haiku writing. Someone else will have to plan the weekend sprees and all-night bashes. So you give up ownership of the partytime file:

```
[maddog@shamet maddog]$chown root partytime
```

This command changes the ownership of partytime to root. If you want to change it back, you can use the `chown` command, but you have to do it as root.

Files and users all belong to *groups*. In the partytime example, the group is users. Having groups enables you to give large numbers of users — but not all users — access to files. Group permissions and ownership are handy for making sure that the members of a special project or workgroup have access to files needed by the entire group.

To see which groups are available to you on your system, take a look at the /etc/group file. To do so, use the more command. You see a file that looks somewhat like this:

```
root::0:root
bin::1:root,bin,daemon
...
nobody::99:
users::100:
floppy:x:19:
.....
your-user-name::500:your-user-name
```

where *your-user-name* is the login name you use for your account. Please remember that the file won't look exactly like this, just similar. The names at the beginning of the line are the group names. The names at the end of the line (such as root, bin, and daemon) are user-group names that can belong to the user-group list.

To change the group that the file belongs to, log in as root and use the chgrp command. Its syntax is the same as that of the chown command. For example, to change the group that partytime belongs to, you would issue the following:

```
[maddog@shamet maddog]$chgrp newgroupname partytime
```

Red Hat assigns a unique group to each user. For instance, when you add the first user to your system, that user gets the user ID and group ID of 500. The next user receives the user ID and group ID of 501, and so on. This gives you a lot of control over who gets access to your files.

Making Your Own Rules

You, as the owner of a file, can specify permissions for reading, writing to, or executing a file. You can also determine who (yourself, a group of people, or everyone in general) can do these actions on a file. What do these permissions mean? Read on (you have our permission) for the scoop:

✔ **Read permission** for a file enables you to read the file. For a directory, read permission allows the ls command to list the names of the files in the directory. You must also have execute permission for the directory name to use the -l option of the ls command or to change to that directory.

✔ **Write permission** for a file means you can modify the file. For a directory, you can create or delete files inside that directory.

✔ **Execute permission** for a file means you can type the name of the file and execute it. You can't view or copy the file unless you also have read permission. This means that files containing executable Linux commands, called *shell scripts,* must be both executable and readable by the person executing them. Programs written in a compiled language such as C, however, must have only executable permissions, to protect them from being copied where they shouldn't be copied.

For a directory, execute permission means that you can change to that directory (with cd). Unless you also have read permission for the directory, ls -l won't work. You can list directories and files in that directory, but you can't see additional information about the files or directories by just using an ls -l command. This may seem strange, but it's useful for security.

The first character of a file permission is a hyphen (-) if it is a file or d if the file is a directory. The nine other characters are read, write, and execute positions for each of the three categories of file permissions:

✔ Owner (also known as the user)

✔ Group

✔ Others

Your partytime file, for example, may show the following permissions when listed with the ls -l partytime command:

```
-rw-rw-r--
```

The hyphen (-) in the first position indicates that it is a regular file (not a directory or other special file). The next characters (rw-) are the owner's permissions. The owner can read and write to the file but can't execute it. The next three characters (rw-) are the group's permissions. The group has read-only access to the file. The last three characters (r--) are the others' permissions, which are also read-only.

[-][rw-][r--][r--] illustrates the four parts of the permissions: the file type followed by three sets of triplets, indicating the read, write, and execute permissions for the owner, group, and *other* users of the file (meaning *everyone else*).

You can specify most file permissions by using only six letters:

✔ *ugo,* which stands for — no, not that awful car — user (or owner), group, and other

✔ *rwx,* which stands for read, write, and execute.

These six letters, and some symbols such as = and commas, are put together into a specification of how you want to set the file's permissions.

The command for changing permissions is `chmod`. The syntax for the command is

```
chmod <specification> filename
```

Change the mode of partytime to give the user the ability to read, write, and execute the file:

```
chmod u=rwx partytime
```

That was easy enough, wasn't it? What if you want to give the group permission to only read and execute the file? You would execute the following command:

```
chmod g=rx partytime
```

Note that this last command does not affect the permissions for owner or other, just the group's permissions.

Now set all the permissions at once. Separate each group of characters with a comma:

```
chmod u=r,g=rw,o=rwx partytime
```

This command sets the user's permissions to just read, the group's permissions to read and write, and the other's permissions to read, write, and execute.

You can set the permission bits in other ways. But this way is so simple, why use any other?

Bossing Linux Around

Issuing commands can be simple or complicated. That's because Linux is a powerful operating system and can do just about anything that you want it to. We introduce Linux commands in this chapter, and describe more complex commands in Chapter 10.

A *command* is just a program that you run in order to get something done. For instance, you use the `ls` command to list files and the `mount` command to make a floppy or CD-ROM drive accessible. Linux provides a rich and varied set of standard commands that you use to manage your system.

Tweaking Linux Commands

Most Linux commands are flexible and can be modified to perform special tasks. You can use two devices to alter a command: command options and standard input and standard output redirection. You find out about command options first.

You can use *command options* to fine-tune the actions of a Linux command. We introduce the ls command earlier in this chapter so you can see the results of actions taken on the file system. To see how its options work, in the next example you try out the ls command several times, with different options.

Use the mkdir command to make a new directory called gregger and then use the cd command to change your working directory to that new directory:

```
[maddog@shamet emptydirectory]$ mkdir gregger
[maddog@shamet emptydirectory]$ cd gregger
```

At the Linux prompt, type ls as follows:

```
[maddog@shamet gregger]$ ls
[maddog@shamet gregger]$
```

That didn't do much, did it? It seems as if the account has no files. You may need an option. Try the -a option and see what happens:

```
[maddog@shamet gregger]$ ls -a
.  ..
[maddog@shamet gregger]$
```

Remember to type the commands and options exactly as shown. For example, the ls -a command has a space between the command and the option, and no space between the hyphen and the letter *a*.

Notice the two files (they're actually directories, but in Linux all directories are just files) that the ls command displayed. What? All you see are dots? Well, the single dot represents the directory you are in; the double dot represents the parent directory, which is typically the one above the directory you're in. (Linux creates these filenames and puts them into the directory for you. If you just installed your directory, all you have are files that begin with a period.)

Next, create a few additional files in the gregger directory, by using the touch command:

```
[maddog@shamet gregger]$ touch file1
[maddog@shamet gregger]$ touch .dotfile
```

Now if you use the same ls command (without the -a option), you see the following:

```
[maddog@shamet gregger]$ ls
file1
[maddog@shamet gregger]$
```

And if you redo the ls command with the -a option, you get this:

```
[maddog@shamet gregger]$ ls -a
.       ..        .dotfile  file1
[maddog@shamet gregger]$
```

The ls command by default doesn't list files that begin with a period. By adding the -a option, you modify the action taken by ls to print every filename whether or not it begins with a dot.

The ls command has many options, and you can use more than one at a time. Want to see how? Modify the -a option by adding l to it. The command line becomes:

```
[maddog@shamet gregger]$ls -al
 total 5
drwx------ 3(username)(groupname)(filesize) Jan 10 14:33 ./
drwxr-xr-x 6 root    root    (filesize) Jan 04 22:15 ../
-rw-rw-r-- 1(username)(groupname)(filesize)Jun18 11:30 .dot-
           file
-rw-rw-r-- 1 username)(groupname)(filesize) Apr 13 17:40
           file1
```

As you can see, instead of just listing the filenames, the l option shows a more detailed listing of files. If long listings don't fit on a single line, Linux just wraps them to the next line.

Most of the time, Linux doesn't care about what order you type the options and therefore considers ls -al and ls -la to be the same. Multiple option choices aren't available with all commands, however, and work only with commands that have single letters to specify their options.

The ls command lists files in alphabetical order as the default, but you can tailor the output. For example, ls -alt displays the files in order by date and time, with the most recent first; ls -altr reverses that order.

Piping: Oh Danny Boy, the Pipes. . . .

Many Linux commands generate a lot of output, and if it all went to standard output as output to the screen, without some type of control, it would scroll past. For example, type the following:

```
ls -al /etc
```

This command lists all the files in your /usr directory. Because this directory holds a truckload of files, the information scrolls down your screen faster than you — or any Evelyn Wood graduate — can read it. You can, however, correct this.

With a process called *piping,* Linux uses the output from one command as the input for another. It's not as confusing as it sounds. In the last example, you had too much information — or *output* — to fit on one lonely screen. You can take that information and put — or *input* — it into a program that divides the information into screen-sized pieces and then displays them.

To do this, you use the more command, which is an appropriate name for this tool. You *pipe* the list command's output to the more command. But how do you pipe? You use the | character on your keyboard. We bet you were wondering what the heck that key was for. Type the command as follows:

```
ls -al /etc | more
```

Linux doesn't care if spaces surround the | character, but you may want to use them for clarity and to get in the habit of including spaces because they are important at other times.

When you press Enter, the information appears one screen at a time with the word *More* appearing at the bottom of each screen except the last one. To move to the next screen, press the spacebar. When you finish with the last screen, the more command takes you back to the Linux prompt. The more command can do even more. When the screen halts with the word *More* appearing at the bottom, you can type some commands to the more program:

- ✔ **q** to get out of the more command without wading through all those screens
- ✔ **h** to see a list of all commands available in the more command

Note that if you press Enter after one screen at a time, Linux shows you the next entry in the list, not the next screen.

Note that some commands to the more program (such as the b command) don't work when you're piping input into the program, as opposed to using more with a file.

Everyone makes mistakes. Everyone changes his mind from time to time. For those reasons, you need to know how to delete text from the Linux command line. If you want to start over, press Ctrl+U to remove everything you have typed on the command line — if you have not yet pressed Enter. The Backspace key erases one character at a time. The left- and right-arrow keys move the cursor along the line of characters without erasing; when you get to the place you want to change, use the Backspace key to erase mistakes and retype changes. In most cases, the up- and down-arrow keys jump the cursor back and forth through the last few commands.

Linux sometimes uses a command called less, which duplicates the functionality of the more command. Originally, the less command was designed to be more robust than the more command, but the more command caught up and they are now almost the same. Some Linux systems display text with the less command instead of the more command, which most UNIX programs use.

The less and more commands have two apparent differences. One, the less command requires a q command to get back to the Linux prompt, even when you are at the end of the last page. Two, the more command always says *More* at the bottom of a screen, whereas less has just a : character at the bottom of the screen to indicate that it's waiting for you to input the next command. The companion CD-ROM (CD1), which is a Red Hat distribution, uses more instead of less as a default.

Chapter 10

Avoiding Shell Shock

· ·

In This Chapter

▶ Discovering the bash shell

▶ Experimenting with wildcards

▶ Using bash history to find files

▶ Banging around to find files

· ·

*I*magine that you are in a foreign country and don't know the language, so you hire an interpreter to accompany you. You tell the interpreter what you want to do and where you want to go. Assuming that nothing goes wrong with your flight, the interpreter then decides what steps to take (hire a taxi or take the subway, for example) and in what order. When you to talk to a foreigner, the interpreter translates your statements into that country's native language.

Shells (also known as *command interpreters*) do much the same thing. They take the English-like commands that you type in, gather resources (such as file names and memory), and supply lower-level computer statements to do what you want.

Many shells have evolved throughout the history of UNIX and Linux. Their history and derivation is discussed in the "A shell for all seasons" sidebar later in this chapter. For now, we'd like to simplify the issue of which shell is best and suggest a shell for you to use.

We recommend *bash* because it is widely available and has more features than you'll ever need as a user. If you go on to become more of a programmer or if you really enjoy investigating shells, you may want to try the popular zsh or the even more popular Tcl/Tk or Python, all of which have graphical interfaces.

Bashing Ahead!

The first thing that you need to do before continuing with this chapter is to make sure you're using the bash shell. If you're using Linux without X and you're logged in as a general user (rather than as the superuser, root), you're probably at a *shell prompt.* If you're using X, you must log in and use the window manager to launch a terminal emulator window, which generally contains a shell prompt. If you aren't familiar with this process, check out Chapter 11.

Your shell prompt should look something like this:

```
[maddog@shamet maddog]$
```

The most important element is the $ at the end of the line. This *prompt* is the shell's method of saying, "Okay, I'm finished with the last thing, so give me something else to do." The information contained within the square brackets ([ ]) tells who you are logged in as, the name of the computer that you are logged in, and the last part of the directory that you are in; for instance, if you are in your home directory, /home/me, the *me* part of the directory displays.

If you are logged in as root or have become a superuser through the use of the su(1) command, the $ is replaced with a # sign, which indicates that the user is root or otherwise has become a superuser.

To make sure that your default shell is the bash shell rather than one of the other shells, type the following:

```
[maddog@shamet maddog]$ bash
```

After you press Enter, Linux comes back with one of two responses. If bash wasn't installed properly, you see the following:

```
command not found
```

If you didn't install your own Linux system, you should find the person who did and throttle him within an inch of . . . no, no. You should find the person who installed your Linux system and kindly ask them to help you use the bash shell as your default shell.

If you're lucky, you see the following:

```
[maddog@shamet maddog]$
```

Geez. Linux didn't seem to do much. It did, though. You're definitely in the bash shell and ready to see its power.

If you're logged in as superuser or root (a # appears at the end of your shell prompt), change over to a nonsuperuser account. No examples in this chapter require superuser privileges. And because you're experimenting with shells, limiting potential damage is a good idea. Remember, it's not called *superuser* for nothing.

Commanding Linux

Commands can contain one, two, or all three parts, but the first part — the command name — must always be present. Linux commands three major parts, namely:

- ✔ The command name
- ✔ Options to the command (telling the command how to change its actions for a specific execution)
- ✔ Input or output files, which supply data or give the command a place to put output data, respectively

Regular expressions: Wildcards and one-eyed jacks

If you had to type every filename for every command, Linux would still be useful. But something that makes Linux more useful is the capability to use a few special characters — called *metacharacters*, *pattern-matching characters*, *wildcards*, or *regular expressions* — to supply filenames. Just as you can substitute wildcards for any card of your choice in a poker game, Linux pattern-matching characters can be substituted for filenames and directory names, much like DOS wildcards.

Three of these special pattern-matching characters follow:

- ✔ * (asterisk)
- ✔ ? (question mark)
- ✔ \ (backslash)

The asterisk matches at least one character in any filename. For example, *
matches the following filenames:

- ✔ a
- ✔ acd
- ✔ bce
- ✔ moody

You'll probably use * the most in the command `ls -l *`.

The question mark matches any single character. The string of characters `a?c`,
for example, match the following:

- ✔ abc
- ✔ adc
- ✔ aac
- ✔ afc
- ✔ a9c

The question mark and the asterisk can be helpful for identifying a particular
type of file, if you're careful about naming your files. For example, text editor
files usually have the .txt extension, and Microsoft Word files have the .doc
extension. Linux doesn't care what the name of a file is, but some programs
work only with a particular type of file.

Now suppose you followed the convention of naming all your text files with
the .txt extension, and you want to see all the text files in a directory. You can
use the `ls` command like this:

```
ls -l *.txt
```

The screen displays all the files in this directory with the .txt extension.
Notice that we didn't say that the command shows you all text files or that it
shows only text files. If you want to name a graphics file with a .txt extension,
Linux happily obliges you. For your own sanity, however, be diligent in
naming files. Some programs (such as those that create audio files or picture
files) strictly enforce a naming convention on files they create, but Linux
itself doesn't care.

What do you do if the * is part of the filename you're trying to match? How
can you tell the shell that you want only the file that contains * and not all
the other files? The backslash character prevents the shell from interpreting
the * as a metacharacter and expanding it — in Linux lingo, the backslash
escapes the meaning of the special character. For example, `hi*est` matches a
file named *highest,* but `hi\*est` matches only the *hi*est* filename.

If you want to delete the file hi*est, then enter the command:

```
rm hi\*est
```

The backslash tells the shell to treat the asterisk as a character and not to expand it to mean zero or more characters.

Although more regular expression characters are available, the ones listed in this section are enough for you to work with for a while.

I command you

To see how the three parts of a command work together, suppose you type the following Linux command at the shell prompt:

```
ls -l *
```

When bash looks at that line, it performs the following steps:

1. bash creates a new environment for the `ls` command to be executed in and determines what should be *standard input* and *standard output* to the command. Standard input is normally the keyboard, and standard output is normally the video screen. (You find out more about environments in a moment.)

2. bash expands * to match all the filenames in that particular directory. By *expanding* the filenames, we mean that certain special characters are used to indicate groups of filenames. When these characters are used, the computer sees what filenames match up with these special characters and supplies the filenames to the command, instead of the special characters.

   For example, suppose you have the files ert, wert, uity, and opgt in your current directory. If you type

   ```
   ls -l *
   ```

   to the `ls` command, it looks like you typed

   ```
   ls -l ert opgt uity wert
   ```

   Note that the shell puts the names in alphabetical order before giving them to the command.

3. Next, bash searches the PATH environmental variable looking for a command called `ls`. The PATH variable holds the names of directories that contain commands you may want to execute. If the command you want is not in the list, you have to explicitly tell the shell where it can find the command by typing either a complete or relative pathname to the command.

4. bash executes the ls command in the new environment, passing to the command the -l argument and all the filenames it expanded, due to the use of the * character in the command.

5. After ls runs, bash returns to the current environment, throwing away all the side effects that occurred in the new environment, such as an environmental variable changing its value.

In Step 1, we mentioned the *environment.* A shell operates in an environment just like humans live and work in an environment. We expect to have and use certain things in our human environment. Suppose you leave your office for a few days, and someone else steps in to use it. At first, this newcomer uses your environment as you arranged it. The person probably appreciates the fact that the phone works, office supplies are in the desk, and so on. But after a while, the newcomer starts moving and changing things, and maybe even drinking decaffeinated coffee out of your coffee mug! When you come back from your trip, everything is changed. You can't find things easily, and green stuff is growing in the bottom of your mug. Wouldn't it have been nice if that person had left the office (your environment) exactly as you had arranged it?

Bash creates an environment for commands to operate in. When a new command is executed, bash creates a clean copy of the environment, executes the command in it, and then throws away that environment, returning to the environment it started with.

Now look at a more complex example than just the one command ls -l *:

```
cd /usr/lib
ls -l * | more
```

In this case:

1. bash creates a new environment for the ls command to be executed in and determines what should be the input (called *standard input* in technical jargon) and the output (called *standard output* in nerd-speak) to the command. You can call this new environment child number 1; the old environment is its parent.

2. bash creates another new environment for the more command to be executed in, called child number 2, and determines what should be input and output to the more command. Because the pipe | symbol is used between the ls -l * command and the more command, the output of the ls -l * command is sent to the input of the more command. The output of more is sent to the output of the parent bash shell. The parent shell is the one into which you have been typing commands and information, and the output of that original bash shell is the screen.

3. bash expands * to match all the filenames in that particular directory, as before.

4. Next, in the child 1 environment, bash searches the PATH environmental variable looking for a command called ls. The same process occurs for the more command in child number 2.

5. bash executes the ls command in the child number 1 environment, passing to the command the -l argument and all the filenames it expanded, due to the use of the * character in the command.

6. more sees the output of ls -l * as its input, and puts its output to the screen.

7. After ls runs, bash returns to the parent environment, throwing away all the side effects that occurred in the child number 1 environment.

8. more sees the end of its input from ls, puts the last of its data out to the screen, and terminates.

9. bash returns to its parent environment, throwing away all the changes that more may have made to the child number 2 environment.

The original bash shell is called the *parent,* and the two new environments that bash created are called *children,* or *child number 1* and *child number 2.*

Putting the output of one into the standard input of the other, as demonstrated with the command

```
ls -l * | more
```

is called *piping.* The | symbol is called — you guessed it — the pipe symbol.

Editing the Command Line

One of the most useful bash features is *command-line editing,* which is the capability to change parts of a command line without having to retype the entire command. Suppose you type the following line:

```
[maddog@shamet maddog]$ ls -l * | more
```

You actually meant to use the less command, not the more command, but you pressed Enter anyway.

You groan. You press Ctrl+C to halt the command. You would really like to reexecute the command, changing *more* to *less,* without having to type the entire command. Easy; just do the following:

```
[maddog@shamet maddog]$ ^more^less
```

This line resubmits the command to bash with more changed to less, as follows:

```
ls -l * | less
```

Output appears. If you have to stop the less command, press Q.

Note that the shell redisplays the first command with the change, and then the command is reexecuted. How does the shell know about the first command? History. bash remembers all the commands you have typed (to a certain extent) and allows you to edit and resubmit them. Awesome!

We say "to a certain extent" because bash remembers only a certain number of commands, depending on a parameter in the environment. After bash holds that many previous commands, it throws away the oldest ones as you type in newer ones. Normally, this parameter is large (perhaps 1,000 commands), so bash will essentially remember every command that you enter. (We can't imagine ever wanting to be able to recall more than the last thousand commands that we entered.)

Bang-bang

The fact that the shell remembers the command lines you type is useful for reexecuting commands at a later time. Simple *reexecution commands* are represented by exclamation points. In computerese, an exclamation point is called a *bang,* and two exclamation points are called — you guessed it — *bang-bang.*

Here are two key ways to use the exclamation point:

- ✔ !! reexecutes the last command.
- ✔ !<partial command line> reexecutes the command line that started with *<partial command line>*.

Here's an example. Type !cat on the command line as follows (*cat* is the *<partial command line>* mentioned in the preceding list):

```
[maddog@shamet maddog]$ !cat
```

bash searches backward through the previously executed commands in this session, looking for the first occurrence of a command line that starts with the letters *cat.* After the program locates the command, it is reexecuted.

A little timid about this? Perhaps your memory of which command you typed and when is a little faulty. Add :p to the command line to see what history finds. The command looks like this:

```
[maddog@shamet maddog]$ !cat:p
```

Linux sees the :p in the command and returns

```
cat /etc/passwd
```

which now becomes the last `cat` command in bash's history. Thus, to run the command that `!:p` found, enter bang-bang, like this:

```
[maddog@shamet maddog]$ !!
```

While using history to find and reexecute command lines, you can also make additions to the command line. Starting from the beginning with our example, if you type the following:

```
[maddog@shamet maddog]$ cat /etc/passwd
```

the file /etc/passwd is output to standard output, which in this case is the screen.

When you reexecute the preceding command by typing `!!`, you can also send the output to the `sort` command by using the pipe symbol:

```
[maddog@shamet maddog]$ !! | sort
cat /etc/passwd |sort
[maddog@shamet maddog]$
```

Linux pulls the /etc/passwd file from the disk and passes it to standard output, feeds it into the standard input of `sort`, and then outputs it to the screen in sorted fashion.

The bash shell also makes use of the up-arrow and down-arrow keys to reuse commands. The up-arrow key sequentially returns commands starting from the most recent. The down-arrow key, not surprisingly, goes forward in time. This is bash's most convenient feature.

This history command displays all the commands that you have used up to the Red Hat default of 1,000. You can use the history command to perform a sort of archaeological dig. For instance, if you want to see all the commands of a certain type that you have used, then you can pipe the output of the history command to the grep filter. To find all the times that you have entered the `ls` command, you can use the command: history | grep ls.

Several shells (such as csh, bash, tcsh, and zsh) have this type of simple editing, but bash also has more elaborate editing.

A shell for all seasons

When Ken Thompson and Dennis Ritchie first started writing UNIX, they wanted to investigate lots of new ideas in using computers. One of the ideas they explored was making the human interface to the computer changeable and adaptable to the specific needs of the application.

This human interface (or more specifically, what humans interact with most) is typically called a *command interpreter* because it looks at each command as it is typed and converts it into something the computer can follow as an instruction. Most computer systems back then had the command interpreter built into the operating system, which meant the user couldn't change it. (DOS is constructed this way.) The UNIX developers wanted to separate the command interpreter from the rest of the operating system. Because the functionality desired was both a command interpreter and a complete environment, it was called a *shell*. The first command interpreter for UNIX was called the Bourne shell, often abbreviated as sh.

Later, when UNIX escaped from Bell Labs and fled to the University of California, Berkeley, the developers decided to extend the shell. They made it more of a programming language and included some features found in the C language. The resulting shell was the C shell, abbreviated csh (pronounced "sea shell," of course).

Both the Bourne shell and the C shell existed for many years. The Bourne shell version was available on both System V and Berkeley-based systems. The C shell was used only on Berkeley systems — AT&T was paranoid about having a shell on its system that was created by long-haired college students. The researchers at Bell Labs fought to add the C shell, and eventually it was ported to System V, too.

Next, enter GNU, a collection of software based on UNIX and maintained by the Free Software Foundation. (GNU, by the way, stands for GNU's Not UNIX.) The GNU project decided it needed a shell free of royalty restrictions. Unfortunately, at the time, the C shell was still under restrictions from AT&T. So the GNU folks decided to create their own royalty-free, GPLed shell. Their new shell would be compatible with the Bourne shell, incorporate some of the C shell idea, and have some interesting new features. They called their shell bash, for Bourne Again SHell.

Meanwhile, innovation stirred at AT&T. David Korn, a researcher there, merged the best of the Bourne shell, C shell, and any other shells he could find, and made the resulting shell even better for programmers by implementing several programming features. The most notable addition was *functions* (which helps to divide large shells into smaller, easier-to-maintain ones). His shell was named the Korn shell (abbreviated ksh). Eventually, this shell also developed graphical features and was adopted by the Open Software Foundation folks as part of their Common Desktop Environment (dtksh).

As the price of computers dropped and freely distributable versions of UNIX (netBSD, FreeBSD, and Linux) made their way across the Internet, new shells evolved from the old ones and other shells started to appear, such as:

- **tcsh:** A C shell with filename completion and command-line editing

- **ash:** A System V–like shell

- **zsh:** Like ksh, but with built-in spelling correction on the command-line completion, among other useful features

- **pdksk:** A public domain reimplementation of the Korn shell

- **Perl:** Practical Extraction and Report Language

(continued)

> ✔ **Tcl/Tk:** A string-oriented language with a graphical interface toolkit
>
> ✔ **Python:** A powerful scripting language with a built-in graphical interface
>
> So why do we have all these shells (and shell-like languages)? They are examples of how separating the command interface from the operating system can allow the language to grow and improve. They are also examples of how specialized languages can be combined with other shells and programs to do really powerful work. If only one shell existed, under the control of one person or organization, innovation would certainly take much longer.

Back to the future

Linux offers a handy tool for rerunning long commands that you've already entered. Press Ctrl+P, and the display scrolls through the commands that you've entered, one command at a time in reverse order, showing the most recent command first. When the command you want appears on the screen, just press Enter to run it.

Interpreting File Names

Suppose your mind has been wandering, and although you do remember that a file in /etc contains passwords, you can't remember whether the file is in /etc/passwd, /ctc/password, or whatever. You may want the command interpreter to choose the proper spelling of the filename for you, rather than type what you think it may be.

You can first list the files in the /etc directory, and then use more to view the specific file you want to see (/etc/passwd):

```
[maddog@shamet maddog]$ ls /etc/pass*
/etc/passwd
[maddog@shamet maddog]$ more /etc/passwd
```

Or you can use a shortcut with bash by pressing the Tab key after you think you have a unique match:

```
[maddog@shamet maddog]$ more /etc/pass<TAB>
```

The shell automatically expands the name of the file to /etc/passwd and then hesitates to see whether you want to accept the command:

```
[maddog@shamet maddog]$ more /etc/passwd
```

When the shell automatically expands a filename and then hesitates, waiting for you to confirm a command by pressing the Enter key, this action is known as *command completion*. Now you can press the Enter key to execute the command.

But wait! What happens if you have two files, one /etc/passwd and the other /etc/password? When you press the Tab key, the system rings the bell, and the name doesn't expand. Press the Tab key a second time, and bash shows you all the possible expansions of that argument. If a huge number of expansions result, bash warns you:

```
[maddog@shamet gifs]$ ls p<TAB><TAB>
There are 255 possibilities. Do you really
wish to see them all? (y or n)
```

By the way, using the ls command and then pressing the Tab key twice is an interesting way to get a complete listing of every executable command available in your PATH. The command completion works not only for the filename arguments but also for the commands themselves. For example:

```
[maddog@shamet maddog]$ lp<TAB><TAB>
lpq          lpr       lptest
lpqall.faces    lprm      lpunlock
```

Here is another example:

```
[maddog@shamet maddog]$<TAB><TAB>
There are 1455 possibilities. Do you really
wish to see them all? (y or n) y
```

Stand back, because the shell now lists all 1,455 commands in your PATH!

Another useful command completion is the tilde (~), known to your business manager as the *squiggly thing*. When you use this symbol in a command line, it represents your login directory.

Suppose you are in the /etc directory, and you want to put a copy of the passwd file (which normally resides in the /etc directory) into your own login directory. You can type the entire pathname to your directory, or you can just type the following:

```
[maddog@shamet /etc]$ cp passwd ~
```

If you are root and want to put the passwd file into someone else's directory, you can type the following, for example:

```
[root@shamet /etc]$ cp passwd ~maddog
```

A copy of passwd goes into the login directory of maddog, assuming that maddog is a valid login name with a valid home directory.

Chapter 11

Scripting Your Act

● ●

In This Chapter

▶ Writing a simple shell program

▶ Writing a not-so-simple shell program

▶ Finding out about multitasking

● ●

*A*fter you get the hang of working from within a shell, you can branch out to writing shell scripts. And if you're good at it, you can move to Hollywood and find fame and fortune. You probably never anticipated that you could gain so much from purchasing this Linux book, eh?

The bash shell that comes standard with all Linux distributions provides you with a powerful programming environment. Shell programming is also called scripting and is typically used to perform repetitive administrative tasks. This chapter describes how to get started in the exciting world of writing scripts. Send your dues to the Screen Actor's Guild right away!

Starting Out with a Simple Shell Script

In Chapter 10, we show you *interactive shell functions,* a fancy term that simply means that you type something and the computer executes it immediately. After a while, you may notice that you're typing a certain series of commands over and over. Wouldn't it be nice to put all those commands in a file and execute them all at once? Well, you can!

For the rest of this section, you work on creating shell scripts, which contain a series of commands that are executed every time you type the name of the script as a command. First you create a simple shell script and later you create a more complex one.

Suppose you want to periodically generate a report, showing who owns the login accounts. You can simply print the /etc/passwd file, but that file has a lot more information in it than you need. Plus, you are an organized person and prefer to format the report yourself rather than use the password file's layout.

First, look at the following entry in the passwd file:

```
maddog:eyrtwuir:500:500:Red Hat Linux
              User,,,,:/home/maddog:/bin/bash
```

Each grouping of characters between the colons is called a *field*. For the report, you want only the first and fifth fields. The cut command is the way to go. The man page for the cut command shows that the command to get the first and fifth fields is as follows:

```
cut -f 1,5 -d: /etc/passwd
```

The *man pages* are terse but complete descriptions of commands. To get to the man page for the cut command, type man cut on the command line.

You use the -f option for the cut command to list the fields you want printed, in this case the first and fifth fields. You use the -d option to specify the delimiter for the field, which in this case is a colon. The preceding command gives lines of output formatted like this:

```
maddog:Red Hat Linux User,,,,
```

Maybe you'd prefer to replace the colon with a hyphen, adding a space on each side to make the report easier to read. The stream editor sed is your ticket to formatting happiness. You can send the output of cut directly to sed with the following command line:

```
cut -f 1,5 -d: /etc/passwd | sed -e 's/:/ - /'
```

The pipe symbol, |, takes the output of the cut command and feeds it to the sed command. Look at the part of the command line to the right of the pipe symbol, and you can see that the -e option of the sed command tells the command to use the next string of characters (in this case, what appears between the two apostrophes, or single quotation marks) as a command for the sed stream editor. (The command here is basically the same as the s command in the ed and ex text editors, which you can read about in Chapter 9.) The command finds the string of characters between the first and second slash marks and replaces them with the characters between the second and third slash marks.

Note the single quotes around 's/:/ - /'. These quotes instruct the shell to think of the entire string of characters as one *thing,* and present the string to the sed editor as the thing that -e has to work with. Without the single quotes, the shell would conclude from the blanks in the string that three different things are in that string of characters: s/:/, -, and /. In shell statements, unquoted blank space (called *white space*) is considered a separator.

Continuing with your report, you want some type of header that states the subject of the report and the date. You can use the echo command (for the header) and the date command (for the date):

```
echo Report of login names and users on the Linux system
date
echo =========================================
cut -f 1,5 -d: /etc/passwd | sed -e `s/:/ - /'
```

These four lines are not difficult to type, but having to remember them and retype them each time you run the report is a nuisance. We like to save time whenever we can, and our memory cells seem to be dropping like . . . ah, we forget. For those reasons, we want to use our favorite text editor to type the lines in a file.

Our favorite editor is vi. If you want to use another editor, we won't stop you. But be sure to name your file *quagmire* so that the rest of the example will work.

In the following example, we use vi to edit a file named quagmire, entering the commands that we typed before into that file:

```
[maddog@shamet maddog]$ vi quagmire
a
echo Report of login names and users on the Linux system
date
echo =========================================
cut -f 1,5 -d: /etc/passwd | sed -e 's/:/ - /'
<ESC>
:wq
```

The last line, :wq, writes the file to the disk and quits the editor.

Now you must tell Linux that executing the file is okay. To do this, you have to change the file permissions to execute:

```
chmod ugo+x,ugo+r quagmire
```

For more on permissions, check out Chapter 9.

Your quagmire file was probably created with the owner's (u), the group's (g), and the rest of the world's (o) permissions of at least read (r), if not read and write (rw). The owner (that's you), the people in the group, and the rest of the world should be able to read (r) and execute (x) the shell file, or *shell script*.

Just because a shell can be read does not mean that it can be executed. You must explicitly tell the system that executing it is okay.

Now, type the following:

```
./quagmire
```

and you see your report run before your eyes! Type

```
./quagmire | more
```

and you see that your quagmire program acts like any other program. It allows piping to other programs, including the printer (if you have one available to your system):

```
./quagmire | lpr
```

But notice that for your program, you have to type . / in front of the filename. If you don't include . /, you get the following message:

```
bash: quagmire: command not found
```

You receive this message because your current directory, where the quagmire shell script resides, is not in the list of directories contained in the PATH variable. If you type the following:

```
echo $PATH
```

you probably see a line that looks something like this:

```
/usr/local/bin:/bin:/usr/bin:/usr/X11R6/bin:/usr/bin/mh:/home
             /maddog/bin
```

A colon separates each *path* of a directory, so Linux searches for valid commands in these directories (in order): /usr/local/bin, /bin, /usr/bin, and so forth. The directory that is most interesting to you is probably at the end of the line. It should be something like /home/<*your user name*>/bin. Likewise, you should have a bin directory in your login directory. If you don't, create one now, as follows:

```
[maddog@shamet maddog]$ mkdir ~/bin
```

Then move your quagmire file to the bin directory in your login account:

```
[maddog@shamet maddog]$ mv quagmire ~/bin
```

Now you can execute the quagmire program just like you can any other program:

```
[maddog@shamet maddog]$ quagmire
Report of login names and users on the Linux system
Sun Jul 6 08:57:01 EDT 1997
=============================================
```

(continued)

```
root - root
bin - bin
daemon - daemon
adm - adm
lp - lp
sync - sync
shutdown - shutdown
halt - halt
mail - mail
news - news
uucp - uucp
operator - operator
games - games
gopher - gopher
ftp - FTP User
nobody - Nobody
maddog - Red Hat Linux User,,,,
. . .
[maddog@shamet maddog]$
```

You just wrote a program. It's a simple program, but as far as Linux is concerned, it's as much a program as any other.

What you just wrote is called a *shell program,* or a *shell script.* In many cases, shells are more efficient than writing many hundreds of lines in C or Fortran. Shells are fairly easy to write, fairly easy to change, and even experienced C and Fortran programmers use them every day instead of writing more complex programs with those other languages. Systems administrators wouldn't survive without scripting languages such as shell.

Moving On to More Flexible Shell Scripts

The program in the previous section always works on the same file, which is hard-coded into the script. For the rest of this chapter, we show you how to create more flexible shell scripts, ones that can generate different filenames as needed and automatically adapt to being run on different dates.

Suppose you want to keep monthly copies of the passwd file and see the differences between those copies. First, write a program that saves a copy of the passwd file and stores it in a directory:

1. **Use the** `cat` **command to create a script in your ~/bin directory called genreport.**

   The genreport script is simple. It copies the file /etc/passwd to standard output by using the `cat` command; the redirection symbol puts it into a file.

2. **When choosing a filename that the script will generate when it is executed, start with the name *passwd* but attach the year and the month
to it.**

For example, the passwd file for July 2000 would be passwd200007, and
the one for August 2000 would be passwd200008.

To create these files, execute the date command inside the shell script
line and use its output to add to the word *passwd*. If you use the backward single quote (called accent grave) around the date command, it
generates the numbers *200007* (if it is July 2000, for example) that will be
added to the string of characters *passwd*. The accent grave tells Linux to
"execute what is between the accent grave symbols as a Linux command
and use the results of that command as a string in the larger command."
Therefore, the date command generates the string *200007,* which is
added to the name *passwd* to create *passwd200007*.

If you're searching your keyboard for that accent grave character, you
may find it under the tilde (~) character usually found in the upper-left
of the keyboard under the Esc key.

3. **When you make this file in your bin directory, don't forget to change
its permissions to make it executable.**

This is the program that we generated and an example of it being run:

```
[maddog@shamet bin]$ cat ~/bin/genreport
cat /etc/passwd > passwd`date +%Y%m`
<CTRL+D>
[maddog@shamet bin]$ chmod u+rx ~/bin/genreport
[maddog@shamet bin]$ cd
[maddog@shamet maddog]$ mkdir reports ; cd reports;
[maddog@shamet maddog]$ genreport
[maddog@shamet reports]$ ls
passwd200007
[maddog@shamet reports]$
```

Note that on the second line, we typed two accent grave characters, not
apostrophes.

Single commands that are not separated by a pipe symbol — that is, their
standard output won't be fed to the standard input of the next command —
may be placed on the same line and separated with a semicolon (;). This
shortcut is useful in interactive mode because you don't have to press Enter
and wait for a response; however, it seldom saves any time in scripts. In
scripts, putting commands on separate lines is better because they're easier
to change later if necessary.

Suppose you run the program on the first day of the month over several
months' time. You accumulate several copies of the passwd file, each with
changes as login accounts are added and deleted.

Just a few good commands

Shell programming depends heavily on the many hundreds of specialized programs that come with most UNIX systems. Of these many hundreds, perhaps only 20 or 30 are used in day-to-day scripting, but the others are there just in case, and most, if not all, are documented in a section of one of the man pages.

Jon still remembers the day he began to feel comfortable with UNIX (*long* before Linux was available). He was trying to do something with a shell script, utilizing the 20 to 30 commands he knew. Finally the thought occurred to him that although he was not sure that UNIX had the command he needed, there was a strong probability that it did. So he started going through the manual pages looking for a command that might help. Sure enough, he found one. From that day on, he felt comfortable with UNIX, even though he kept learning more about it every day. From time to time, he still goes through the reference pages of the manual, one by one, to find out about new commands and to refresh his memory on old ones.

Each of these commands typically does one thing very well, and you can put them together with pipes and shell-script glue to solve a larger problem. Becoming familiar with them takes time and practice, but after you do that, your abilities expand a thousand fold.

Eventually the reports directory looks somewhat like this:

```
[maddog@shamet reports]$ ls
passwd200007 passwd200009 passwd200011 passwd200001
passwd200008 passwd200010 passwd200012 passwd200002
[maddog@shamet reports]$
```

To simulate running your genreport program over several months, follow these steps:

1. **Create a directory called reports, and change to that directory.**

2. **Execute the genreport program once.**

3. **Create seven copies of the report file for different months.**

   To do so, change the name of each new file to a different date. This action creates eight total files (the original and seven copies). The files have the same contents, but that's okay for now.

   ```
   cp passwd200007 passwd200008
   cp passwd200007 passwd200009
   cp passwd200007 passwd200010
   cp passwd200007 passwd200011
   cp passwd200007 passwd200012
   cp passwd200007 passwd200101
   cp passwd200007 passwd200102
   ```

4. **Write a shell script that shows you the accounts that were added and deleted from month to month.**

   One way to write this script is to create a program that allows you to supply the names of two of the files to see whether any accounts have been added or deleted. The second way is more automated: Have the program look through all the files to see whether any accounts have been added or deleted. Later in this chapter, you find out how to provide that level of automation.

Passing information to your shell

The shell program can get several pieces of information from the arguments you use when you invoke the shell. To illustrate the presence of arguments on the command line and the capability of the shell to access them, use a text editor to create a small, simple shell called *stuff* and put it in the bin directory of your login account (remember to change the shell's mode to be executable by you, the owner):

```
[maddog@shamet reports]$ cat > ~/bin/stuff
echo The zeroth argument $0
echo The first argument $1
echo The second argument $2
echo The third argument $3
echo The fourth argument $4
echo The number of expanded arguments $#
<CTRL+D>
[maddog@shamet reports]$ chmod u+x ~/bin/stuff
```

Okay, you have enough lines to put into the shell. Note that each line ends with either a number or the character #, preceded by a dollar sign. These are special names inside the shell that will have values assigned to them, according to what you type on the command line as a command name and as arguments when you invoke the shell.

You should still be in the reports directory, but just to make sure you are, change directories to your reports directory. Then execute the stuff shell script that you just created:

```
[maddog@shamet maddog]$ cd ~/reports
[maddog@shamet reports]$ stuff
The zeroth argument /home/maddog/bin/stuff
The first argument
The second argument
The third argument
The fourth argument
The number of expanded arguments 0
[maddog@shamet reports]$
```

Note that the *zeroth* argument (called $0) is the full pathname for the executed shell command. When executing the command name by itself on the line with no additional arguments or options, the zeroth argument is the only argument that receives information.

Now supply a wildcard on the shell command line as follows:

```
[maddog@shamet reports]$ stuff *
The zeroth argument /home/maddog/bin/stuff
The first argument passwd199707
The second argument passwd199708
The third argument passwd199709
The fourth argument passwd199710
The number of expanded arguments 8
[maddog@shamet reports]$
```

The shell expands the wildcard to include all the filenames that match the * wildcard, which in this case means all the files in the directory. The $# argument reports that eight arguments match the wildcard. Only four of the filenames are printed, however, because you requested only four arguments — filenames in this case — in your shell script.

To see that eight arguments really are on the command line, type the following command:

```
echo *
```

The echo command echoes whatever follows it on the line. If you type echo Hi there and press the Enter key, Hi there appears on the next line. If you type the command line echo 5342 and press Enter, 5342 appears on the line.

But when you type echo * in your reports directory and press Enter, something different from * appears on the next line. What appears is the name of every file or directory in the reports directory. This happens because the bash shell sees the * as a regular expression and expands it to match every filename or directory name in the directory that does not begin with a period. That expanded line is then presented to the echo command.

The same thing happens to your stuff shell script or any other shell script that has a regular expression passed to it as an argument. The *shell* — not the command or shell script you invoke — expands the regular expression. Because you created eight filenames in the reports directory, you know that eight arguments are on the line (for the eight names in your directory) and not just the four you printed.

Now add the proper regular expansion to cover all the files called passwd2000*xx;* six exist:

```
[maddog@shamet reports]$ stuff *2000*
The zeroth argument /home/maddog/bin/stuff
The first argument passwd200007
The second argument passwd200008
The third argument passwd200009
The fourth argument passwd200010
The number of expanded arguments 6
[maddog@shamet reports]$
```

Only four files are returned in your four arguments $1 through $4 because the shell script asked for only four to be printed.

The final step causes wildcard expansion of the 2001 years:

```
[maddog@shamet reports]$ stuff *2001*
The zeroth argument /home/maddog/bin/stuff
The first argument passwd200101
The second argument passwd200102
The third argument
The fourth argument
The number of expanded arguments 2
[maddog@shamet reports]$
```

Only two of the four arguments are filled. Likewise, the $# argument reports that only two files were expanded and placed on the command line.

Controlling the flow

One series of commands is typically used only in a shell script to make decisions instead of on the command line (typed in one line at a time). These commands are *flow control,* or *conditional,* statements and are found in many computer languages in different forms. The simplest one in the bash shell language is if. The if statement is usually written as follows:

```
if list1
then
list2
fi
```

Or, for more complex conditions,

```
if list1
then
list2
[elif list3
then
list4]
{and so on...}
fi
```

Seems ugly, doesn't it? But it isn't too bad. Note that overall it begins with `if` and ends with `fi`, which is the backward spelling of `if`. Who says computer programmers have no sense of humor?

The *list* statements represent other shell commands, statements, and so forth that should be tested to see whether they are true or false *(list1 and list3)* or executed *(list2 and list4).*

So what are some examples of *list* statements? You see one in the next example, which is a test to see whether a file exists. In this case, the built-in function test `-e` sees whether a filename exists; if it exists, `echo` says so. You can try out this example on the command line without putting it in a shell. Make sure that you have spaces in front of and behind each left bracket (`[`) and right bracket (`]`). A small `>` appears after the first line, to indicate that the shell is expecting you to type some more:

```
[maddog@shamet reports]$ if [ -e /etc/passwd ]
> then
> echo file exists
> else
> echo file does not exist
> fi
file exists
[maddog@shamet reports]$
```

Now, to test to see whether the `if` statement can detect the passwd filename, type the name incorrectly:

```
[maddog@shamet reports]$ if [ -e /etc/password ]
> then
> echo file exists
> else
> echo file does not exist
> fi
file does not exist
[maddog@shamet reports]$
```

You can create other simple tests, such as:

- ✔ -f for finding out whether a file exists and is a regular file, not a directory or device file
- ✔ -d for finding out whether a file exists and is a directory
- ✔ -r for finding out whether a file exists and is readable

In the manual pages, you can read more about tests to perform on filenames. You can even combine tests to check for many conditions at one time.

Putting your ideas together

Are you ready to put the concepts from the first shell script together with the concepts from the second shell script? The result is a program that selects two passwd files from different months and compares them. The program tests to make sure that all the filenames are typed correctly on the command line and then extracts the information from the files, compares them, and prints the differences, if any.

You should use a text editor to create a file called passdiff in your ~/bin directory, putting the following lines in it:

```
# Shell comments start with a pound sign (#) on a line.
# Anything following a # is ignored by the shell and is
# used only by humans to understand what is going on
# in the script. Use comments liberally.
#
# if the number of arguments is not equal to 2
if [ $# != 2 ]
# then
then
# echo a usage message
echo Usage: passdiff file1 file2
# and exit with an error code of 9
exit 9
fi
# if the first argument is not a file
if [ ! -f $1 ]
# then echo message that the first argument is not a file
then
echo $1 is not a file
# and exit with an error code of 9
exit 9
#
fi
# test the second argument the same way
if [ ! -f $2 ]
```

(continued)

```
then
echo $2 is not a file
exit 9
fi
# Now use the cut and sed statements, which we used
# before to create the login-name/description. But this
# time, store the contents in files called
# /usr/tmp/quagmire.?.$$ where the ? matches any digit
# and the $$ assumes the process number of the shell to
# create a unique filename. Two files with unique
# filenames will therefore be generated temporarily in
# /usr/tmp: quagmire.1.<processnumber> and
# quagmire.2.<processnumber>
# There is a difference in Linux (as in most programming
# systems) between a single quote (that symbol below the
# double quote on a U.S. keyboard) and accent grave`,
# that symbol below the tilde (the squiggly thing) on a
# U.S. keyboard. In the following lines, the ` symbol is
# a single quote, which turns off the shell's regular
# expression matching and allows the sed command to see
# the regular expression (if any).
cut -f 1,5 -d: $1 | sed -e 's/:/-/' \ >/usr/tmp/quagmire.1.$$
cut -f 1,5 -d: $2 | sed -e 's/:/-/' \ >/usr/tmp/quagmire.2.$$
# use the diff command to compare the two files generated.
# diff creates output lines with a < symbol pointing to
# extra lines from the first file and a > symbol pointing
# to extra lines from the second file. The results are
# placed in a third temporary file created
# using the process number as before.
diff /usr/tmp/quagmire.1.$$ /usr/tmp/quagmire.2.$$ \
            >/usr/tmp/quagmire.3.$$
# now we echo whether or not there were any extra
# login names
echo password file $1 had these extra login names:
# if there are any extra ones from the first file, print
# them to standard output
# We have to use single quote marks around the `^<`
# argument to tell the shell script this is an argument to
# the grep command, and not a redirection symbol telling it
# to take the file of /usr/tmp/quagmire.3.$$ and feed it
# through standard input
grep `^<` /usr/tmp/quagmire.3.$$
# now we echo whether or not there were any extra
# login names
echo password file $2 had these extra login names:
# if there are any extra ones from the second file, print
# them to standard output. (Note the use of single quotes
# in the line below.)
grep `^>' /usr/tmp/quagmire.3.$$
# remove all temporary files from /usr/tmp. The ? matches
# all three digits.
rm /usr/tmp/quagmire.?.$$
# exit with a successful error code.
exit 0
```

Remember to save the file. Change its mode to read and execute by typing the following:

```
chmod u+rx ~/bin/passdiff
```

Time to take the program on a test run. To do that, you need to make some of the files in the reports directory different. Add one more line to passwd200008, as follows:

```
baddog::502:502:A BAD Red Hat Linux
        User,,,,:/home/baddog:/bin/bash
```

Then add one more line to file passwd200010:

```
bulldog::501:501:Yet Another Red Hat Linux
        User,,,,:/home/bulldog:/bin/bash
```

Now, cross your fingers and test the program! Oops. Uncross your fingers and type the following:

```
[maddog@shamet reports]$ passdiff
Usage: passdiff file1 file2
[maddog@shamet reports]$
[maddog@shamet reports]$ passdiff passwd200008 pass20010
pass20010 is not a file
[maddog@shamet reports]$
[maddog@shamet reports]$ passdiff passwd200008 passwd200010
password file passwd200008 had these extra login names:
< baddog - A BAD Red Hat Linux User,,,,
password file passwd200110 had these extra login names:
> bulldog - Yet Another Red Hat Linux User,,,,
[maddog@shamet reports]$
```

Multitasking

When executing programs on a Linux system, being able to take advantage of its *multitasking* capabilities — that is, running multiple programs at the same time — is beneficial. This process is also called *job control*. Windows NT does this, Windows 95 and Windows 98 seem to do it, and UNIX systems have been doing it for almost 30 years. Most of this job control capability is due to the shell being able to launch background jobs and manage them.

For example, perhaps you have a task that will be running a long time, with little or no human input needed. When you start that task, all you have to do is put an & (ampersand) sign at the end of the line, and the job starts running in the background.

Deciphering bash

Linux is known for its *cryptic* command names, error messages, and documentation. We prefer to think of the command names as *terse* — a lot of meaning in a small space. The man page on bash, however, is more than 60 pages long, with no examples and no cheery dialog to entertain you.

From that lengthy page count, you can surmise that shell programming involves a lot more than we can tell you in these few pages. Entire books have been written just on shell programming. What we show you in this book, however, should help you write a few short scripts to make your life easier.

For example, if you start ical (a really nice graphical calendar program on the CD-ROM [CD1] that comes with this book), you probably want it to run a long time, and yet you want to type other commands at the same time. (For more on the ical program, see Chapter 14.) To put ical into the background (assuming you have X running), you can start ical by typing the following command into a terminal emulator:

```
[maddog@shamet maddog]$ ical&
[1] 2449
[maddog@shamet maddog]$
```

The number in brackets is the job number, followed by the process ID number. The *job number* is the number that the shell gives the ical program to keep track of the ical job. The *process ID number* is the number that the entire operating system uses to keep track of the ical program.

To find all the programs running under the shell you're currently using, you can use the jobs shell command, as follows:

```
[maddog@shamet maddog]$ jobs
[1]+ Running          ical &
[maddog@shamet maddog]$
```

This information tells you that ical is job number 1, is running fine (thank you), is not waiting for any input from the console, and is having a great old time.

On the other hand, you can have another job (such as largejob) that you put temporarily into the background by simply putting the & at the end of the line:

```
[maddog@shamet maddog]$ largejob &
```

When you type **jobs** as a command in this case, you see that largejob was stopped, waiting for input or for some other reason:

```
[maddog@shamet maddog]$ jobs
[1]- Running          ical &
[2]+ Stopped (tty output)  largejob
[maddog@shamet maddog]$
```

You can bring largejob into the foreground by typing `fg %2` and giving it
some more input, and then put largejob back into the background by pressing Ctrl+Z and typing **bg**. Whew. Here's how it looks:

```
[maddog@shamet maddog]$ fg %2
largejob
MADDOG tries hard.
<CTRL+Z>
[2]+ Stopped          largejob
[maddog@shamet maddog]$ bg
[2]+ largejob &
[maddog@shamet maddog]$
```

You can have dozens or even hundreds of background processes. If they all
accepted data from the keyboard at the same time, how would you know
which program is receiving the data? Therefore, each program has to wait
until you recognize it, bring it into the foreground, enter the necessary data,
and then put it back into the background, where it blissfully keeps running
until it terminates or again needs input from the keyboard (or standard input,
as you have come to know it). Now you know why largejob was waiting to
accept such valuable and timely input.

Chapter 12

Managing the Linux File System

. . . .

In This Chapter

▶ Making your files available to Linux by mounting a file system

▶ Dismounting a file system

▶ Playing inspector to search for other users

▶ Experiencing the joys of configuration files

▶ Rehabilitating corrupted files

▶ Increasing disk space with a new drive

▶ Using more floppies

▶ Adding a CD-ROM drive

. . . .

*M*anaging the Linux file system is not a simple job. It is one of the more important ones for maintaining and updating your Linux system. You have the responsibility of creating the Linux file system and ensuring that users (even if you're the only user) have access to secure uncorrupted data. With a little work, you can quickly master the basics.

The tasks associated with file system management include the following:

▸ Diagnosing hardware failures

▸ Preventing file corruption

▸ Blocking user errors

▸ Connecting and configuring new hardware

▸ Managing disk resources

Linux performs some of these tasks automatically, thank goodness. Others you must do manually as needed. In this chapter, you discover the ins and outs of managing your Linux file system — the easy way.

Mounting and Dismounting

Files are important to Linux and other UNIX-like operating systems in ways that are different from their importance to DOS, Windows, and Macintosh operating systems. In Linux, *everything* is stored as files in predictable locations in the directory structure — Linux even stores commands as files. Like other modern operating systems, Linux has a tree-structured, hierarchical, directory organization called a *file system*.

All user-available disk space is combined in a single directory tree. The base of this system is the *root directory* (not to be confused with the root user), which is designated with a slash, /. A file system's contents are made available to Linux by merging the file system into the system directory through a process called *mounting*. This is just like mounting a horse except that no horse is involved.

File systems can be mounted or dismounted, which means that file systems can be connected or disconnected to the directory tree. The exception is the *root file system,* which is always mounted on the root directory when the system is running and cannot be dismounted. Other file systems may be mounted as needed, such as ones contained on another hard drive, a floppy disk, or a CD-ROM.

Mounting a file system

Here's the command syntax for manually mounting a file system:

```
mount block-special-file mount-point
```

Block-special-file is the *device driver* file for the partition of the disk drive (such as a hard drive or a CD-ROM drive) where you have created a file system, and *mount-point* is the directory where the file system is mounted. Want to see the mount command assign the first floppy drive, /dev/fd0, to the /mnt directory? Hey, did we promise you a good time or what?

```
mount /dev/fd0 /mnt
```

A file system can be mounted in only one place at any given time. The directory where the file system will be mounted *(mount-point)* must exist before you issue the mount command. Otherwise, the command won't work. If you need to create the directory, use the mkdir command, like this:

```
mkdir /canadianpolice
mount /dev/fd0 /canadianpolice
```

The first command makes a new directory called /canadianpolice. The second command mounts /dev/fd0 — the file system on the disk in the floppy drive — onto that new directory.

A directory that is used as a mount point is just like any other directory. It can store files and other directories. However, any files or directories that are stored in a directory that is used as a mount point will not be visible or usable until the file system mounted on that directory is unmounted.

When you're finished or fed up with the file system that you mounted on /canadianpolice, you must dismount it by using the umount command. The syntax for the umount command is

```
umount name
```

where *name* is either the name of the *block-special-file* (/dev/fd0) or the name of the directory that is the *mount-point* (/canadianpolice).

Sleuthing for other file users

Because Linux is a multiuser operating system, sometimes more than one user is logged in to the system at the same time. If this is the case, multiple file systems might be mounted and in use. The umount command works only on inactive file systems. If one of the files in the file system is open or the file system is the current directory, an error message says that the device is busy.

How do you find out which files are being used and by whom? You use the fuser command. (Get it? Find user — fuser.) This command returns a lot of information, identifying which processes are using a particular file or file system and which user is using them. If you use fuser with a filename, it returns information on just that file. If you invoke fuser with the block special filename, fuser reports on all the files in that file system.

The fuser command has two options that you may find useful:

- ✔ -u displays user names along with process IDs.
- ✔ -m enables you to specify the file system by name.

fuser is a character-cell, or text-based, program. By running fuser with the -u option, you can get the process number of programs using the file system, along with the user name of the person using those programs. For example:

```
[maddog@shamet p3ch0920]$ /usr/sbin/fuser -u /home
/:          492r(maddog)   503r(maddog)
  504r(maddog)   508r(maddog)   580r(maddog)
  581r(maddog)   585r(maddog)   586r(maddog)
  598r(maddog)   599r(maddog)   601r(maddog)
  879r(maddog)  1287r(maddog)
[maddog@shamet p3ch0920]$
```

Here you can see that maddog (that dirty dog!) has a series of programs using the /home file system. If you want to see what those programs are, you can use the ps command, which shows the process numbers and names of the processes running in the system:

```
[maddog@shamet p3ch0920]$ps ax |grep 601
 601 p0 S  0:00 /opt/applix/applix
[maddog@shamet p3ch0920]$
```

We ran ps ax to see all the processes in the system in extended mode so that you can see additional information about them instead of just their names. Then, by using the grep command with the process number 601 as an argument, we isolated one line from the output of the ps command. You can see that the program running is the /opt/applix/applix program. This is just one of the programs that you have to shut down to unmount the root file system.

By repeating the ps and grep commands, but substituting other process numbers for 601, you can see all the processes and know which programs to shut down. You can then ask the people running those processes to quit their programs, or you can use the kill function of fuser on the file system.

To use the kill function of fuser, you simply use the -k flag on fuser when you list the file systems that you're trying to unmount. For example, the

```
fuser -ku /home
```

command kills all the processes that are using the home file system for any reason. After all the programs are shut down and no one else is using the file system, you can unmount the file system.

Configuring file systems

Having to manually mount all the file systems every time you boot the system would quickly become annoying. To avoid this, you can have the system execute the required mount commands when you boot. The information needed to execute the required mount commands is in the standard Linux file system configuration file located at /etc/fstab. The entries in the file usually follow this format:

```
block-special-file mount-loc type opts dump-freq passnumber
```

Here is a breakdown of this entry:

- *block-special-file* is the name of the device file that is used to mount a file system. A device such as a hard drive handles data in chunks and thus the term block is used. A block device file such as /dev/hda1 refers to the first partition on an IDE drive.

✔ *mount-loc* is the directory where the file system will be mounted. If the directory is on a partition used for swapping, use `swap` for *mount-loc*.

✔ *type* is the kind of partition. For a native Linux file system, *type* is `ext2`.

✔ *opts* is the field for listing options, separated by commas. The options may include any of the following:

- `rw` — Allow the file to be read and written to (read-write mode).

- `ro` — Allow the file to be read only (read-only mode).

- `dev` — Treat special files in this file system as special files.

- `nodev` — Treat special files in this file system as filenames.

- `exec` — Permit execution of binary files from this file system.

- `noexec` — Prevent the execution of binary files from this file system. This option is useful for file systems that should only store data to prevent programs from being introduced by system crackers or to prevent people from trying to execute programs that were meant to run on a different system, such as MS-DOS.

- `auto` — Allow the file system to be mounted with the `-a` option to the `mount` command.

- `nouser` — Forbid a non-superuser from mounting the file system.

- `async` — Write data to the file system asynchronously. The system is faster, but you can lose data if a system failure occurs.

- `sync` — Write data to the file system synchronously.

- `suid` — Permit the suid (set user ID) access mode (the default).

The `suid` access mode enables an executable program with the suid (or setguid) permission bit set to take on the personality and permissions of the owner (or the group) of the executable program. This can be a security hole; specifying the `nosuid` option prevents files in this file system from having the set user ID (or setguid) access take effect.

- `nosuid` — Do not permit the `suid` access mode.

- `noauto` — Do not automatically mount this file system when the `-a` option is used with the `mount` command.

- `usrquota` — User quotas may be put into effect.

- • grpquota **Group quotas may be put into effect.**
- • defaults **A combination of** rw, suid, dev, exec, auto, nouser, **and** async.

✔ *dump-freq* is the frequency with which the file system may be backed up by the dump utility (not all systems use this).

✔ *pass-number* is a decimal number specifying the order in which fsck, the file system check utility, checks the file systems. A pass-number of 1 (one) indicates that this file system should be checked first. This pass-number is assigned to root. All other file systems should have a higher number. Two file systems on different drives can be checked at the same time to speed things up, but file systems on the same drive should have different pass-numbers. For a swap device, the pass-number should be 0 (zero), which disables fsck checking.

Following are examples of some typical /etc/fstab entries:

```
/dev/hdb1   /    ext2  defaults  1  1
/dev/hdb3  none swap  sw     0  0
/dev/hda1  /w95 msdos noauto   0  0
```

The first line enables the mounting of the first partition of the second IDE disk as the root file system. It is a Linux native file system and uses the rw, suid, dev, exec, auto, nouser, **and** async options. The first entry in the /etc/fstab file also indicates that the root file system should be dumped (backed up) once a week (use the man dump command for details on dump). Finally, the first entry of the /etc/fstab file indicates that the root file system should be the first file system to have fsck performed on it after booting the system.

The second line shows that the third partition of the second IDE disk is a swap partition and has the format of a swap file. (The swap partition is used for temporarily storing chunks of your random access memory [RAM] when it fills up. Having swap space enables your computer to run programs that take up more space than you have memory for.) You should never back up the swap partition or perform the fsck command on it.

The third line of the /etc/fstab file points to the first partition of the first disk, which is a file system to be mounted on the /w95 directory. This file system probably holds Microsoft Windows 95 files, and you can read and write to it. Because the noauto option is used, the -a option of mount won't automatically mount the file system. You should never use dump to back it up, nor should you do a file system check on it.

After you set up the /etc/fstab configuration file, file systems can be mounted automatically at boot time. In addition, after the /etc/fstab file is set up, the mount **and** umount **commands require only** *mount-point* or *block-special-file* as their argument.

Normally, most of the /etc/fstab file is set up during installation, so you have to update it only when you add new disks or disk partitions.

Red Hat and other vendors have created graphical interfaces for updating the /etc/fstab file so that you don't have to edit the file with a text editor (although you still have this option). On the accompanying CD-ROM (CD1), you can update the file with a program called linuxconf, as follows:

1. **log in as root or superuser.**

2. **Type** startx **to make sure that X Window System is operating.**

3. **Type** linuxconf **in a terminal emulator window.**

   The window, shown in Figure 12-1, appears.

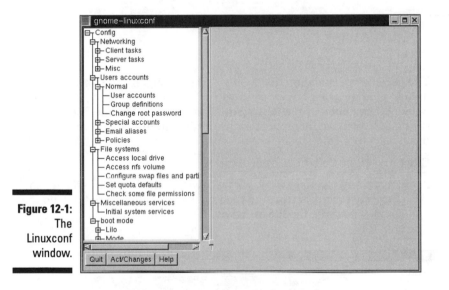

Figure 12-1:
The
Linuxconf
window.

4. **Click the File Systems menu.**

5. **Click the Access local drive menu.**

   The dialog box, shown in Figure 12-2, appears in the right pane of the linuxconf window.

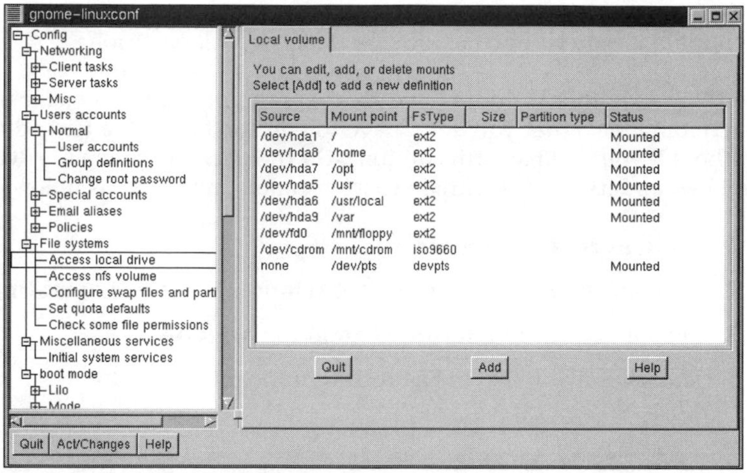

Figure 12-2:
The Access
local
drive/Local
volume
dialog box.

6. **Click any of the local mounts.**

   The Volume specification dialog box shown in Figure 12-3 appears. It indicates what type of file system you selected, what device it is, and where it is mounted. By choosing other tabs in the Volume Specification dialog box, you can fill in most of the options in the /etc/fstab file without having to memorize a lot of obscure options.

7. **Click Accept or Cancel as appropriate.**

   If you make any changes, they will be saved to the /etc/fstab file when you click the Accept button and then click the Quit button. Clicking the Cancel button leaves the file as it was.

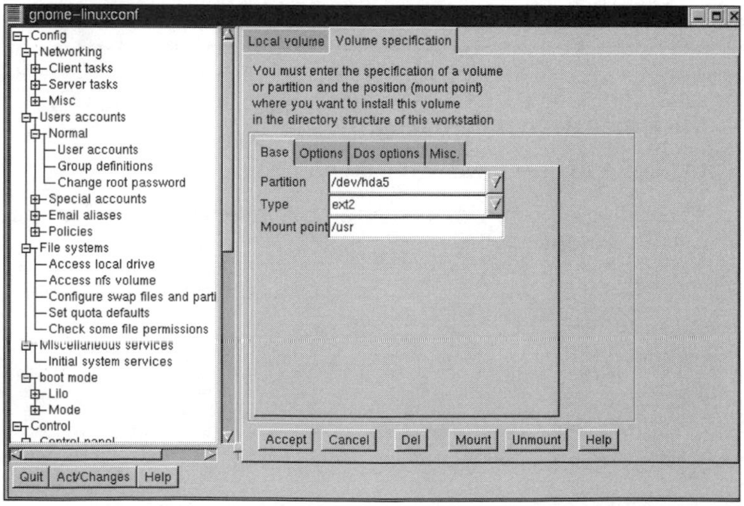

Figure 12-3:
The Access
local drive/
Volume
specifica-
tion dialog
box.

Reforming Corrupted File Systems

File systems can become corrupted by anything, from turning off your computer without shutting down Linux properly to a driver error or a hardware crash. The fsck utility can check the file system's consistency, report errors, and make some repairs. Normally, the fsck program is called automatically as the system boots. Therefore, if your system crashes, fsck runs on all file systems that were mounted when the system crashed.

The repairs that fsck can perform are limited to *structural* repairs of the file system and its data components. The fsck utility can't help if you have corrupted data in a structurally intact file. Also, remember that except for the root file system, fsck runs on only unmounted file systems. You must make sure that the system is in single-user mode to use fsck on the root file system.

Here's the syntax for the `fsck` command:

```
fsck (options) filesystem
```

filesystem names the block special file where the file system resides. If *filesystem* is omitted, the fsck utility checks all the file systems listed in the /etc/fstab file configuration file. If the fsck utility finds any errors, it prompts you for input on what to do about the errors. For the most part, you simply agree with whatever the program suggests.

The `fsck` command has the following options:

- ✔ `-p` Preen the file system. Perform automatic repairs that don't change the contents of files.

- ✔ `-n` Answer no to all prompts and only list problems; don't repair them.

- ✔ `-y` Answer yes to all prompts and repair damage regardless of how severe.

- ✔ `-f` Force a file system check.

Many people run the `fsck` command with the `-y` option. If you run `fsck` with the `-p` option, Linux performs some steps automatically. Lost files are placed in the lost+found directory, zero-length files are deleted, and missing blocks are placed back on the list of *free blocks,* which are blocks still available for filling with data, among other things.

Suppose your electricity goes out and your system crashes. When the system reboots, you see messages similar to the following:

```
/dev/hda5 was not cleanly unmounted, check forced
/dev/hda5: Deleted inode 1456 has zero dtime. FIXED
/dev/hda5: Deleted inode 14577 has zero dtime. FIXED
/dev/hda5: Deleted inode 123753 has zero dtime. FIXED
Fix summary information? Yes
/dev/hda5: 46906/308400 files (1.6% non-contiguous), 767485/
          1228801 blocks
```

And a little later, you see something like this for each one of your file systems:

```
fsck.ext2 -a /dev/hda7
/dev/hda7 was not cleanly unmounted, check forced
/dev/hda7: Deleted inode 1324 has zero dtime. FIXED
/dev/hda7: Deleted inode 15987 has zero dtime. FIXED
Fix summary information? Yes
/dev/hda7: 47266/356000 files (1.6% non-contiguous), 765217/
          1283507 blocks
```

The information that is shown above is from fsck running with the `-a` option, which answers all the questions with yes. For the most part, fsck corrects any errors that occur when the power fails or when something breaks inside your computer, causing it to crash. After fsck runs, it reports whether it modified any file systems.

Adding More Disk Storage

Eventually, you're likely to want to add more hard disk storage to your Linux system to hold more programs, to hold more data, or to enable more users to log in. You usually increase disk storage by adding one or more disks at a time; each disk can have one or more disk partitions.

The disk partition is Linux's basic file storage unit. First, you create the file systems on the disk partitions, and then you combine the file systems to form a single directory tree structure. The directory tree structure can be on one disk or spread across many.

You can define disk partitions when adding a new disk or sometime later. In most cases, Linux defines disk partitions during the original Linux installation. You may divide a disk into one, two, four, or more partitions, each of which may contain a file system or be used as a swap partition. Swap partitions allow very large programs or many small programs to run even if they take up more memory than you have as RAM in your computer. The total of all your swap partitions and RAM is called *virtual memory*.

After you create a disk partition, you must create a file system. The file system occupies a single space on the disk that has a unique block special file (device) name. This unique name accesses the file system regardless of whether the data is stored on all or only part of a physical disk or is an aggregation of multiple physical disks.

Linux developers are constantly supporting new file systems. The following file system types are the major ones:

- **Local:** ext, ext2, hpfs
- **NFS:** nfs
- **Samba:** SMB
- **CD-ROM:** iso9660
- **DOS:** msdos, umsdos, vfat
- **Other:** sysv and minix

If you want to add one of these types of file systems, you have to make a new partition, which may mean adding a new disk drive, which just so happens to be the subject of the next section.

Adding a Disk Drive

The first step to increasing your disk space is to add a new disk drive. The following tasks are required to add a disk to your system (regardless of whether the disk is SCSI or IDE) and make it accessible to users:

- Attach the disk drive to your computer system.
- Provide a suitable device driver for the disk's controller in Linux. Completing this task may mean rebuilding the kernel of the Linux operating system (see Chapter 14 for details).
- Define at least one partition.
- Create the block special files for the partition(s).
- Create a Linux file system(s) on any partition(s) to be used for user files.
- Enter the new file systems into /etc/fstab, the configuration file.
- Mount the file systems (you may have to make a directory for a mount point).

The following sections guide you through the process of configuring a hard disk, a floppy drive, and a CD-ROM drive after they are physically installed.

Configuring a Hard Drive

The business of adding a hard disk to your microcomputer can be broken down into two steps:

- ✔ Physically adding the hard drive
- ✔ Logically making Linux aware of it

The first step is beyond the scope of this book, because your drive may be either IDE or SCSI, and the setup of the physical disk is dependent on the rest of the hardware in the system. We suggest that you consult the hardware manual that came with your system or have a reseller install your new hard disk. The Linux system is complicated by the fact that several operating systems — such as DOS, Linux, and SCO UNIX — may share the same hard disk.

To complete all the steps necessary to install and configure your new disk, you must know the total formatted drive capacity and the number of heads and cylinders, among other details. You can usually find this information in the documentation or from the manufacturer.

You may want to keep a record of the data from the partition table (as displayed by fdisk), such as

- ✔ Partition numbers
- ✔ Type
- ✔ Size
- ✔ Starting and ending blocks

Installing a drive

After the drive is attached to the system, Linux should recognize it when you boot. To review the booting messages in a slower fashion than they're displayed, use the dmesg command. If you added a new IDE drive, look for the mention of a new hdx drive, where the *x* is replaced with the letter *b, c, d,* or *e*. This information tells you that your kernel saw the new hard disk as it booted, and rebuilding the kernel is not necessary in order to add this drive. Likewise, if you're adding a new SCSI disk drive, you see a boot message indicating a new disk drive that has the designation sdx, where the *x* is a letter. In either the IDE or SCSI case, you may see other messages with additional information.

The messages for an IDE drive may look like this:

```
hdb: HITACHI_DK227A-50, 4789MB w/512KB Cache,CHS=610/255/63
```

And sometime later, a message appears that looks like the following, which describes the existing partitions on the new disk (if any):

```
hdb: hdb1 hdb2 < hdb5 hdb6 hdb7 hdb8 >
```

A SCSI disk drive has messages that look like this:

```
SCSI device sdb: hdwr device= .......
  sdb: sdb1
```

If you see these messages, the kernel has seen your new disk, and you don't have to rebuild the kernel to use the new disk.

The Linux distribution on CD1 features block special files for each of eight IDE disks (had–hdh) with nine partitions each (1–9). Linux also has block special files for seven SCSI hard disk drives (sda–sdg), which can have eight partitions each (1–8). In addition, Linux has a block special file for a SCSI CD-ROM (scd) with eight partitions (0–7). If you have lots of disks, or if your Linux distribution doesn't have enough block special files for your disk, you may have to create one or more additional block special files for the device, like this:

```
cd /dev; makedev sdg
```

This command creates the block special files for SCSI disk 7. Note that in both IDE and SCSI disks, the letters and disk numbers correspond: *a* is for the first disk, *b* is for the second disk, and so on.

If you add a SCSI disk drive with a lower ID number than one you already have, the new disk drive takes on that number. Suppose you have SCSI disk drives with hardware ID numbers of 0, 2, and 3. Linux gives these disks the names sda, sdb, and sdc, respectively. You make your partitions and your file systems, and create your entries in /etc/fstab to show where you want the file systems mounted. Now you get a new disk drive and set the hardware ID number to 1. When you reboot, the new disk drive gets the sdb designation, and the disk drives with ID numbers of 2 and 3 are renamed to sdc and sdd, respectively. You must now, at the very least, change your /etc/fstab table. For this reason, we recommend adding SCSI disk drives to your system, starting with ID 0 and working up the number chain, with no gaps in the numbering.

Partitioning a drive

After you've created block special files, you can use fdisk to partition the drive. The command to call this utility is `/usr/bin/fdisk`. For example, if you want to invoke fdisk for partitioning the first SCSI disk on your system, you type the following command:

```
/sbin/fdisk /dev/sda
```

To format the common IDE disk, you use the following command:

```
/sbin/fdisk /dev/hda
```

To find out how to use fdisk, refer to Chapter 5. Using fdisk is not too difficult; you can partition the drive fairly easily.

Making the file system

Every disk partition is simply an empty space with a beginning and an end. Unless the partition is being used for swap space, you have to put some type of file system on the partition before it can become useful. The mkfs (for make file system) command is used to create the file system on the partition. Normally, the file system is a native Linux file system, which at this time is called ext2. The Linux version of mkfs has been nicely streamlined and requires hardly any input. To create a file system on the disk drive partition sda1, for example, you enter the following command:

```
mkfs -t ext2 /dev/sda1
```

Or, for an IDE drive, enter this command:

```
mkfs -t ext2 /dev/hda1
```

If you want to create an MS-DOS file system on the disk partition, you use this command:

```
mkfs -t msdos /dev/sda2
```

You can continue to execute mkfs commands to create file systems for every partition on your new disk. Or you can leave some partitions without file systems (for future use), as long as you remember to perform the mkfs command on them before trying to attach them to your file system by using the mount command or the /etc/fstab table.

Congratulations! Your disk has been physically added to your system and partitioned, and you've added file systems to it. Now the disk is ready to join the rest of the file system — simply use either the mount command or the /etc/fstab file, which we describe earlier in this chapter.

Living with Floppy Disks

Floppy disks are treated a little differently than hard disks, mostly due to their size and fragility. They are not normally mounted and used for hours and days on end to hold gigabytes of data. More often, floppy disks are used to transfer data to other computers or to back up a few files.

Although you can create Linux file systems on floppy disks, using them in other ways is more advantageous. For example:

- ✔ Floppy disks can be mounted as DOS file systems, which can then be accessed with the standard Linux utilities such as `cp` and `ls`.

- ✔ Floppy disks can be used as raw devices with commands such as `tar` and `cpio`.

- ✔ Floppy disks can permit the use of special utilities that read and write to DOS disks.

On Linux systems, the block special file for the first floppy drive is /dev/fd0. The default density is 1,440 kilobytes. We assume that you're using standard, 3½-inch, preformatted floppy disks.

The following commands mount a floppy disk and write a DOS file to it, (replace `any-dosfile.txt` with a real filename):

```
mount /dev/fd0 /mnt/floppy
cp any-dosfile.txt /mnt/floppy
umount /mnt/floppy
```

These commands are one way to move files back and forth to an MS-DOS (Windows 3.1, 95, 98, or NT) machine. You can add the files to a floppy disk, insert the floppy in the MS-DOS machine, and the MS-DOS machine can read the files from the disk. Likewise, by mounting a floppy disk created on an MS-DOS machine, you can read and manipulate the files by using Linux.

The mtools package installed on your system enables you to access DOS disks and files without first mounting the floppy disk and adding it to your file system. Table 12-1 presents some mtools commands, which are probably familiar to DOS users.

Table 12-1	The mtools Utilities
Command	*What It Does*
Mformat	Formats a floppy disk in DOS format
mlabel	Labels a DOS floppy disk
mcd	Changes the current directory location on a DOS floppy disk
mdir	Lists the directory contents on a DOS floppy disk
mtype	Displays a DOS file's contents
mcopy	Copies files between a DOS floppy disk and Linux
mdel	Deletes files on a DOS floppy disk
mren	Renames files on a DOS floppy disk
mmd	Creates a subdirectory on a DOS floppy disk
mrd	Removes a directory from a DOS floppy disk
mattrib	Changes DOS file attributes

Configuring a CD-ROM Drive

You treat CD-ROM drives similar to — but not exactly like — hard or floppy disk drives. The block special file for CD-ROMs in Linux is usually /dev/cdrom, /dev/hdc, /dev/hdd, or /dev/sr0, depending on factors such as the type of CD-ROM, how it is connected to the controller, and its drive number.

The most common type of CD-ROM drive is ATAPI, and Linux usually recognizes ATAPI CD-ROM drives at boot. SCSI CD-ROM drives are normally recognized as the kernel boots. If you installed the system from CD1, Linux will have recognized the CD-ROM drive, which is probably called /dev/cdrom.

We mentioned that CD-ROM drives are not exactly like other disk drives because CD-ROMs are read-only (which means that you can't change their contents) and typically have only one file system to a disk. Therefore, you don't partition a CD-ROM drive, nor do you make a file system before mounting it. The manufacturer already did these things. You simply have to determine where you want to mount the CD-ROM and which drive you want it attached to. We assume that your CD-ROM drive is /dev/cdrom, which is really just a pointer to another special device file. This extra pointer (called a *link*) enables you to call the CD-ROM by the name /dev/cdrom, instead of having to call it /dev/scda on some systems (because it happens to be a SCSI device) and /dev/hdc on other systems (because it happens to be an IDE-based device).

Here is the command to mount a CD-ROM on your Linux system:

```
mount -r -t iso9660 /dev/cdrom /mnt/cdrom
```

The Linux system dismounts file systems automatically when you shut down the machine and — if you have put all the necessary information into the /etc/fstab file — automatically mounts them when you start up the system. So as far as disk systems go, you should be all set.

Chapter 13

Revving Up the RPM

- -

- -

*T*his chapter introduces the Red Hat Package Manager (RPM). Red Hat developed RPM in conjunction with Caldera Systems. It provides a mechanism for installing, updating, and removing software automatically. Without RPM, Linux would be not be where it is today and is a big reason why Red Hat is the de facto Linux distribution leader.

Introducing RPM

One of the primary systems that sets the Red Hat Linux distribution apart is its Red Hat Package Manager (RPM). When Linux distributors such as Red Hat create a system like RPM, they provide value to their customers and make Open Source software profitable. Some of the first Linux systems required the user to install all software via the tape archive system (tar), which was a bear to modify. RPM, on the other hand, accelerates like crazy as you wind out its engine, and yet is quite easy to manage.

All the software that was installed during the Red Hat installation process is stored in RPM form. The /mnt/cdrom/RedHat/RPMS directory contains all the RPM packages. You can also install, update, or uninstall software. As of this writing, RPM is the most popular system for installing, modifying, and transporting Linux software.

The package-management concept has been around for quite a while, with all the major UNIX vendors supplying their own systems. The idea is to distribute software in a single package and have a package manager do the work of installing or uninstalling, and managing the individual files. The Linux world has benefited greatly from this system that simplifies software distribution.

Taking a Look at What RPM Does

RPM performs three basic functions: installing, upgrading, and removing packages. In addition to these functions, it also can find out all sorts of information about installed and yet-to-be-installed packages (and also washes windows). Here is a brief rundown of each function:

✔ **Installing packages.** RPM installs software. Software systems such as Netscape Communicator have files of all types that must be put into certain locations to work properly. For instance, under Red Hat, some of the Netscape files need to go into the /usr/bin directory. RPM does that organizational stuff automatically. Not only does RPM install files into their proper directories, but it also does such things as create the directories and run scripts to do the things that need to be done.

✔ **Upgrading packages.** RPM can update existing software packages for you. Gone are the days when updating a system was worse than going to the dentist. RPM keeps track — in a database of its own — of all the packages that you have installed. When you upgrade a package, RPM does all of the bookkeeping chores and replaces only the files that need replacing. It also saves configuration files that it replaces.

✔ **Removing packages.** The package database that the RPM keeps is also useful in removing packages. RPM goes to each file and removes it. It also removes directories — when no files from other packages occupy them — that belong to the package.

✔ **Querying packages and files.** RPM can also give you a great deal of information about a package and its files. You can use the query function to find out the function of a package and what files belong to it. It can also work on the RPM packages themselves, regardless of whether they have been installed.

✔ **Verifying packages.** Installed packages can be validated. RPM can check an installed package against a checksum (a computered fingerprint) to see if and how it has been changed. This feature is very useful for security reasons. If you suspect that a file or system has been hacked, you can use RPM to find out how it has changed.

Enough car talk. The following sections describe using RPM.

Installing a RPM package

When you install your Red Hat Linux system, all the software that is copied to your hard disk comes from RPM packages. When you want to add additional software from the CD1 or a Red Hat mirror (www.redhat.com/mirrors.html), you can do so by using the rpm command; a mirror is a Web or FTP site where an exact image of a central software distribution is kept. If you want to add the HTML-based HOWTO documents, then log in as root and mount the CD-ROM and the package, as follows:

```
mount -r -t iso9660 /dev/hdc /mnt/cdrom
rpm -ivh /mnt/cdrom/RedHat/RPMS/howto-html*
```

The i parameter tells rpm to install the RPM package, the v tells it to be verbose, and the h creates a simple progress meter. After this process is complete, you can view the documents with your browser.

Sometimes forcing the installation of a package is necessary. Sometimes the RPM database that keeps track of installed packages can become corrupted and refuse to install a package for you. The following command forces the installation of a package:

```
rpm -ivh --force /mnt/cdrom/RedHat/RPMS/
```

Updating a RPM package

When you obtain a newer version of a Linux package, you may want to update your existing software. The update function is a way of doing so. To upgrade Samba, for instance, simply enter this command:

```
rpm -U samba*
```

Sometimes RPM balks at installing or upgrading a package. Typically, RPM looks at an installed package and decides that you aren't allowed to install the same, or older package, over it. You can override RPM and force it to install or upgrade a package by using the −force parameter:

```
rpm -U --force samba*
```

Removing a RPM package

You can remove a package by using the erase function (-e):

```
rpm -e samba
```

This command removes the Samba software. Sometimes, however, other package files occupy the same directories of the package that you want to delete. In these cases, you get a message saying that the directory cannot be deleted because it is not empty.

Getting information on a RPM package

After installing the HTML HOWTO documents, you can find out information about the files and the package by using the RPM query function. The command is as follows:

```
rpm -qi howto-html
```

This command returns the information about the RPM package and a short description of its function:

```
Name:           howto              Relocations: (not relocateable)
Version:        6.0                Vendor: Red Hat Software
Release:        4                  Build Date: Mon Mar 29 21:44:10
                                   1999
Install date:   Fri Apr 30        Build Host:
                16:45:59 1999      porky.devel.redhat.com
Group:          Documentation     Source RPM: howto-6.0-4.src.rpm
Size:           11370265          License: distributable
Packager:       Red Hat           <http://developer.redhat.
                Software          com/bugzilla>
URL:            ftp://sunsite.unc.edu/pub/Linux/docs/HOWTO
Summary:        HOWTO documents from the Linux Documentation
                Project.
Description:
Linux HOWTOs are detailed documents which describe a specific
aspect of configuring or using Linux. Linux HOWTOs are a
great source of practical information about your system. The
latest versions of these documents are located at http://
sunsite.unc.edu/linux.
```

Install the HOWTO package if you want to be able to access the Linux HOWTO documentation from your own system:

```
Name:           howto-html        Distribution: Manhattan
Version:        5.2               Vendor: Red Hat Software
Release:        2                 Build Date: Fri Oct 2
                                  00:43:18 1998
Install date:   Sat Mar 20        Build Host:
                16:59:17 1999     porky.redhat.com
Group:          Documentation     Source RPM:
                                  howto-5.2-2.src.rpm
Size:           11483727          License: distributable
Packager:       Red Hat Software  <bugs@redhat.com>
Summary:        html versions of the HOWTOs
Description:
These are the html versions of the HOWTOs. You can view them
with your favorite Web browser.
```

You can find out what files are in the package and where they live by using the query listing function:

```
rpm -qpl howto-html
```

This function returns a long list of HOWTO files that sit in the /usr/doc/HOWTO/ other-formats/html directory. Here is a sample of that listing:

```
/usr/doc/HOWTO
/usr/doc/HOWTO/other-formats
/usr/doc/HOWTO/other-formats/html
/usr/doc/HOWTO/other-formats/html/3Dfx-HOWTO-1.html
/usr/doc/HOWTO/other-formats/html/3Dfx-HOWTO-10.html
...
```

Later, you can check the state of the installed files by using this command:

```
rpm -qls howto-html
```

Any files that have been changed are listed as *changed* or *not installed*. Otherwise, they are listed as *normal*.

```
normal    /usr/doc/HOWTO
normal    /usr/doc/HOWTO/other-formats
normal    /usr/doc/HOWTO/other-formats/html
normal    /usr/doc/HOWTO/other-formats/html/3Dfx-HOWTO-1.html
normal    /usr/doc/HOWTO/other-formats/html/3Dfx-HOWTO-10.html
...
```

The all option -a is another useful query function that lists every RPM package installed on your system. The following command lists all of your installed packages:

```
rpm -qa
```

Here is a sample of that display:

```
setup-2.0.2-1
filesystem-1.3.4-4
basesystem-6.0-4
ldconfig-1.9.5-15
...
```

These packages were installed during the Red Hat installation process in Chapter 1.

If you pipe the output to the grep command, you can find a specific package or packages:

```
rpm -qa | grep -i howto
```

You can determine what RPM package a file belongs to, as follows:

```
rpm -qf `rpm -qla |grep -I bash` | more
```

You can find out information about an uninstalled package, as follows:

```
rpm -qpi /mnt/cdrom/RedHat/RPMS/filesystem*
```

This command uses RPM to display the description of the bash, an example of which follows this paragraph. You can substitute various other options like the file listing l option with the i option to gain other information about the package. More options are listed in the man page.

```
Name:          filesystem       Relocations: (not relocateable)
Version:       1.3.4            Vendor: Red Hat Software
Release:       4                Build Date: Sun Mar 21
                                14:06:24 1999
Install date: (not installed)  Build Host: porky.devel.
                                redhat.com
Group:         System           Source RPM: filesystem-1.3.4-4.
               Environment/Base src.rpm
Size:          81958            License: Public Domain
Packager:      Red Hat Software <http://developer.redhat.com/
                                bugzilla/>
Summary:  The basic directory layout for a Linux system.
```

```
Description:
The filesystem package is one of the basic packages that is
installed ona Red Hat Linux system. Filesystem contains the
basic directory layout for a Linux operating system, includ-
ing the correct permissions for thedirectories.
```

If you want to see what packages an installed package depends on, then use
this command:

```
rpm -qR kernel
```

It shows that the kernel package requires the initscripts package, as shown
here:

```
initscripts >= 3.64
/bin/sh
```

Verifying RPM packages

The RPM can verify information about installed packages and their files. This
is a very useful system administration tool. For instance, if you're in doubt
about the Samba configuration file, then you can run this command:

```
rpm -V samba
```

The Samba RPM package keeps a checksum and compares the state of the
installed files against it. The command returns

```
S.5....T c /etc/smb.conf
```

which means that the smb.conf file has been changed. Please consult the
RPM man page for information about the meaning of the result.

Comparing RPM Packages to Tar Files

Until the advent of the RPM (and the Debian package manager on Debian
Linux systems), Linux software was distributed via tar archives, which are
sometimes referred to as tarballs, or more descriptively as hairballs. The tar
mechanism stores one or more files in a single file in a tar format. Typically,
the tar file has the file suffix of .tar; if the tar file is compressed, it should
have a suffix like .tgz or .tar.gz. Using the tar-based distribution system is suf-
ficient if your software does not change often and you are young. However,

when you need to upgrade or change software, or work with complex software systems, it becomes quite difficult to work with tarballs. Rather than spending your life spitting up hairballs, systems like RPM greatly simplify your life.

Some software is still distributed exclusively via tar archives. Use the commands described in the backup section to employ tar distributions and read any documentation that comes with such software. Installing tar archives in a common location is best so that you do not lose track of them. The /usr/local directory tree is generally considered to be the best location.

Part IV
Using Red Hat Linux

The 5th Wave   By Rich Tennant

"Okay - this is an example of some of the
bootup problems you'll incur with Linux."

In this part . . .

You have finished your initial journey and have Linux up 'n running. You've looked at the map enough to know where you are. Now, the big question is what do you do with it.

Well, one thing that you can do is use the computer to warm your feet while you watch the screen saver kick in. You can also tell all of your friends that you have a "Linux box" at the next party you go to. Wow, that'll make you popular. Or, you can actually use your new Linux box to get things done.

Chapter 14 pushes you out the door into the wonderful world of the GNOME windows environment. GNOME is a friendly 'lil guy who likes to put a friendly face on Linux. With GNOME you can set up the "look and feel" of Linux so that you feel comfortable and at home.

In Chapter 15, you discover how to use the file manager to open, close, and find Linux files among other things. From there you move on to use a few of the many utilities that come with GNOME. Atta boy GNOME.

Chapter 16 introduces you to the world of Linux applications. Linux is not just for nerds anymore. You can purchase full-fledged desktop productivity programs such as Applixware and StarOffice. These programs include powerful, full-featured word processors, spreadsheets, and more. For instance, this book was written almost entirely on Applixware Words.

Chapter 14

Getting to Gnow GNOME and X

● ●

In This Chapter

▶ Introducing the X Window System

▶ Introducing GNOME and Enlightenment

▶ Configuring GNOME

▶ Managing windows

▶ Understanding the virtual desktop

▶ Closing and killing windows

▶ Stopping X

▶ Logging out and locking GNOME

● ●

*I*n 1984, MIT Project Athena was trying to develop a computer system that could deploy over thousands of computers tied together by networking. Bob Scheifler (of MIT) and Jim Gettys (of Digital Equipment Corporation) built on earlier work performed at Stanford University by Brian Reid and Paul Ascente (of Digital Equipment Corporation). Brian and Paul's work was called W, so of course Bob and Jim named their work X. This work, along with the work of thousands of other people and companies, eventually developed X Window System, the graphical interface to the Linux operating system as well as to many other operating systems.

More recently, the fine GNU people (technically the GNU Project) have introduced the GNU Network Model Environment — GNOME. GNOME is a graphical desktop environment that is easy to work in and modify to your own taste. The Enlightenment window manager is used together with GNOME and X to give you a complete graphical environment. Enlightenment provides the "look and feel" for your system. The line between where GNOME starts and Enlightenment ends can get blurry. To keep things simple, in this book the combination of GNOME/Enlightenment is referred to as simply GNOME.

In this chapter, you find out some basic ways to work in X and GNOME. You start by learning some of each system's basics. Then you mess with the GNOME *panel* and desktop; the panel is similar to the menu bar on a Windows computer. Later, you fool around with simple maneuvers, moving windows, changing their size, bringing them to the forefront, and hiding them in the background. You finish by locking your screen, logging off GNOME, and stopping X altogether.

Introducing the Amazing X Window System

X (also designated as X11 or X Window System) has three main parts:

- A graphics server
- A set of graphics libraries
- A set of graphics clients who normally use the graphics libraries

The *graphics server* is a program that talks to the video card, keyboard, and mouse on your system. It receives commands from the set of graphics libraries that are incorporated into programs. Sometimes these programs are executed directly on the same system where the graphics device resides; other times, these programs talk across a network to a graphics device on another system. Using X, you can run your program in one part of the world and someone can see the output of it in another part of the world over the Internet. Kewl.

The server program, often called *X Server,* is not part of the operating system, as it is in some other operating systems. Instead, X Server is a *user-level* program — a special and complex one.

Three main types of programs use X:

- Window managers
- Terminal emulators
- General applications

But I don't do windows!

Window managers like Enlightenment are programs that receive commands indirectly from the user through mouse clicks and keystrokes. The window manager passes those commands to the set of graphics libraries mentioned in the previous section. The graphics libraries then communicate with the X server to manipulate windows on the graphics device, which is usually your screen.

The window manager acts like a playground monitor; it's the central point of control for the major windows seen on the screen (and even some windows that can't be seen). It blows a whistle when a window gets unruly. The window manager can serve also as a desktop, where you can use it to launch applications. A window manager isn't necessary, but it would be difficult to use more than one or two applications at once without also using a window manager. (The applications would need to be written to allow resizing, window positioning, and so on.)

Here are some typical window manipulations:

- ✔ Move a window around a screen
- ✔ Make a window smaller or larger
- ✔ Overlap a window with another one
- ✔ Bring an overlapped window into full visibility (called *raising* a window)
- ✔ Send a window into less visibility (called *lowering* a window)
- ✔ Make a window very small but still accessible (called *iconifying* a window)

Window managers may also maintain an *icon bar,* which keeps icons easy to find and manage, as well as performs other functions. But the most important thing to remember about window managers in X is that they are just user-level programs like any other — they are not part of the system. You have a choice of window managers, and each has different capabilities, although a discussion of those window managers and capabilities is outside the scope of this book.

With these smarts, why should I play dumb?

The second main category of program under X is the *terminal emulator,* a program that emulates dumb character-cell terminals. You may be wondering why you would want to simulate a dumb, inexpensive terminal when you paid a lot of money for a neat graphics monitor. Shouldn't every program be graphical?

In the early days of X, few graphical programs were available. Most programs were written to run on character-cell terminals and did not include the libraries that create graphical programs on X Server. Therefore, to run both character-cell and graphical programs, the dumb terminal had to be emulated through software. The main terminal emulator in Linux is xterm. The xterm program simulates both a Digital VT102 and a Tektronix 4014 terminal. Most character-cell programs were written to drive these terminals.

If you start xterm, it usually executes a shell and gives you a command-line prompt. You type commands, and the results are output to the window containing xterm. You can use xterm to start the execution of a totally graphical-based program such as xedit or xfig by typing the name of that graphical-based program on the command line presented by xterm.

Now the good stuff!

The third main type of program is the *general application,* and this can range from text editors such as xedit (which looks a lot like a terminal emulator but is much different) to applications such as xfig (which manipulates images) and xpaint (which enables you to draw objects) to games such as Doom. These programs would be impossible (or at least very hard) to run on a character-cell terminal.

Two interfaces in one

The Linux operating system comes with two, two, two interfaces in one. Linux makes use of both a command-line interface (like that found in MS-DOS) and the X graphical interface. X is said to "sit on top of" the command-line operating system. This allows total access to the operating system through a command-line interface as well as through a graphical interface. (Some operating systems provide you with only a graphical interface.)

The *Red Hat Linux For Dummies* CD1 includes several window managers including GNOME/Enlightenment, KDE, and the previous Linux standard Fvwm95. GNOME/Enlightenment is the default used in this book. KDE is similar to GNOME in that it is a modern system but we leave it up to you to explore. You can also use good old Fvwm95 to start applications (and stop them of course), move windows, shrink windows, expand windows, and do everything but wash windows. Just think, you can use your system without ever typing a command line!

If X does not automatically start when you boot your computer, then you need to do so manually. From the command line, simply enter the command startx. If X fails to start, consult Chapters 5 and 6.

Gnowing GNOME

Log in to your Linux computer. You should see the GNOME environment, as shown in Figure 14-1. GNOME consists of three major elements: the desktop, standard applications, and the Panel. The desktop is simply the space where you do your work. Standard applications include things like the GNOME File Manager, Help Browser, and such. The Panel is the menu bar that appears on the bottom edge of your screen.

The desktop comes pre-configured with several icons that are links to the GNOME File Manager, Red Hat Web sites, the Linux Document Project (LDP), and GNOME. In Figure 14-1, you can see these icons along the left-hand edge of your screen. By default, the GNOME File Manager and Help Browser start when you log in. The File Manager is, of course, a graphical system for working with files and directories in your home directory as well as the entire file system. The Help Browser provides an excellent introduction to GNOME and Enlightenment.

The GNOME Help Browser provides a comprehensive and easy to follow tutorial, and will take you through all the basics of GNOME and Enlightenment. The Help Browser also provides a good reference.

The GNOME Panel is the menu bar along the bottom of the desktop, providing a location to place common menus and applets for easy starting or viewing. The Panel also gives you a view of the virtual desktop (described later in this chapter) and windows that are minimized.

By default, Red Hat places icons for accessing the GNOME Help Browser, Configuration tool, a terminal emulation program, and Netscape Communicator 4.7. You can start any of those programs by clicking their icon. There is also a simple clock placed at the far right of the Panel.

Another important element of the Panel is the Main Menu Button at the far left, which is used to access all of the standard GNOME applications and configuration tools. Click the Main Menu Button, which looks like a small footprint located in the lower left-hand corner of the screen. The menu shown in Figure 14-2 appears.

Figure 14-1:
The first login window and your environment.

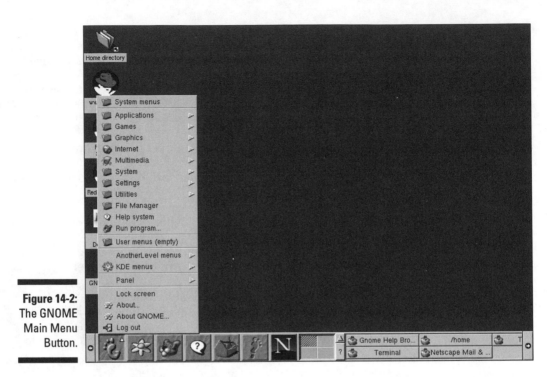

Figure 14-2:
The GNOME
Main Menu
Button.

The submenus are pretty much self-explanatory. For instance, the System menu contains programs used to configure GNOME and other systems tied to GNOME and X. The Multimedia menu provides access to your CD player and such. One submenu that you should really pay attention to is Panel, as described in the following section.

Playing with the panel

The Panel submenu is used to modify the configuration and behavior of the Panel itself. Click the Panel submenu to see the menu shown in Figure 14-3. Click the Add applet submenu to see another menu of applets that you can add to the Panel. Choose Utility⇨AfterStep Clock and you get the — in my opinion — attractive clock applet added to the panel.

If the default Panel doesn't give you enough space, then you can also add new Panels by using the Add new panel menu. Choose Panel⇨Add new panel and you get the choice of adding a new panel across the top of the Desktop or a minimized one in the upper right-hand corner. You can use the new Panel just like the original.

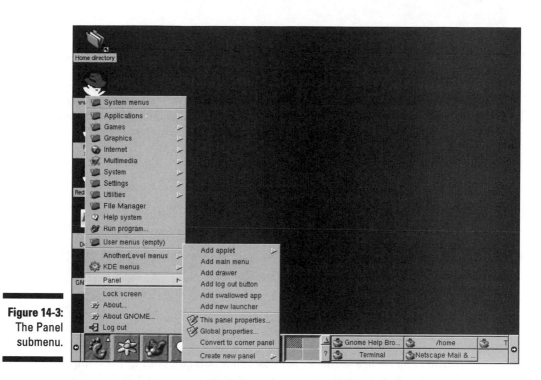

Figure 14-3:
The Panel
submenu.

Onc of the other interesting functions of the Panel menu is the Add new launcher function. Choose Main Menu Button⇨Panel⇨Add new launcher buttons. The Create launcher applet appears as shown in Figure 14-4. By entering the name and location of an application, you can add a new applet to the Panel that *launches,* or starts, that application.

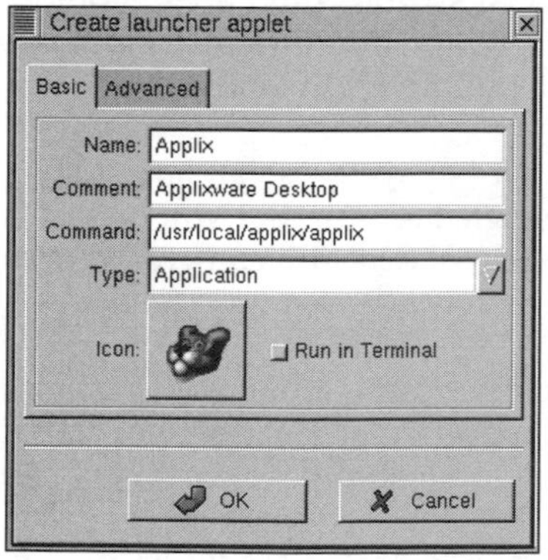

Figure 14-4:
The Create
launcher
applet.

Try it. For instance, if you download the Applixware Office suite (which includes a full-fledged word processor, spreadsheet, etc.), you can add an applet for it. From the Create launcher applet, add the name, any comments, and the command to launch the program. Applix will install by default into the /usr/local/applix directory so enter the pathname, including the program name, `/usr/local/applix/applix` to the Command entry box. GNOME gives you a few pages of standard icons that you can use to distinguish your new applet.

Once you are finished editing the Create launcher applet window, click OK, and it is added to your panel, as shown in Figure 14-5.

Figure 14-5:
The Applix
launcher
applet
added to
the Panel.

You can create a launcher for any application on your Linux computer. Simply enter the appropriate application name and pathname as described above.

Working on your virtual desktop

I think you can see at this point that you could have lots and lots of windows on the screen. You might even lose a window behind other windows. Do you wish that your monitor was larger just so you could open more windows and do more things at one time? Or maybe you don't want to close down or minimize one application before going to another application.

Well, monitors are expensive, and a lot of systems can have only one graphics card, so you are stuck using a single monitor. But you do not have to be stuck with one *screen*. X, with the help of GNOME, can give you both virtual screens and virtual desktops.

A *virtual desktop* enables you to have a screen full of applications. By clicking a button or moving your cursor to a particular location, you can display an additional entire screen of different applications.

A *virtual screen* is when the screen of one desktop is larger than your monitor, and you can't see the entire desktop at one time. As you move your cursor to one side of the monitor or the other, you automatically pan over that virtual screen.

It's usually confusing to have both virtual screens and the virtual desktop turned on at the same time, so I recommend that you go with the virtual desktop. Both, however, are explained in this section.

Towards the middle of the Panel is the *virtual desktop display* and it controls which virtual desktop space you're in.

You may notice that the upper-left block in the virtual desktop display seems to be colored or seems to contain some smaller blocks. That upper-left block represents the virtual desktop you are in right now.

Getting to know (and configure) GNOME

Now that you are familiar with the basics of what GNOME can do, it's time to briefly describe how you can modify it. There are two configuration systems that you need to pay attention to. The first is the GNOME Control Center system. The second is the Enlightenment Configuration system.

The GNOME Control Center is started by clicking the Main Menu button and choosing Settings➪GNOME Control Center. The screen shown in Figure 14-6 starts. The Control Center lets you modify all the basic properties of GNOME. For instance, choose Desktop➪Background and you can set the color, and other aspects of the Desktop. Choose Desktop➪Screensaver➪Xjack and you switch from the default random screen saver to the "All work and no play makes Jack a dull boy" screen saver. Not a bad selection for those long winters spent at remote resorts!

Figure 14-6:
The GNOME Control Center window.

```
Control Center                                        _ □ ×
 File   Help
┌ Desktop
│  ├ Background
│  ├ Screensaver
│  ├ Theme Selector
│  └ Window Manager
├ Gnome Edit Properties
├ Mime Types
┌ Multimedia
│  ├ Keyboard Bell
│  └ Sound
┌ Peripherals
│  ├ Keyboard
│  └ Mouse
├ Startup Programs
└ URL Handlers

Background
```

The Control Center also lets you configure things other than maniacal rantings. I'll leave it to you to explore the wonderful world of setting your keyboard bell and such. This system gives you lots of flexibility.

You can reach the Enlightenment window manager by positioning the mouse cursor over a blank part of the desktop and clicking both the left and right mouse buttons. A menu appears and you click the Enlightenment Configuration item. The Enlightenment Configuration Editor window appears, as shown in Figure 14-7.

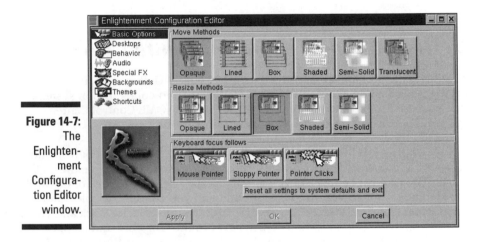

Figure 14-7: The Enlightenment Configuration Editor window.

The important menus are the Basic Options and Behavior. The Basic Options lets you change the style of how windows appear as they are moved and resized. More importantly, the Basic Options menu lets you change the way windows are controlled by the movement of your mouse. This is called keyboard focus.

By default, you have to click a window to bring it to the surface (also known as focus). You can change it so that merely moving the mouse cursor to a window focuses it. The Sloppy Pointer option works more-or-less in between these two options.

The Behavior menu gives you the ability to control your keyboard focus. Keyboard focus is a way to create shortcuts by assigning certain keys to launch applications. There are too many options and combinations to describe here, so give it a try. The Miscellaneous section provides control over things like how long it takes for Tooltips to appear and for keyboard focus to take affect.

The other options provide control over the remaining look and feel of your desktop. You can control the number of virtual windows displayed, your audio system (if you have one), and other such things.

Teaching GNOME Some Tricks

GNOME performs all of the basic graphical functions that you expect a GUI to do. You can move windows, resize them, and minimize them and such. This section describes those basic functions.

Before doing something to a window, however, you have to get its attention. When a window has your attention, it's said to have *focus*.

Depending on how you've set up GNOME, you can give a window focus with GNOME in several ways:

- Click the window's name, which is in the icon bar at the bottom of the screen.
- Click the window's title bar, which is at the top of the window.
- Click the window itself, which typically also makes the window the top-most one.
- If you're working in an office with many people, then you can shout, "Hey you, wake up!"

We'll stick with the Red Hat/GNOME default of having to click a window to focus it.

Moving day

To move a window, click and hold the left mouse button anywhere on the title bar. As long as you hold down the left mouse button, the window can move anywhere that you move your mouse. Release the button and the window will stay there. Note that the title bar is the "bar" along the top of any window where the window name is located.

Resizing to your heart's content

Sometimes a window is a little too big or a little too small. Life would be much easier if you could just nudge that window into shape. To do just that, you can position the mouse cursor on either the lower left or right corner of a window until the cursor changes into a double-sided arrow. Left-click the mouse and pull the window's outline to your desired size. Release the mouse button and your window takes the new size.

Another way to resize a window is to click the far upper left-hand corner. A menu appears. Click the Window Size submenu and another menu appears that allows you to toggle either the height, width, or entire window between its normal (default) size and the entire desktop.

Making a molehill out of a mountain

You can minimize (iconify) a window by clicking on the bold, underscore button towards the upper-right corner. Doing this removes the window from the desktop and places it in a storage area on the right-hand side of the Panel.

Now that I have you clicking away through the menu, do you want to know an easier way to minimize a window? Look back at Figure 14-7. See those squares in the title bar? Click the one that is the third from the right (it looks like an underscore character) and your program is minimized.

Making a mountain out of a molehill

You can return the window to the desktop by clicking on the icon that corresponds to the window on the Panel. You also have the option of completely closing the application by right-clicking its icon in the Panel and choosing either Close or Nuke in the menu that appears. The difference between the two is that Nuke will close the program if it does not respond to the Close command. Nuke isn't as nice as Close and potentially could cause problems if you are running a program like a database that is actively manipulating data.

You're probably thinking, "If the underscore-looking button to the right of the title bar minimizes a window, one of those other buttons probably maximizes a window." Or maybe you're thinking, "I sure hope I can take a break soon." Okay, you're first hunch is right. Check out those buttons to the right of the title bar. The Maximize button is the one in the middle; it looks like a square. It is similar in action to the cascade button in Windows. Stay tuned to find out about the X button to the right of the Maximize button.

Closing Your Windows

Now that you've put a lot of windows on the screen, how can you get rid of a few or all of them? Well, you can put them in the background by reducing them to icons, or you can be more drastic and kill them. Here are a few ways to do so:

  ✔ First, take advantage of any exit buttons or menu options that the application gives you.

- Click the Close button (the X), which is in the upper-right corner of the window's title bar, to kill the window.

- Click the upper-left corner of the window and then click either the Close or Annihilate options in the menu that appears.

- Close attempts to contact the application and ask it nicely to stop itself. Annihilate doesn't care what the application thinks and stops it immediately.

- Click the Title bar to get to the menu described in the previous two steps. The menu works exactly as described in those steps. This is just another way to get to it.

Going out to lunch

You can save the time of logging out of your X/GNOME desktop by using the screen lock. Click the Main Menu Button and choose Lock Screen and the screen saver is displayed. To return to productive life and your desktop, press any key, or wiggle your mouse and then enter your password in the X Screensaver window.

Locking up the shop

When you've finished for the day and want to go home (or just upstairs) you need to log out. Click the Main Menu Button⇨Log out. The Really log out? screen appears; click Yes to finish your day.

You also have the option of using this window to halt or reboot your Linux computer. A root password prompt appears before the computer is halted or rebooted.

Stopping X

When you can't get your applications to respond to you, you can simply stop the X Window System, which will kill all the programs running under it. To stop the X Window System, press the Ctrl+Alt+Backspace keys all at once. If you started X manually, you can then log out of the account. If X is started automatically at boot time (as this book assumes), then you will get the X login screen and you can log back in.

Chapter 15

Gnowing More Graphical Stuff

● ●

In This Chapter

▶ Using the GNOME File Manager

▶ Viewing images with GNOME

▶ Marking time with the Linux calendar

▶ Counting away with the Linux calculator

▶ Grooving to tunes

● ●

*I*n this chapter, you see — and hear — a few useful programs under the X Window System. Although space prohibits us from showing you all the programs that run under the X Window System, the programs mentioned here give you a good idea about how the others work.

Becoming a GNOME File Manager

Being the boss doesn't make you a bad person. It's just a job. Right? Well that little GNOME guy is a good worker and doesn't eat much. Just press a key here, click a button there, and you're its manager. It even comes with its own file manager that saves you work and makes room for those long lunches.

The GNOME File Manager follows in the tradition of all good file managers; it graphically displays the files and directories on your computer. You can copy, move, delete, and execute files by pointing and clicking. You can also create directories, view file details, and the like. Not a bad deal considering it works for free.

Waking up the little guy

Red Hat Linux configures the GNOME File Manager to start automatically when you log in. The File Manager appears toward the end of the login process, as shown in Figure 15-1. Should you want to start it manually — after you've closed it, for instance — then choose Main Menu Button⇨File Manager.

The main menu follows the familiar File, Edit, and so on format and does all the things that you would expect such a menu to do. The menu immediately below the main menu enables you to quickly move up one directory (Up) and redo previous moves (Back and Forward). It also lets you rescan a directory, go to your home directory, and change the way icons appear. The rescan function, for instance, is useful if you create a new file via a terminal screen. The file doesn't show up in the File Manager until you move to another directory and return or else rescan.

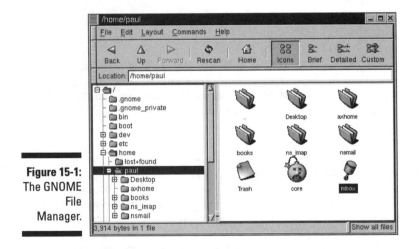

Figure 15-1:
The GNOME
File
Manager.

Putting him through his paces

Most people use file managers to do the basics: copying, moving, and deleting files and such. We cover those things here and leave the rest (advanced functions) for you to explore on your own.

Moving files and directories

Moving a file or directory is as simple as clicking it and holding down the mouse button, and then dragging the mouse cursor over the directory that you want to move it to. Release the button, and you have moved your file or directory.

You can move multiple files by clicking and holding the mouse button and then dragging the mouse cursor over the files that you want. The mouse cursor creates a rectangular outline and highlights all the files within that box. Next, click anywhere within the box and drag the mouse cursor to the desired directory. Release the mouse button and the files move to the specified directory.

Copying files and directories

Copying a file or directory is a bit more complicated than moving one. Rather than simply clicking an icon and dragging it someplace, you have to right-click the file or directory icon and choose from the menu that appears, as shown in Figure 15-2. The menu lists all the options available from the File Manager. Choose Copy and another dialog window appears. Within that window, you can manually enter the pathname of where you want to copy the file, or you can use the Browse function. If you choose Browse, yet another window appears, and you can click and go.

You can copy multiple files and directories in the same manner that you move them. You trace a box around the files you want to work with by clicking and dragging the mouse cursor (an action called a *lasso* by some). Next, right-click any of the highlighted icon names (but not the white space around the icon and names themselves), and you get a menu similar to the one just described; this menu has only three options: Copy, Move, and Delete. Choose Copy and follow the directions described in the preceding paragraph.

Deleting files and directories

Deleting files and directories is much the same as copying them. You right-click the desired file or directory icon, and the same menu appears that you get when copying. Choose Delete and a prompt appears verifying if you really want to delete that file or directory. Exercise your normal caution and click Yes if you mean it.

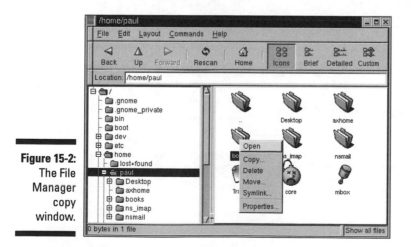

Figure 15-2:
The File
Manager
copy
window.

Deleting directories is a little more complicated, of course. When you choose to delete an entire directory, and it's not empty, a prompt appears to delete it recursively (which means it deletes all subdirectories, too). Answer Yes and every file and directory within that directory is removed.

Finally, you can delete multiple files and directories. Again, lasso the desired files and directories by clicking and dragging the mouse cursor. Right-click the icons or icon names (but not the white space around the icon and name). The simple menu, as described previously, appears. Select Delete and then answer Yes in the confirmation window.

You can change the confirmation behavior of moving, copying, or deleting functions. Choose Edit⇨Preferences and select the Confirmation tab in the Preferences window. You can then toggle various options that control such behavior.

Creating directories

To create a new directory, choose Directory. The Create a New Directory dialog box appears; enter the name of the new directory. Linux creates the directory in the current working directory, which is the directory that the File Manager currently shows.

Viewing files and directories

By default, files and directories display in iconic — symbolic — form. The only information that an icon shows is the name and whether an item is a file or directory. You can see more information by clicking the Brief, Detailed, or Custom buttons that appear below the main menu, as shown in Figure 15-3.

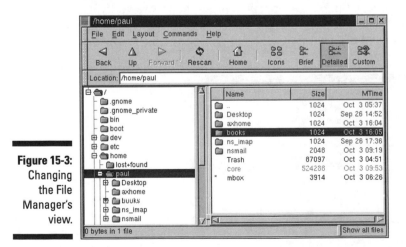

Figure 15-3: Changing the File Manager's view.

The following bullets describe the differences between these views:

- ✔ **Icons view:** Displays the symbol (icon) and indicates whether an item is a file or directory. Regular file icons take several forms, but text and configuration files look like pieces of paper with a corner folded, and executable files look like pistons. Links, devices, and so on take other forms. Directories take the form of a partially open file folder. Icons are also evenly placed across the entire File Manager screen.

- ✔ **Brief view:** Shows files and directories on individual lines. Directories appear as smaller (closed) file folders. Regular files use various characters such as asterisks (*) and exclamation points (!) before the filename to represent executable files. Text and word processing files, however, use no such characters and show only the filenames.

- ✔ **Detailed view:** Displays the size and time stamp of each file and directory as well as their names.

- ✔ **Custom view:** Allows you to choose what file attributes to display. You can select the attributes by choosing Edit⇨Preferences and selecting the Custom View tab. From there, you can add and delete the attributes from a list of possible attributes.

You can reach these same views by clicking the Layout button and then clicking the radio buttons for Icon View, Brief View, Detailed View, or Custom View.

Finding files and directories

You can search for files and directories by using the File Manager's Find command. Choose Commands⇨Find File. In the Find File window, enter the directory in which you want to start your search (your current directory is the default) and the filename to look for.

Running programs and scripts

GNOME is such a hard worker that it happily launches commands for you. Choose Commands⇨Run Command and enter the name of the command in the Enter Command to Run dialog box. For instance, enter the xclock command, and the X xclock appears on your desktop.

Viewing Graphics in GNOME

GNOME comes with a nice, simple graphics viewer called GQview. You start it by choosing Main Menu Button⇨Graphics⇨GQview. You can see all the usual suspects through this guy: TIF, GIF, JPEG, and so on. The graphics files in your current directory appear in GQview's mini-file managers. Just click the graphics image that you want to view, and it appears, as shown in Figure 15-4.

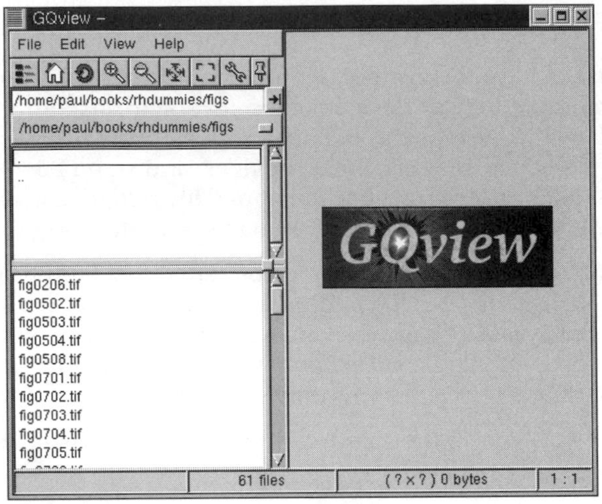

Figure 15-4:
The GQview
program.

You can perform simple graphics manipulations on the image, such as zooming in and out. Try GQview; it's simple and effective.

Checking Out Some Handy Linux Programs

GNOME not only does the work described in the previous sections of this chapter, but it also works overtime. Several nice programs are bundled along with Red Hat Linux. See the following sections for a description of a couple of particularly useful ones.

Coordinating with ical

ical is a nice calendar that's available on Linux. You can use it not only to display your own calendar but also to combine other calendars, such as your boss's calendar or a calendar of holidays. You set up calendar items to recur daily, weekly, or monthly — all with different alarm settings. The ical program includes excellent online documentation under the Help key, so we don't go into a lot of detail about the program.

To take the calendar program out for a spin, follow these steps:

1. **Start the calendar program.**

   Choose Main Menu Button➪AnotherLevel menus➪Misc➪ical. Or type **ical** in a terminal emulator program. When you start the calendar either of these ways with the X Window System working, a screen similar to Figure 15-5 appears.

   We use a shorthand method for showing menus. When you see a line such as Start➪Programs➪Egad, it means to click the Start button, and then click the Programs menu, and then click the Egad menu item.

2. **Click the lower-left area of the calendar, under the Prev, Today, and Next buttons.**

   This step creates a new *notice entry,* as shown in Figure 15-6. Notice entries are messages to you and typically have no specific timeframes. You can think of them as sticky notes that you put up on the wall. Because it has no time associated with it, you can't set an alarm to remind you of a notice entry.

3. **Type some text as a reminder.**

4. **Customize the notice, if you want.**

   Using the Repeat menu at the top of the screen, select whether the notice should be repeated, when it should be repeated, how many times it should be repeated, and so on.

Figure 15-5:
The ical calendar program.

Calendar							_ □ ×
File Edit Item Repeat List Options							Help

⇦　October　⇨ ⇦ 1998 ⇨

Sun	Mon	Tue	Wed	Thu	Fri	Sat
				1	2	3
4	5	6	7	8	9	10
11	[12]	13	14	15	16	17
18	19	20	21	22	23	24
25	26	27	28	29	30	31

Prev	Today	Next

8:00
9:00
10:00
11:00
12:00
13:00
14:00
15:00
16:00
17:00

Calendar

File Edit Item Repeat List Options   Help

	October	1998		8:00

Sun	Mon	Tue	Wed	Thu	Fri	Sat
			1	2	3
4	5	6	7	8	9	10
11	12	13	14	15	16	17
18	19	20	21	22	23	24
25	26	27	28	29	30	31

9:00

10:00

11:00

12:00

| Prev | Today | Next |

13:00

14:00

15:00

16:00

17:00

Main Calendar [Owner maddog]

Figure 15-6:
The ical pro-
gram with
one notice
window
selected.

Now that you've created a notice on the calendar, you're ready to find out how to make an appointment. An appointment has all the attributes of a notice (it can be repeated, edited, and so on), but it also has alarms that remind you of the event. Follow these steps to schedule an appointment:

1. **Find the timeframe for your appointment and then click the horizontal box that appears to the right of it.**

2. **Type the information for the appointment.**

If you want to move the box to a different timeframe, move the cursor to the middle of the appointment box and then click and hold the middle mouse button. Positioning squares appear, as shown in Figure 15-7. Drag the appointment box to another timeframe and then release the button.

If you want to make the appointment longer, move the cursor to the black sizing box in the middle of the lower line of the appointment box. Click and hold the mouse button; drag the positioning squares to make the box bigger or smaller.

3. **Click the Repeat menu at the top of the screen and choose a repeat scheme that meets your requirements.**

4. **To close the calendar program, choose File⇨Exit.**

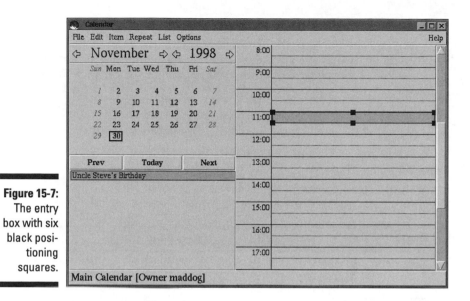

Figure 15-7:
The entry
box with six
black posi-
tioning
squares.

Processing with your Linux calculator

Red Hat Linux provides you with a handy scientific calculator that can emulate a TI-30 or an HP-10C. Whether you're predicting the location of the next
meteorite to hit Earth or trying to balance your checkbook, look no further
than Linux.

To use the calculator in TI-30 mode, follow these steps:

1. **Choose Main Menu Button⇨AnotherLevel menus⇨Utilities⇨Calculator.**

   The calculator appears, as shown in Figure 15-8. Note that the calculator
   also goes by the nickname xcalc(1).

Figure 15-8:
xcalc, the
calculator.

2. Activate the buttons and calculate away.

You activate the buttons by using the keyboard or the mouse. The keyboard equivalents of special functions are not intuitive, so we provide Table 15-1 for reference. We extracted this information from the manual page for the xcalc program, which you can see in its entirety by typing the following at the command prompt of an xterminal window:

```
man xcalc
```

3. When you're tired of all those numbers, click the kill icon.

The kill icon looks like an X Window System icon and appears in the upper-left corner of the title bar.

Table 15-1	Calculator Key Mappings			
TI Key	*HP Key Accelerator*	*Keyboard*	*TI Function*	*HP Function*
SQRT	SQRT	r	squareRoot()	squareRoot()
AC	ON	space	clear()	clear()
AC	<-	Delete	clear()	back()
AC	<-	Backspace	clear()	back()
AC	<-	Control-H	clear()	back()
AC	n/a	Clear	clear()	n/a
AC	ON	q	quit()	quit()
AC	ON	Control-C	quit()	quit()
INV	i	i	inverse()	inverse()
sin	s	s	sine()	sine()
cos	c	c	cosine()	cosine()
tan	t	t	tangent()	tangent()
DRG	DRG	d	degree()	degree()
e	n/a	e	e()	n/a
ln	ln	l	naturalLog()	naturalLog()
y^x	y^x	^	power()	power()
PI	PI	p	pi()	pi()
x!	x!	!	factorial()	factorial()

TI Key	HP Key Accelerator	Keyboard	TI Function	HP Function
(	n/a	(	leftParen()	n/a
)	n/a	)	rightParen()	n/a
/	/	/	divide()	divide()
*	*	*	multiply()	multiply()
-	-	-	subtract()	subtract()
+	+	+	add()	add()
=		=	equal()	n/a
0..9	0..9	0..9	digit()	digit()
.	.	.	decimal()	decimal()
+/-	CHS	n	negate()	negate()
n/a	x:y	x	n/a	XexchangeY()
n/a	ENTR	Return	n/a	enter()
n/a	ENTR	Linefeed	n/a	enter()

Follow these steps to multiply 5 times 3:

1. **Choose Main Menu Button⇨AnotherLevel menus⇨Utilities⇨Calculator.**

2. **Click the AC calculator button.**

   AC stands for All Clear.

3. **Click 5, * (asterisk), 3, and then = (equal sign).**

   The number 15 appears in the display.

4. **Click AC to clear the display.**

Using your Linux calculator is a lot like using a physical calculator, except that you use the mouse rather than your fingers to select buttons.

You can also operate the calculator with the keyboard, as follows:

1. **If necessary, start xcalc.**

   See Step 1 in the preceding list.

2. **If necessary, press the Backspace key to clear the display.**

3. **Type 5*3= using the keyboard.**

For the numbers and asterisk, you can use the keyboard or the numeric keypad. Note that the Enter key on the numeric keypad has the same function as the = key on the main keyboard.

Pressing the Backspace key once is the same as clicking CE (Clear Entry) on the calculator. Pressing the Backspace key twice is the same as clicking the AC (All Clear) calculator button.

4. **After you've had enough calculating, exit xcalc by right-clicking the AC button.**

Setting Up Your Sound System

Imagine that you're sitting alone, working at your computer. Feeling lonely? Want a little company? Well, we can't provide a pal, but we can show you how your system can provide some tunes.

First, we assume that your computer has a working sound card installed, and that it's a sound card that's supported by Linux. (Assuming a lot, aren't we?) You can configure and test the sound card at the same time by following these steps:

1. **Make sure that you're logged on as root or superuser.**

2. **Mount the companion CD-ROM (CD1).**

3. **Install the following packages:**

   rpm -ivh /mnt/cdrom/RedHat/RPMS/sox-12*

   rpm -ivh /mnt/cdrom/RedHat/RPMS/awesfx*

   rpm -ivh /mnt/cdrom/RedHat/RPMS/playmidi-2*

   rpm -ivh /mnt/cdrom/RedHat/RPMS/sndconfig*

4. **At the superuser prompt, type** /usr/sbin/sndconfig.

   A dialog box similar to the one in Figure 15-9 appears, showing that the hardware will be probed in case your card is Plug and Play.

5. **Click the Ok button.**

   The dialog box shown in Figure 15-10 appears.

   If the card is Plug and Play and is the only Plug-and-Play card in your system, the /etc/isapnp.conf file is rewritten, updating all Plug-and-Play information about your system.

   If your sound card is one of several Plug-and-Play devices, you must edit /etc/isapnp.conf to uncomment all the other Plug-and-Play cards in your system by removing the # sign in front of the cards you have.

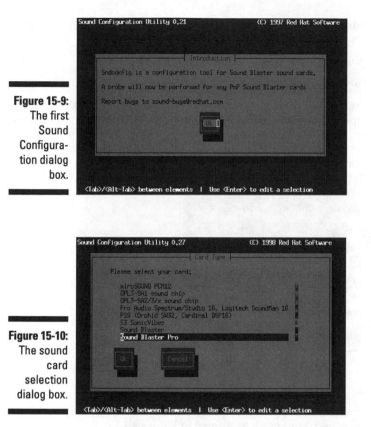

Figure 15-9:
The first
Sound
Configura-
tion dialog
box.

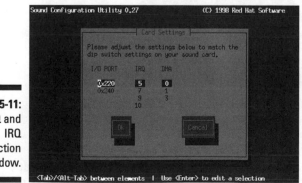

Figure 15-10:
The sound
card
selection
dialog box.

6. **Select the name of your card or a compatible card.**

7. **Press the Tab key until you reach the Ok button, and then press Enter.**

The Card Settings dialog box may appear, if required, as shown in
Figure 15-11.

Figure 15-11:
The I/O and
IRQ
selection
window.

8. **Enter the information for the I/O port address, the interrupt request, and the 8-bit and 16-bit DMA numbers, which you obtain in Chapter 3.**

   To move between the columns, press the Tab key.

9. **Press the Tab key until you reach the Ok button, and then press Enter.**

   The next window, shown in Figure 15-12, is a warning, telling you that a file will be updated and the current file will be copied to a backup before it is changed. You usually can ignore this message.

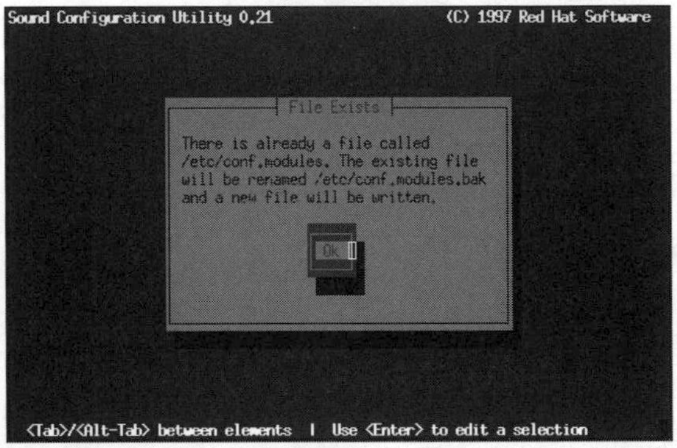

Figure 15-12:
The warning
message.

10. **Press Enter.**

    The SoundCard test dialog box informs you that Linux will play a sound sample to test the sound card, as shown in Figure 15-13.

Figure 15-13:
The test for
sound.

11. **Press Enter to hear the sound test.**

    The final screen of sndconfig (Figure 15-14) acknowledges that you heard the sound test sample. This sample solves the burning question of how to pronounce the word *Linux*.

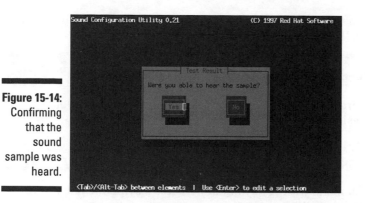

Figure 15-14:
Confirming
that the
sound
sample was
heard.

If you heard the sound sample, your sound card is now functional. Yippee!

If you didn't hear the sound test sample, make sure that you have compatible speakers or earphones plugged into your sound card output. If you do, then one of the following reasons may explain why you didn't hear the sound:

✔ You chose the wrong sound card.

✔ You entered the wrong parameters for the right sound card.

✔ Someone else's stereo is way too loud.

You can go back and re-execute the sndconfig program to try other settings for your sound card.

The world's most intelligent music machine

Everyone wants a little music in his or her life, right? That's why you bought a $2,000 computer instead of a $300 stereo system. So, in this section, we give you all the steps to set up Linux to play music CDs.

You can also use the CD player that comes with the GNOME multimedia application. You start the simple player by choosing Main Menu Button➪ Multimedia➪CD Player.

First, you need to make sure that Linux recognizes the CD-ROM drive when you run xplaycd, the CD player program. Type the following:

```
cd /dev
ln -s device cdrom
```

where *device* represents the place in the Linux file system where your CD-ROM drive resides. We typed this:

```
cd /dev
ln -s hdc cdrom
```

The `ln` (link) command with `-s` (symbolic) creates a symbolic link from `cdrom` in `/dev` to `hdc` in `/dev`.

If you have a SCSI CD-ROM drive, your command may be as follows:

```
ln -s scd0 cdrom
```

Creating the symbolic link is all that you *should* have to do, but Red Hat V5.1 requires that you follow a few more steps. Like a lot of programs in Linux, xplaycd is a work in progress. It has a small feature (that is, bug) in which it writes information to one place and reads it from some other place. To correct this problem, type the following commands as root (or superuser):

```
cd /usr/local/lib
mkdir cddb
chmod 777 cddb
ln -s cddb /var/lib/cddb
```

All you need to do now is run xplaycd. You can do this either by typing **xplaycd** into a terminal emulator, such as xterm, or by choosing Start⇨Programs⇨Utilities⇨Sound⇨XPlayCD. With either method, a window like the one shown in Figure 15-15 appears.

One file, two names

Normally, every file in a Linux file system has one directory entry. Sometimes, however, giving the same file two names is useful. In fact, the `ln` command was created for this very reason.

Unfortunately, the `ln` command does not work across file systems. In other words, a directory entry in one file system (on one disk partition) can't point to a file in another file system (on another disk partition). To solve this problem, the symbolic link was created, in which the directory entry is a full (or relative) pathname to the file.

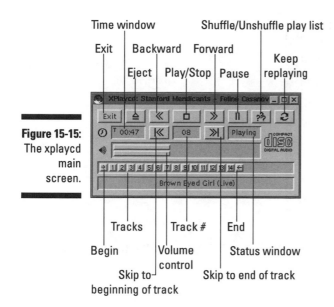

Time window

Shuffle/Unshuffle play list

Exit | Backward | Forward

Eject | Play/Stop | Pause

Keep replaying

Figure 15-15:
The xplaycd main screen.

Tracks | Track # | End

Begin

Volume control

Status window

Skip to beginning of track

Skip to end of track

If you've used a CD player, most of these symbols will be familiar. In addition, we label most of the elements in Figure 15-15. Here are the details on a few of them:

- ✔ If you click the Time window, the display shows the time remaining for the song. Click again to see the total time the disk has been playing, and click yet again to see the time remaining on the total disk.

- ✔ The volume control bars in the middle of the screen are normally used to — guess what — control the volume of the two sound channels. Your system may not allow you to use the volume control bars on the xplaycd front panel. You may also have to start xmixer to control the volume. (We cover xmixer in the next section.)

- ✔ To program the order in which tracks are played, drag a track button to where you would like to have that song played in the sequence.

- ✔ To change where the CD starts and stops playing, drag the Begin and End buttons, respectively.

- ✔ To skip a song, move the song after the End button.

You can create a database of CDs and song titles as follows:

1. Right-click anywhere on the xplaycd window.

A screen similar to Figure 15-16 appears. Your screen, however, will be empty.

Figure 15-16:
The xplaycd
editing
dialog box.

Media editor

Title: The Ale is Dear

```
1 — More Beer Polka
2 — Robert, Me Brother
3 — Ashlyn's Song
4 — Greg's Best
5 — Gravel Crawl
6 — Matt's Brew
7 — The Ale is Dear
8 — Incredible Brew
9 — Radman's Keg
10 — He's No Relation, He's My Brother
11 — Rocky Road to Dublin
12 — Clandestine
```

More Beer Polka

| OK | Apply | Undo | Cancel |

2. **Click in the Title field and type the CD's title (and artist if you want).**

3. **Press Enter.**

   The title appears in the field.

4. **Click in the area after the number 1.**

   This area corresponds to track one of the CD.

5. **Type the name of the track and then press Enter.**

   The selection automatically moves to track two.

6. **Repeat Step 5 until you finish typing the last track.**

   After pressing Enter the last time, the selection automatically returns to the first entry.

   If you make a mistake while typing, use the Backspace key and retype to correct your mistake. If you make a mistake in some entry, you can click that entry to select and then change it.

7. **When you're finished, click the OK button.**

   The data is applied to the database, and you quit the window. The Apply button applies the data to the database but does not close the window. Undo restores the data in the database to the window, eliminating any changes you have made. Cancel makes the window go away without applying any changes you have made.

8. **If you see a window asking for a music category, choose None (the default).**

   This xplaycd feature is under construction, so choose None.

Now when you play the CD, the names of the songs appear in the CD window as the songs play.

Xmixer: Sounds for the rest of us

As mentioned in the preceding section, the xplaycd program controls may not affect the volume of the music coming from your sound card. This process is usually controlled by the xmixer program. Depending on how the hardware of your computer is put together, the xmixer program may use different inputs for the CD music. So, you may have to experiment a little by moving the sets of slider bars until you get the volume of sound you want.

Figure 15-17 shows the xmixer window with all its buttons and slider bars. These controls may or may not match the capabilities of your sound card; the xmixer application is written for sound cards in general, as opposed to being written for a specific sound card.

Note that for xmixer to work, you must have a sound card, a cable must attach the CD-ROM drive to the sound card, and the headphones must be plugged into the sound card (not the CD-ROM).

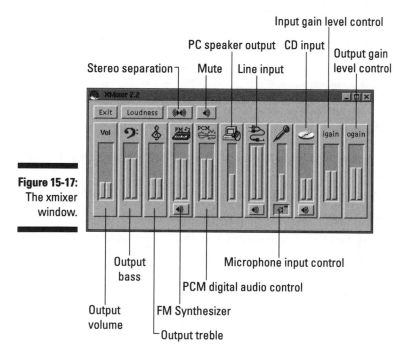

Figure 15-17:
The xmixer
window.

Most of the xmixer controls are labeled in Figure 15-17. Here's a little additional information:

- ✔ The Loudness control boosts the bass slightly for when you want low volume output (when your parents are home, the baby is asleep, or you have new batteries in your hearing aid).

- ✔ The Stereo Separation control is for cards that try to convince you that they have stereo separation capabilities.

- ✔ Each slider is made up of two columns, one for the left channel and one for the right channel. Place the cursor directly over one of the columns and drag to move the column up or down. Move the cursor between the two columns to move both columns at the same time.

We find it easier to use the middle mouse button to grab the top of the column. To do so, move the cursor to the top of a column, click and hold down the middle mouse button, and then move the mouse to pull the column up and down. If your mouse has only two buttons but you requested three-button emulation when installing your system, hold down both buttons at the same time to simulate the middle mouse button.

If you didn't ask for three-button emulation but want it now, follow these steps to do so:

1. **Become root or superuser.**

2. **Execute the following:**

   ```
   /usr/sbin/mouseconfig
   ```

3. **Tab until the cursor is over Emulate Three Buttons and then press the spacebar.**

   An asterisk (*) appears in the window.

4. **Tab to the Ok button and then press the Enter key.**

   You have installed three-button emulation for your mouse.

5. **Restart X Server to enable the emulation.**

This chapter highlights just a few of the applications on the companion CD-ROM. Two other applications, for example, are gimp and xpaint. Note that applications may be graphical applications that use the X Window System or character-cell applications that use the command line.

Chapter 16

Using Linux as Your Workstation

● ●

In This Chapter

▶ Getting work done with Linux

▶ Obtaining and installing Applixware Office

▶ Using Applix Words

▶ Introducing StarOffice

▶ Checking out Citrix Terminal Server

▶ Exploring the Wine Windows Emulator

▶ Taking a look at Linux applications

● ●

*L*inux is a great operating system with a large base of applications. Major desktop productivity applications, like the Applixware and StarOffice desktop office suites, have moved Linux into the realm of everyday use. You can also use Windows applications on your Linux computer with the help of emulation and other tools. Put together, these packages provide powerful, inexpensive methods for getting your day-to-day work done. Linux isn't just for us nerds any more.

Introducing Applixware

Applixware Office is a desktop productivity suite that does nearly everything that Microsoft Office does, for less. Within the suite is:

- ✔ **Applix Words:** A full function *what-you-see-is-what-you-get* (WYSIWIG) word processor. Applix Words comes with many functions that you would expect — formatting, cutting and pasting, graphics, spell check, and more.

- ✔ **Applix Spreadsheets:** A full-function spreadsheet program used by Wall Street Brokers.

- ✔ **Applix Presents:** A graphics program with all the bells and whistles for creating presentations. You can also import and export Microsoft PowerPoint files.

✔ **Applix Graphics:** Your personal graphics tools for creating anything from a novice drawing to a masterpiece. This program provides your creative side with a tool for creating graphics.

✔ **Applix Data:** A SQL database viewer. This program provides you with a graphical interface to your SQL databases.

✔ **Applix Mail:** An e-mail client that converts documents into an outgoing message.

✔ **HTML Editor:** An editor that creates Web pages. You can create simple Web pages from this editor.

How good is Applixware? Can it get the job done? Well, we wrote this book using Words — which is a pretty good test for such an application.

Applixware also has the advantage of running quite nicely on less than top-of-the-line equipment, such as Paul's creaky, old Cyrix P120 (equivalent to a Pentium I 90–120 MHz processor). Not only is Paul writing this book with no problem, but he is also comfortably running several copies of Words, Netscape, and other applications while also downloading a new version of StarOffice (see "A StarOffice is Born" section later in this chapter). It's no doubt that Paul is cheap when it comes to buying computer equipment but he appreciates not having to pay top dollar for a 500MHz chip simply to write down a few words.

Getting Applixware

You can obtain Applixware from your many consumer electronic, computer, or retail stores. They really need your money, so please help them out. You can also order it directly from Applix for $99 ($144 with 45 minutes, or 3 calls, of phone support). They also need your money so that they can battle the great juggernaught from Redmond, Washington.

If you don't want to give anyone your money — except us of course — then Applixware provides a demo version that you can download from its Web site at `www.applix.com/applixware/linux/main.cfm`; click the download button. The demo version works just like the retail one but limits you to one page per document. You're not going to get any real work done with the demo — other than writing a purchase order for the full version perhaps — but it will give you a good flavor of the software.

How do you download something from the Internet if you haven't configured Linux to connect to the Internet? You could use another computer that is connected to download the software. You can also go to Chapter 17, which gives you instructions for connecting to the Internet. After you connect, use the Netscape browser to go to `www.applix.com/download` and click the download Linux button. Read the license agreement and click the Agree button if you agree (does anyone actually read these documents word-for-word?). Click the download button and go take a nap, drink a cerveza, or whatever. You have a lot to download, and depending on your modem, the process may take a while.

Installing Applixware

Once you obtain the Applixware demo via the Internet or the complete package on CD-ROM, installing it is a straightforward process. The demo comes in RPM format (see Chapter 13). To install Applixware, follow these steps:

1. **Log in as the root user and enter the following command (it assumes that you have put the Applixware software into the /usr/local/src directory).**

   ```
   Tar xvf /usr/local/src/applixdemo*
   ```

   (Please note that the pathname you supply depends on where you downloaded the demo to. The following instruction assumes that you downloaded the demo to root's home directory. If you put it some place else, or have a CD-ROM copy, then please make the appropriate adjustments.)

   The Applixware installation and setup system starts its job. A language dialog box appears.

2. **Run the installation script as follows:**

   ```
   /usr/local/src/applix*/install-axdemo
   ```

   A simple informational screen appears.

3. **Press any key to continue.**

   The installation script prompts you to install into the /opt file system.

4. **Press the Return key to continue. Otherwise, you must specify a place to put the file system (the /usr/local file system is a good alternative).**

   If the installation directory does not exist, a prompt appears that enables the installation process to create it. Press the Return key to continue.

   Applixware starts to install. It may take ten or more minutes to complete.

Firing up Applixware

After you install Applixware, you can start it by entering the following command from a terminal window. First, however, fire up a terminal window by clicking the terminal icon on the Gnome/Enlightenment terminal icon desktop — it looks like a computer monitor or TV screen and is located in the middle of the GNOME toolbar located along the bottom of the screen.

```
/opt/applix/applix
```

The Applixware main menu window appears, as shown in Figure 16-1.

This window is the launching point for all five main Applixware components, plus the font installer, the license generator, and the help system, all of which you access from the Tools and Help menu buttons along the top of the window. You use the font installer for installing custom fonts and use the license generator for switching an existing temporary license to a permanent one. If you like the Applixware system and purchase a full-blown license, then you can use this system to convert.

You can add an Applix "launcher" to the GNOME panel by choosing Main Menu Button⇨Panel⇨Add new launcher menus. The Create launcher applet dialog box opens. Enter "Applix" in the Name: box and /opt/applix/applix in the Command: box. You can also select an icon from a standard set of GNOME icons by clicking on the Icon: button. When you are satisfied, click the OK button and your new applet (Icon) appears in the GNOME panel.

Getting Familiar with Applix Words

If you're familiar with Microsoft Word, then you should be able to find your way around Applix Words. The look and feel is a little different, but the idea is the same — plus Words is morally superior to Word because it's not taking over the world. The following sections describe how to use the most common word processing functions. Please experiment with your own test documents and consult the online help for more information.

The main menu items appear at the top of the window, and the next menu bar down, called the *ExpressLine,* doesn't help you check your groceries out any quicker but does contain shortcuts to frequently used functions. The *Ruler* menu bar is third from the top and contains the ruler and font shortcuts. You can hide the ExpressLine and Ruler bars by clicking the View function and toggling its radio buttons. Figure 16-2 shows a sample Words window.

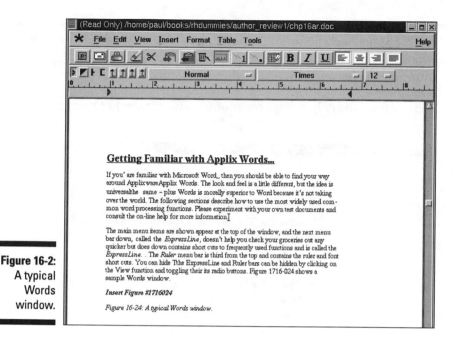

Figure 16-2:
A typical
Words
window.

Using the file menu

As you may expect, you can open, close, and save Words documents with the File menu. The new, open, and save functions work on Applix Words files only; Words files have the *aw* suffix. Other file formats such as Microsoft Word 97 and HTML must be imported and exported. Figure 16-3 shows the various functions of the File menu.

The File menu contains the Import and Export selections. To import a file, follow these steps:

1. **Choose File⇨Import.**

    The Import window pops up.

2. **Double-click any of the directories to browse the Linux file system (directories are distinguished by orange file folder icons).**

3. **Click the file that you want to import.**

4. **Select the file type from the submenu at the bottom of the window.**

5. **Finally, click the Open button.**

    The Import Wizard (Step 1 of 3) dialog box opens up, giving you the option to manually answer questions that the import software has.

6. **It's quickest to allow Applix to use its own best judgement to proceed. Therefore, just click the Next button each time that you are prompted to.**

7. **When the importation has finished, click the Finish button and your file opens, ready for you.**

Please consult the help system for information on the other functions.

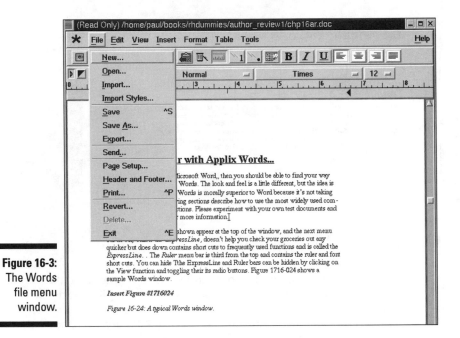

Figure 16-3:
The Words
file menu
window.

Edit this

The Edit menu provides all the functions that you need, such as cut, copy, paste, and delete. You can also access the Find & Replace function from this menu.

The Find & Replace menu enables you to find text strings and replace them with another string, if you want, or delete them. You can search going forward or backward. You can replace one instance as well as all instances. Options include such things as activating case sensitivity (the default is no case sensitivity).

View that

The View menu displays or hides the various menu bars, as described in the beginning of this chapter. You can also have Words display its formatting characters and zoom the display in or out. The zoom function enables you to make smaller fonts more readable without changing the document.

Inserting some stuff

You can use the Insert menu to — yes, you guessed it — insert special characters, objects, files, and macros. Special characters include various symbols that are not part of the normal character set. Objects include graphics, symbols, and figures. You can also insert macros and hyperlinks into your Words documents.

Formatting the stuff

You can format Words documents at the character, paragraph, or document level. You can format a character's font, font size, color, and position, as well as apply bold, italics, and strikethrough.

Table top

You can insert tables into documents. You have control over the number of rows and columns in a table. Words can automatically adjust the row height, or you can do it manually. You can also adjust the overall positioning.

Tools talk

The main function of the Tools menu is to provide access to the spell checker, thesaurus, and change bar. The spell checker is self-explanatory, as is the thesaurus. The *change bar* provides a change-tracking mechanism that works at the line level. For example, if you change a single character or an entire line, then the change bars displays a marker pointing to the line that has changed. This feature could be improved to mark changes in color at the character level.

Help, I need some help!

Applixware provides a pretty good help system. It is similar to other application help systems in configuration, but we've found it to provide the answers to our questions in general. You can use a context-sensitive help feature or look for help on specific topics.

To use the context-sensitive help, follow these steps:

1. **Press the F1 key (or choose Help⇨On Context).**

   The cursor turns into a question mark.

2. **Position the cursor over the menu bar item that you want to find out about.**

   For instance, press F1, position the question mark cursor over File⇨New menu and click.

   The help window pops up, as shown in Figure 16-4, which provides a short description of how to create a new Words document.

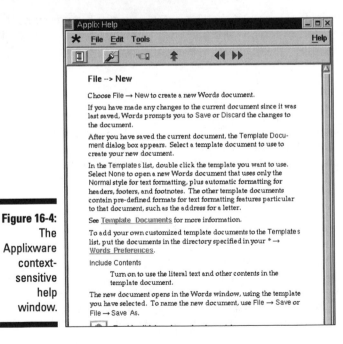

Figure 16-4:
The
Applixware
context-
sensitive
help
window.

You can search for specific topics by following these steps:

1. **Choose Help⇨Search.**

   The Search window pops up.

2. **Enter the name of the topic that you want information on in the search dialog box.**

   For instance, enter the word **delete**, and the Edit->Delete item, shown in Figure 16-5, shows up in the References subwindow.

3. **Click the OK button when your item appears in the reference subwindow.**

   An Applixware Help window pops up, describing how to delete material from a document.

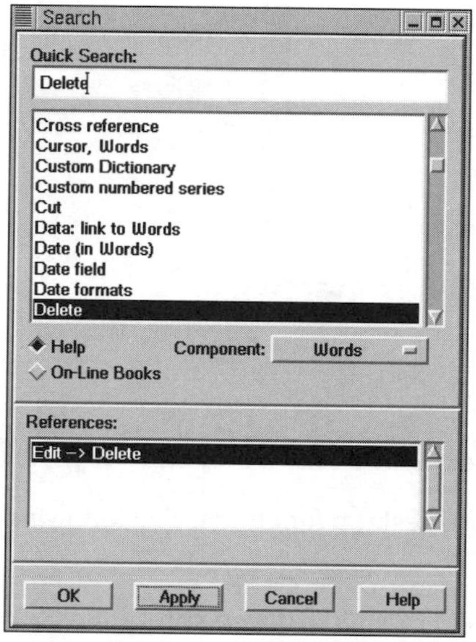

Figure 16-5:
The
Applixware
Quick
Search
window.

Applix help is not case sensitive.

The On Words help function provides more detailed information on selected topics. Choose Help⇨On Words, and the Applix Help window appears. You can find detailed, in-depth information about Words and find out how to work with it and write Web pages. Pretty neat.

We're not done yet! You can also find quick tutorials by choosing Help⇨ Tutorial, such as lessons on formatting and spell checking. These tutorials are a good way to quickly run up that 'ol learning curve. Figure 16-6 shows a sample help window. Help covers several other topics, including the other Applixware functions.

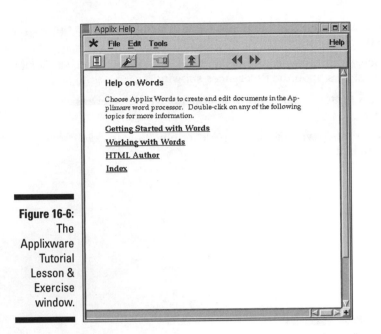

Figure 16-6:
The Applixware Tutorial Lesson & Exercise window.

Applying more functions with Applix

Applixware provides many more desktop functions. The following list outlines Applixware's capabilities.

- ✔ **Spreadsheets.** Spreadsheets is a full-featured spreadsheet program. It is similar to other such tools. If you are familiar with spreadsheet software, then Spreadsheets should be straightforward to use.

- ✔ **Graphics.** This program gives you the ability to create simple drawings. We used it to create several figures in this book.

- ✔ **Presents.** You can create slides and general-purpose presentation graphics with this tool.

- ✔ **HTML editor.** The HTML editor is very simple in its purpose: building Web pages. You enter what you want on the screen, and Applixware saves it in HTML form. The process is as simple as that: You enter it, and Applixware converts it.

- ✔ **SQL database viewer.** If you work with SQL databases — such as Oracle, Informix, Sybase, or Linux's native son, postgresql — then this tool allows you to view and edit the data. Your database must be ODBC-capable in order to use this tool.

✔ **E-mail client.** Applixware Office also provides an e-mail client. However, you'll probably want to stick with your Netscape Messenger client, if only to minimize the number of software packages that you use. Nothing is wrong with this tool, but if you're like us and run the Netscape Navigator browser constantly, then you may as well use Messenger for e-mail.

A StarOffice Is Born

StarOffice is not a Hollywood acting agency but another desktop productivity suite, offered free of charge by Sun Microsystems, Inc. It provides all the functions that you'd expect from such software: word processing, spread sheets, graphics, and more. Our early opinion is that it has more of the look and feel of Microsoft Office 97 than Applixware Office. You can read all about it if you pick up a copy of *StarOffice for Linux For Dummies* by Michael Meadhra (published by IDG Books Worldwide, Inc.).

You can download StarOffice free or order a CD-ROM copy for $9.95 from Sun's Web site at http://www.sun.com/products/staroffice/get.html. Of course, before you can download the free personal-edition copy, you need to connect to the Internet (which we describe in Chapter 17). After you're connected, check it out.

Who's Number One?

Who is better? That question is best left to personal taste and opinion. We have used Applixware extensively in the last six months but have just started using StarOffice. So we can claim ignorance and reasonably bow out of any decisions. However, you can find an informed opinion by checking out *StarOffice for Linux For Dummies.* You can also find a good comparison of Applixware and StarOffice in issue 54 of the *Linux Journal.* The article is posted at `www.linuxjournal.com/issue54/3080.html` and was written by Fred Butzen who is the co-author of *The Linux Network* (IDG Books Worldwide, Inc.).

But What about Corel WordPerfect?

Last, but not least, is the venerable WordPerfect. The former king of DOS word processing is also a prominent Linux player. Corel provides a word processor and an HTML editor, but WordPerfect is not an office suite like the other two systems. We used WordPerfect briefly a couple of years ago, but for reasons unrelated to its usefulness, we didn't spend enough time with it to gain an opinion. You can download a free copy from `linux.corel.com/linux8/download.htm`.

A Window on Linux

One of the really useful tools that we currently use is Microsoft's Windows NT Server 4.0, Terminal Server Edition, with Citrix's MetaFrame. This product displays a full-featured Microsoft Windows NT desktop on your Linux computer. Applications actually run on a Windows NT server but displays on your Linux computer as an X window. You get a virtual Windows NT box running in your Linux box.

Paul uses a Linux computer as his only personal workstation at his job. Most of what he needs to do can be done with Linux. However, certain functions, like his company timesheet, can run only on a Windows computer. By using MetaFrame/Terminal Server, Paul does not need to have a second computer or to bug his coworkers. He simply fires up his MetaFrame client window, connects to the server, and — *voilá* — he has a Windows box within his Linux box. No muss, no fuss.

You can download Citrix's client program from the company's Web site at `www.citrix.com`. Citrix provides a simple Internet-based NT server for demonstration purposes. The Web site offers full instructions.

Days of Wine and Roses

Wine stands for WINdows Emulator. It converts Windows API functions into their X Window System equivalents. You can then run Windows executables on Linux. Pretty sweet.

The Wine home page address is `www.winehq.com`. This site contains not only the latest versions and updates, but also several FAQs. An alternative site is `winebin.netpedia.net`. You can download Wine in RPM format from `www.cse.psu.edu/~juran/wine/`.

Applications Galore!

The list of Linux applications is growing rapidly. Red Hat maintains a Web page for information on Linux applications. The address of that page is `www.redhat.com/appindex/index.html`.

Currently, that Red Hat page lists applications in the following areas:

- ✔ Database
- ✔ Networking

✔ Games

✔ Office Apps and Suites

✔ Graphics

✔ Groupware

✔ Programming and development

✔ Math & Science

✔ Servers

✔ Multimedia

✔ X Window System

✔ Miscellaneous

You can find programs for every major area of interest on this page — systems like Oracle, Applixware, and StarOffice. This list is constantly growing and is a good indication of the overall health and future direction of Linux.

Part V
Going Online

The 5th Wave — By Rich Tennant

"I don't think it's so much the Linux operating system he's fascinated with as it is that its symbol is a small, flightless bird."

In this part . . .

It's time to hit the great outdoors, starting in your back-yard and moving out from there. Chapter 17 shows you how to find an Internet service provider (ISP). Next, it shows how to connect your Linux computer to the Net. From there, you are shown how to protect yourself from the worst aspects of the Net by building a simple, but effective firewall.

Now you're ready for the great mountains, otherwise known as the Web. Chapter 18 shows you how to browse the Web with a program called, naturally, a Web browser. The *Red Hat Linux For Dummies* CD-ROM 1 already contains one of the best Web browsers available, Netscape Communicator.

Okay, now that you're out in the wilds of computerdom, how will you communicate? Smoke signals? Yodeling? E-mail? That's the ticket, and you find out how to send and receive e-mail in Chapter 18 as well.

Chapter 17

Setting Up Your Internet Connection

*O*ne of *the* things to do these days is to ski the Net. You connect to the Internet and tie up your phone line for hours, looking for obscure information and sending e-mail to people you barely know and never speak to on the phone.

Now you, too, can go to a party and drop the casual phrase "I found this while skiing the Net this afternoon . . . [which will draw bored looks] . . . on my Linux system." The mention of Linux immediately shows that you are truly a person of class and standing in the Internet community.

First, though, you have to find a good *Internet service provider* (ISP), hook up your phone to the computer (using a device called a *modem*), and feed a few simple commands to your Linux system (and the networking gods) to make the connection.

Locating Your ISP?

We categorize Internet service providers into those that specialize only in Windows and Windows NT products and those that are good. By *good,* we mean ISPs that can also handle UNIX and Linux accounts.

To find a good ISP, first look in your local Yellow Pages under Internet or Internet Service Providers. List the names and telephone numbers of any ISPs that you find. These companies are probably local companies, which is fine if you want to communicate only from your home. If you do a lot of traveling, you may want to call the following national providers:

AT&T WorldNet: 800-967-5363

IBM Global Network: 800-426-4968

CompuServe: 800-336-6823

Next, talk to some friends who live close to you and ask them which ISP they use and what they think of the service. If a service has overused local access numbers, you get busy signals a lot. Also, ask about the technical help, which in some services is poor or nonexistent.

Finally, call the ISPs and tell them you have a Linux system and are interested in PPP (which stands for point-to-point protocol) services, with e-mail and newsgroups. Find out whether they have access numbers in your local calling area. Otherwise, you'll end up making a long-distance call each time you connect. Check their prices and whether they have unlimited service (a flat rate no matter how many hours you're logged on). A typical price for unlimited service is $20 to $30 per month.

ISPs that host Web pages are a plus, as are ISPs that can filter junk e-mail, or *spam*. Also find out how and what kind of service they provide. Most ISPs are small to medium-sized organizations and cannot afford to staff their lines 24 hours a day, 7 days a week. However, many small ISPs are owned and run by technical people who happen to monitor their systems for what seems like 24 hours a day. They often are logged on while at home and periodically monitor their e-mail — a good indicator is if they have a generic e-mail address such as `help@goodisp.com`. If you get lucky or really do your homework, then you'll connect with one of these ISPs (Southwest Cyberport in Albuquerque, NM is one such place) and get excellent help.

Now is a good time to verify that your own telephone service is billed at a flat rate and not metered.

The Polish connection

A young friend of Jon's from Poland came to visit him. He had obtained a nationwide ISP service to keep in touch through the Internet with family and friends back home. Unfortunately, the closest number to his ISP connection site was a long-distance call from Jon's house. Jon cautioned him to keep his connection time down so that he wouldn't have a lot of long-distance charges. He assured Jon that he would. The month after he went back to Poland, Jon received his phone bill — with $70 in long-distance telephone charges to his friend's Internet provider. Hi Antoni!

Tell the ISP the highest speed of your modem. Any ISP worth its salt handles 56 Kbps modems. You'll probably need to supply a login name and a password for the ISP's server, so you may want to have these written down ahead of time.

After you choose your ISP and arrange payment, the service provides you with certain pieces of information, including the following:

✔ Telephone access numbers

✔ A username (usually the one you wanted)

✔ A password (usually the one you supplied)

✔ An e-mail address, which is typically your username added to the ISP's domain name

✔ A primary Domain Name Server (DNS) number, which is a large number separated by periods into four groups of digits

✔ A secondary Domain Name Server (DNS) number, which is another large number separated by periods into four groups of digits

✔ An SMTP (mail) server name

✔ An NNTP (news) server name

✔ A POP3 or IMAP4 server name, which is used to download e-mail from the ISP's server to your machine

The ISP may also give you software on a CD-ROM or a floppy to help you get your account working, but this software probably works only with Microsoft operating systems. That's okay, because your Linux distribution has more than enough software to use with the Internet and to help you get your account working.

Connecting Your Modem

To use Linux with the Internet, you must have at least one of these devices:

✔ A serial modem (just a regular modem)

✔ An ISDN line

✔ A high-speed (broadband) connector of some type (such as Ethernet, FDDI, a cable modem, DSL, ADSL, or ATM if you're one of the lucky soles to be blessed with such service. US West, where are you?)

For the second and third items, you or someone you know (your boss, your systems administrator, or your 10-year-old) probably arranged for you to get the connection and even set up your computer for it. The serial modem is a device that you may have chosen yourself, or it may have come with your computer, in which case you may have little knowledge of how to use it with Linux. For the rest of this chapter, we assume that you're connecting to the Internet by using a serial modem and a telephone line.

Modems, quite simply, do three main functions:

- ✔ Convert digital information into tones that travel across telephone lines (and vice versa)
- ✔ Dial the telephone number that you want to reach and make the connection with a modem at the other end
- ✔ Negotiate with the modem at the other end about what speed to use when sending bits of information

Sorting through modems

Modems can be either internal or external. An *external modem* stays in its own little box and usually plugs into a wall outlet for power, into the telephone line for the connection, and into a serial connector on the back of your computer. An *internal modem* is usually plugged into a slot on the motherboard inside the computer case. (Some internal modems are built directly onto the motherboard.) To the computer and operating system, an internal modem appears as if it were two or more serial ports. Internal modems draw their power from the computer system, and they plug into the phone jack.

Usually internal modems are less expensive than their external counterparts, but some people like external modems because they can hook them up to different computer systems by simply unplugging the serial line from one system box and plugging it into another.

A third type of serial line modem is a PCMCIA card (sometimes called a PC card). These cards are used most often with laptop computers.

Avoid WinModems. These modems are designed for Windows only. They're cheaper than regular modems because they're lazy (or smart depending on how you look at it) and depend on the Windows operating system to do much of their work for them. As of this writing — as far as we are aware — no Linux drivers exist for such modems.

Finding the serial line

After you connect your modem, you have to tell Linux which serial line (or simulated serial line) the modem is connected to. If you have Windows 95 on your system, you can see which port or COM line the modem is connected to as follows:

1. **Choose Start➪Settings➪Control Panel.**

   The Control Panel window appears.

2. **Double-click the Modem icon.**

   The Modems Properties dialog box appears.

3. **Select the Diagnostics tab.**

   You see your modem listed, with a COM line number beside it. This is the Windows designation for your modem's serial communications line.

The modemtool(8) program, which is included on CD1, tells Linux which serial line has an attached modem. In addition, you can now utilize the linkage between the COM names that Microsoft products use for serial lines (COM0, COM1, COM2, COM3) and the names that UNIX systems tend to use (ttyS0, ttyS1, ttyS2, ttyS3). You can see the modemtool(8) program in action in Figure 17-1.

Figure 17-1: The modem-tool(8) program.

Device	Information
<none>	No Modem
cua0	COM1: under MS-DOS
cua1	COM2: under MS-DOS
cua2	COM3: under MS-DOS
cua3	COM4: under MS-DOS

Configure Modem

Select the device (serial port) to which your modem is connected. If you have no modem, select <none>. (This configuration step simply makes a link from /dev/modem to your actual modem device.)

Ok   Cancel

Another way to determine which serial line the modem is attached to is to use the statserial program. By unhooking everything but the modem from your serial lines, you can issue the statserial command to determine which port your modem is attached to. Each time you execute the program, you provide it with another serial line designation (/dev/ttyS0, /dev/ttyS1, /dev/ttyS2, /dev/ttyS3) and note which of the designations has the Clear to Send and Data Set Ready values set to 1. For example, in Figure 17-2, those values are 0 for /dev/ttyS0.

Sometimes, the program fails to work and displays an error message like the following:

```
statserial: TIOCMGET failed: Input/output error
```

Yet, when you issue the statserial command on a line with a modem on it, the CTS and DSR values are 1, as shown in Figure 17-3.

Figure 17-2:
The output
of the stat-
serial pro-
gram; the
line being
tested
equal to
/dev/cua0.

```
Device: /dev/cua0

Signal  Pin  Pin  Direction  Status  Full
Name    (25) (9)  (computer)         Name
------  ---  ---  ---------  ------  ----
FG       1    -     -          -     Frame Ground
TxD      2    3    out         -     Transmit Data
RxD      3    2    in          -     Receive  Data
RTS      4    7    out         1     Request To Send
CTS      5    8    in          0     Clear To Send
DSR      6    6    in          0     Data Set Ready
GND      7    5     -          -     Signal Ground
DCD      8    1    in          0     Data Carrier Detect
DTR     20    4    out         1     Data Terminal Ready
RI      22    9    in          0     Ring Indicator
```

Figure 17-3:
The statser-
ial program
run on
a line with
an attached
modem.

```
Device: /dev/modem

Signal  Pin  Pin  Direction  Status  Full
Name    (25) (9)  (computer)         Name
------  ---  ---  ---------  ------  ----
FG       1    -     -          -     Frame Ground
TxD      2    3    out         -     Transmit Data
RxD      3    2    in          -     Receive  Data
RTS      4    7    out         1     Request To Send
CTS      5    8    in          1     Clear To Send
DSR      6    6    in          1     Data Set Ready
GND      7    5     -          -     Signal Ground
DCD      8    1    in          0     Data Carrier Detect
DTR     20    4    out         1     Data Terminal Ready
RI      22    9    in          0     Ring Indicator
```

After you know this information, you can execute the modemtool(8) program
and create a link between the device that Linux thinks the modem is attached
to and the designator /dev/modem. See an example in Figure 17-4.

Figure 17-4:
The modem-
tool(8)
program
making
the link
between
/dev/cua2
and /dev/
modem.

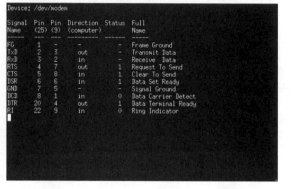

Using modemtool (8)

As mentioned earlier, the modemtool(8) program makes a connection between the special device name /dev/modem and the special device name of the serial line that the modem is attached to (/dev/ttyS0, /dev/ttyS1, /dev/ttyS2, and so on). This way, any programs that need to use the modem do not have to go searching for it. Instead, they talk to the /dev/modem device. In this section, we walk you through the modemtool(8) program.

Remember that when you see a command with a number in parentheses following the command name — for example, modemtool(8) — you type only the command name to run the program, not the number or the parentheses. The number and the parentheses are nomenclature to show that it is a Linux program and that the documentation for it (if any) resides in a particular section of the man(1) pages — section 8 in the case of modemtool(8).

To use the modemtool(8) program, follow these steps:

1. **Log in as root.**

2. **Start X if necessary.**

3. **Start a terminal emulator window and type** modemtool.

4. **Use the arrow keys to highlight the line showing the device to which the modem is attached.**

5. **Use the tab key to highlight the Ok button and press the Enter key.**

Setting Up the Networking Software

You need to have a modem connected and have established an account with an ISP, but that's not all you have to do. You also need to tell the Linux system that whenever you want to connect to the Internet, you really mean that you're going to do the following:

✔ Execute a program called PPP (Point-to-Point Protocol).

✔ Dial your modem to connect to your ISP.

✔ Make the connection.

✔ Negotiate what speed the mutual modems will talk at.

✔ Log on to the ISP's system, giving your username and password.

✔ Start the PPP services on either end, creating an Internet Protocol to flow over the serial line.

To begin setting up your networking, follow these steps to get into the network configuration window:

1. **Log in as root and choose Main Menu Button⟶Systems⟶Control Panel.**

   The control panel appears, as shown in Figure 17-5.

Figure 17-5:
The control
panel for
system
administra-
tion
services.

2. **Click the Network Configuration icon.**

   This icon is generally the fourth icon from the top. (It has a symbolic network symbol on the button. If you hold the mouse cursor over the button, a pop-up message appears, indicating that it is the Network Configuration icon.)

   The Network Configurator dialog box appears, as shown in Figure 17-6. When the Network Configurator dialog box first appears, it doesn't contain any information other than `localhost.localdomain` in the Hostname field. Leave this information alone, because your ISP probably won't supply you with a permanent identity for your system other than your e-mail name and account on the ISP's server.

   Continue to add the ISP contact information

3. **In the Nameservers area, type the Domain Name Server (DNS) numbers that your ISP gave you and then click Save.**

   We filled in the primary DNS and secondary DNS entries in Figure 17-6.

4. **Click the Interfaces tab at the top of the Network Configurator dialog box.**

   The Interfaces tab of the Network Configurator dialog box appears, as shown in Figure 17-7. This tab includes an entry for each hardware interface you will be using for networking.

5. Click the Add button.

The dialog box shown in Figure 17-8 appears. You use this dialog box to select the type of interface you want to add to your system.

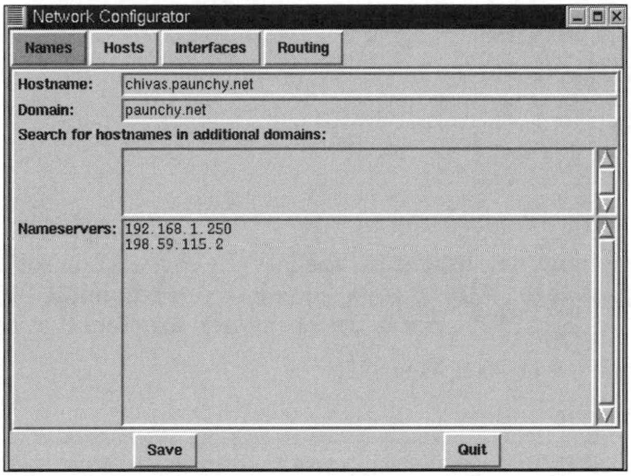

Figure 17-6:
The
Network
Configurator
dialog box
with name
server.

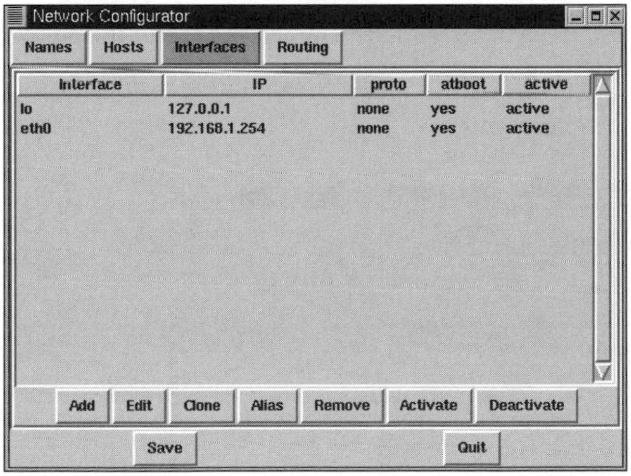

Figure 17-7:
The
Interface
dialog box
as it first
appears.

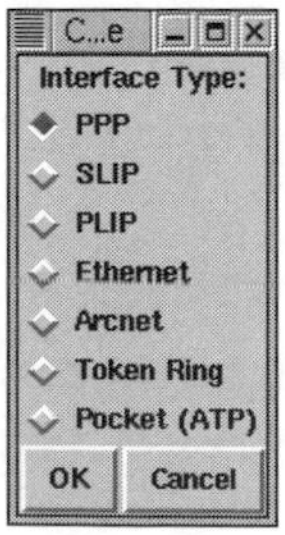

Figure 17-8:
The dialog
box for
selecting
the inter-
face.

6. **Select the PPP option and then click OK.**

   The Create PPP Interface dialog box appears — as shown in Figure 17-9.

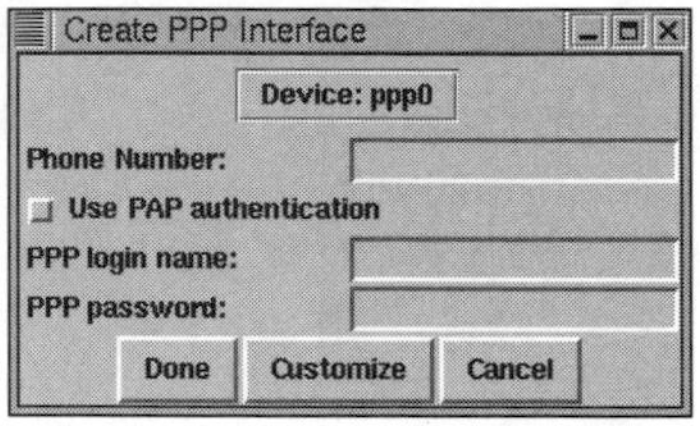

Figure 17-9:
The Create
PPP
Interface
dialog box.

Figure 17-9:
The Create
PPP
Interface
dialog box.

7. **Type the telephone number for the ISP, the login name for the account, and the password. If the account uses PAP (an automatic PPP protocol initiator) to start PPP, click in the check box to select that option.**

   Ask your ISP whether it uses PAP.

8. **Click the Done button.**

   Another dialog box opens asking you if you want to save the configurations. Click on Save if you want to. Otherwise, click on Cancel to forget any changes that you've made.

   The PPP interface is added to the Interfaces tab of the Network Configurator dialog box, as shown in Figure 17-10.

   Continue to check your work.

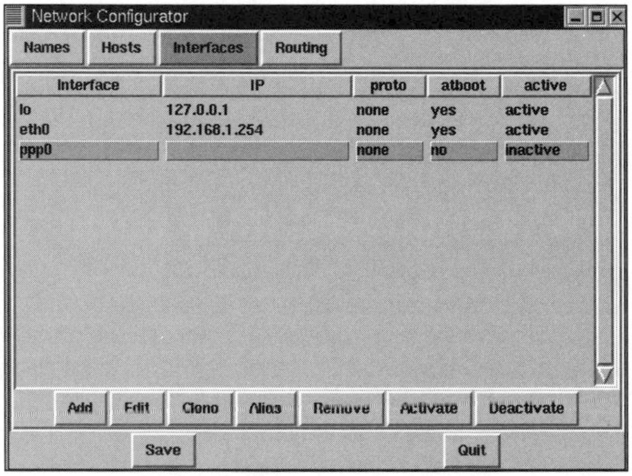

Figure 7-10:
The
Interfaces
dialog box
after you
add the PPP
interface.

9. **Back at the Network Configurator dialog box, highlight the PPP interface by clicking the PPP line and then the Edit button.**

The Edit PPP Interface dialog box appears, as shown in Figure 17-11. Most of the information for PPP has already been entered.

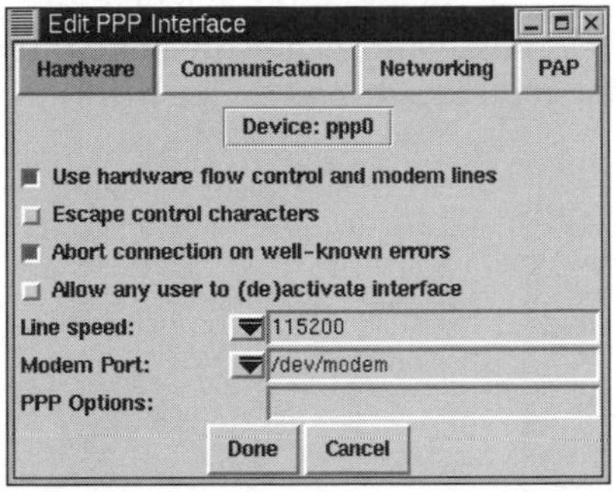

Figure 17-11:
The first dialog box for configuring PPP.

If your system is at home and you have only one telephone line coming into your house, a good option to enable in this dialog box is the Allow Any User to (De)Activate Interface option. This option gives any user the ability to start or shut down PPP services. It's convenient if you, logged in as an average user, can start the PPP program when you want to communicate over the Internet and shut it down (hang up the phone) when you are finished. Otherwise, you have to become a superuser, shut down the PPP account, and then go back to being a normal user again.

10. Click the Communication tab at the top of the Edit PPP Interface dialog box.

The Communication tab appears, as shown in Figure 17-12. You can check out the phone number that the modem will dial. The rest of the entries are mostly for debugging and should be okay for your installation.

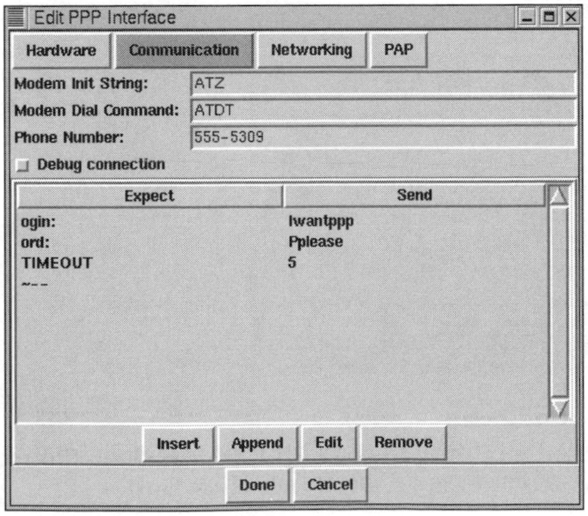

Figure 17-12:
The Communication tab of the Edit PPP Interface dialog box.

11. Click the Networking tab.

The Networking tab, shown in Figure 17-13, appears, with options for telling PPP to redial the modem and remake the connection if the connection is broken. You also have a selection for starting PPP at boot time. If you have only one telephone line, other household members won't appreciate you turning on this setting.

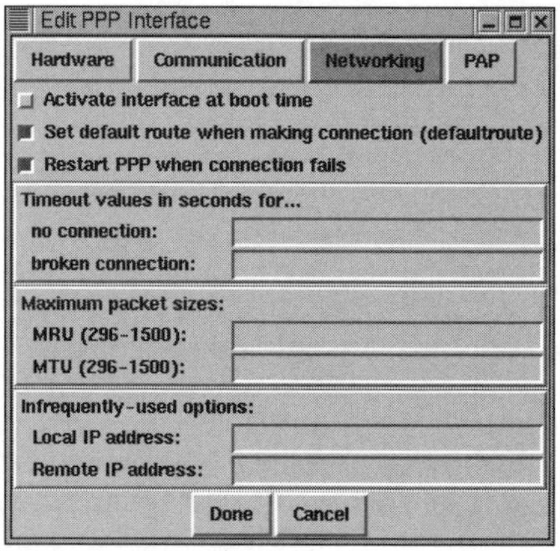

Figure 17-13: Making sure the PPP connection stays connected.

12. Click the PAP tab.

The PAP tab appears, as shown in Figure 17-14, and holds the login names and passwords for the various PPP accounts. It should have all the information it needs for a simple PPP connection.

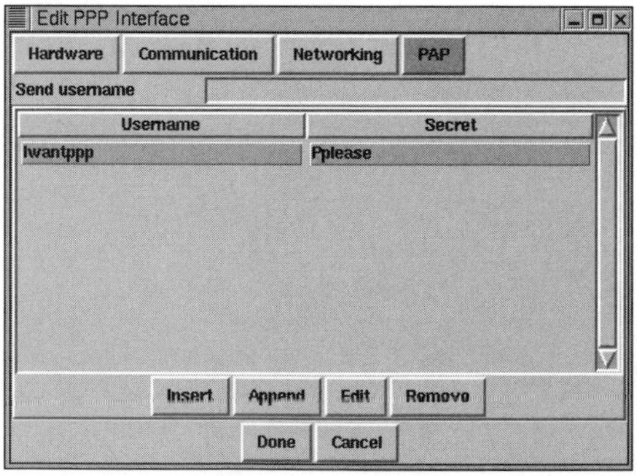

Figure 17-14: The PAP tab with its information filled in.

13. If you've changed anything in the Edit PPP Interface dialog box, click Done. If you haven't changed anything, click Quit.

You return to the Interfaces tab of the Network Configurator dialog box (refer to Figure 17-10).

14. **Click the Save button to save any of the Interface changes you've made.**

15. **Click the Routing tab at the top of the Network Configurator dialog box.**

The Routing tab of the Network Configurator dialog box appears, as shown in Figure 17-15. Leave it blank.

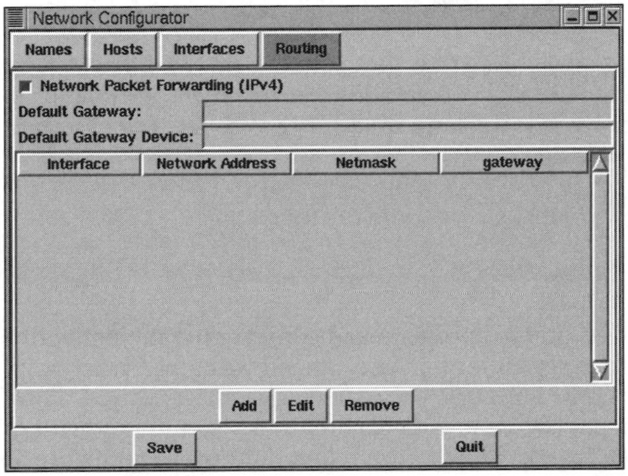

Figure 17-15:
The Routing tab of the Network Configurator dialog box.

The Routing tab is normally filled in with routing information about where to send data going outside your computer and which systems have enough information to send the data on its way to the outside world. However, your ISP automatically supplies this information because the PPP interface is the gateway to the outside world, and the first server it attaches to will route your data on its way. Therefore, leave the Routing tab empty.

16. **If you've made any changes, click Save and then click Quit. If you haven't made any changes, just click Quit.**

Your interface to the outside world is now fully configured.

Firing It Up!

To turn on networking, log in as a regular user. Open a terminal emulator shell by clicking the terminal icon on the GNOME menu bar. From the terminal emulator, type the following at the command line:

```
/sbin/ifup ppp0
```

You should hear a dial tone as your modem picks up the line and then hear your modem dialing the number. After one or a few rings, you hear a scratchy, squawking sound and then silence.

After a few seconds, networking is working, and your computer is connected to the Internet. To test that everything is okay, type the following at the command-line prompt to communicate with a major system at Compaq Computer Corporation:

```
ping gatekeeper.dec.com
```

If you get a message saying that the system is not found, wait a minute more and try again. Eventually, you should receive a message talking about how many milliseconds it takes for a round-trip message. Congratulations, your networking is working!

To turn off networking, simply type the following:

```
/sbin/ifdown ppp0
```

You have now set up the hardware and software to connect your system to the Internet. Your computer has been joined with the Force.

To actually ski the Net, read e-mail, and otherwise interact with others on the Net, check out Chapter 18, where you find out how to configure and use a major Internet tool: the Netscape Communicator program.

Batten Down the Hatches

After you're connected to the Internet, you run the risk of running amok with the bad guys (also known as black hats). You've heard of hackers, Trojan Horses, and such. Unfortunately, they're real, and the Net is a perfect vehicle for them.

Securing your computer

You may think that there's safety in numbers. Literally millions of people, businesses, and organizations are connected at any one time, and what do you — a simple person with a simple computer — have to be concerned about? After all, the bad guys are interested in big money or big publicity.

Well, that line of thinking is all true, and chances are that you'll never suffer anything bad. But that's a risk that you may or may not want to take. Linux offers a rather simple method for protecting yourself. The ipchains RPM that is packaged with Red Hat Linux can be used as a *firewall* — a tool for preventing unauthorized access to your computer.

Linux is a multiuser and multitasking operating system. Unlike Windows, more than one person can be logged in at once. More than one task can be run at once, too. This offers an attractive launching point for black hats. If someone can gain access to your Linux computer while it's on the Net, then that person can use your machine to launch attacks against other machines. You become the proxy that helps the bad guys hide their identities.

Building a simple but effective firewall

The ipchains software is a system that filters IP packets, which are the backbone of the Internet. IP stands for Internet Protocol, in fact. When you're connected to the Internet, all the information (graphics and text) that you send and receive is sent in the form of IP packets. These packets contain the information that you're interested in as well as — and this is how your stuff gets sent around the world — the destination and source address information.

Anyway, all the information that enters and leaves your computer via the Internet is packaged in the form of IP packets. You can use ipchains to accept or deny the IP packets based on their destination and source address and ports. (Oh yeah, ports are another aspect of the Internet Protocol. Suffice it to say that they're used for the internal workings for such things as Web browsing.)

The ipchains firewall that we describe in this chapter allows you to access all the Internet services except FTP. No one can access your machine or even see it. (Tools such as nmap are readily available on the Internet that can be used to scan your computer and find out what type of operating system you have as well as what services it offers.)

FTP is used to transfer files from one place to another. You can modify the rules to allow FTP but that makes it a little more complicated. You can find more extensive and complete rules at Paul's Web site: www.swcp.com/~pgsery/rhbiz/. Look for ipchains.rules and ipchains.reset.

The following steps describe how to protect yourself by building a firewall:

1. **Log in as root and mount the companion CD-ROM (CD1).**

2. **Install the ipchains RPM by typing this:**

   ```
   rpm -ivh /mnt/cdrom/RedHat/RPMS/ipchains*
   ```

3. **Edit a file and call it firewall.on. Put it in the /usr/local/etc directory. Enter the following ipchains rules into it. (The lines preceded by the hash (#) symbol are comments.)**

```
# Flush out all existing rules
ipchains -F
ipchains -X
```

```
# Set default filters to deny everything
ipchains -P input   DENY
ipchains -P output  DENY
ipchains -P forward DENY
```

```
# Allow all internal network traffic
ipchains -A input  -i lo -j ACCEPT
ipchains -A output -i lo -j ACCEPT
```

```
# Allow all private network traffic (Ethernet)
ipchains -A input  -i eth0 -j ACCEPT
ipchains -A output -i eth0 -j ACCEPT
```

```
# Allow all TCP packets out to the Internet
ipchains -A output -p TCP -j ACCEPT -i ppp0 -d 0.0.0.0/0
```

```
# Allow all TCP SYN packets back in (the return packets)
ipchains -A input -p TCP -j ACCEPT -i ppp0 ! -y -s 0.0.0.0/0
```

```
# Allow DNS UDP packets out to the Internet
ipchains -A output -p UDP -j ACCEPT -i ppp0 -d 0.0.0.0/0 domain
```

```
# Allow DNS UDP packets back in from the Internet
ipchains -A input -p UDP -j ACCEPT -i ppp0 -s 0.0.0.0/0 domain
```

4. **Create the file that will be used to turn off the firewall. Call it firewall.off and put it in the /usr/local/etc directory as well.**

```
ipchains -F
ipchains -X
ipchains -P input   ACCEPT
ipchains -P output  ACCEPT
ipchains -P forward ACCEPT
```

5. **Save the files and make them executable by root:**

```
chmod 770 /usr/local/etc/firewall.*
```

To activate your firewall, follow these steps:

1. **Connect your Linux computer to the Internet:**

```
/etc/sysconfig/network-scripts/ifup-ppp
```

2. **After you're connected, turn on the firewall:**

```
/usr/local/etc/firewall.rules
```

3. **Try using the Net to connect to a Web site with Netscape Communicator.**

   Everything should work as usual.

4. **Next, look at the rules that you've set up. Enter the command.**

```
pchains -L.
```

   You should see a list, as follows:

```
Chain input (policy DENY):
target  prot opt     source      destination   ports
ACCEPT  all  ------  anywhere    anywhere       n/a
ACCEPT  all  ------  anywhere    anywhere       n/a
ACCEPT  tcp  !y----  anywhere    anywhere       any ->any
ACCEPT  udp  ------  anywhere    anywhere       domain ->any
Chain forward (policy DENY):
Chain output (policy DENY):
target  prot opt     source      destination   ports
ACCEPT  all  ------  anywhere    anywhere       n/a
ACCEPT  all  ------  anywhere    anywhere       n/a
ACCEPT  tcp  ------  anywhere    anywhere       any ->any
ACCEPT  udp  ------  anywhere    anywhere       any ->domain
```

The first *chain* (which is simply a set of rules used for a common purpose or function) is for incoming — or input — IP packets. You can see that the default policy is to deny all IP packets. The first two rules tell ipchains to allow all internal packets on the logical loopback (lo) and Ethernet (eth0) interfaces. The next rule allows the return packets from outgoing connections to come back in. The last rule allows the incoming UDP domain packets, which are used for domain name service (DNS).

The next chain — forward — denies all packets from being forwarded through your Linux computer. Forwarding is only necessary if you use your computer for routing or other advanced networking functions.

The last chain — output — defines what IP packets are allowed out of your computer. The first two rules are for your lo and eth0 interfaces again and allow all internal traffic. The next rule allows any and all IP packets destined for the Internet to leave through the firewall. The last rule allows domain (DNS) packets to go out to the Internet.

You can make your ipchains rules tighter by allowing only certain types of packets out to the Internet. You can specify certain ports and addresses that are allowable, for instance. This makes your firewall incrementally safer but also more restrictive.

To test your firewall, follow these steps:

1. **Try to Telnet to your ISP or University account; any computer account that's external to your own computer will do.**

   (Telnet is a network program that allows you to connect to a remote computer via and interactively entering commands.)

2. **After you're logged in to your account, try connecting back to your Linux computer.**

   You can find out what your temporary (dynamic) IP address is by entering the following command from your external account if it is a Linux or UNIX computer:

   ```
   who | grep <myloginname>
   ```

   This command should show an IP address in numeric form. For instance:

   ```
   iamme (192.168.1.250) ...
   ```

   Please note that the IP address has been changed to protect the innocent. The address is what is known as a public address and will (should) never exist on the Internet anyway.

3. **Try to Telnet back to your Linux computer:**

   ```
   telnet 192.168.1.250
   ```

If your firewall is set up correctly, then nothing should happen. If you turn off your firewall, however, then you should be able to log in to your Linux computer.

This firewall is simple and effective. But it's by no means the last word in Internet or any other type of security. It will do what it's meant to do: allow you to access the Internet but not allow the Internet to access you.

For more information, search the Internet for security-related topics. The SANS (www.sans.org), USENIX (www.usenix.org), Red Hat (www.redhat.com), and CERT (www.cert.org) Web sites are all good places to start. The companion CD-ROM (CD1) also has some good HOWTO documents on the subject. Numerous books also deal with security, including *Linux Network Toolkit,* by Paul Sery and *Red Hat Linux in Small Business,* by Paul Sery and Eric Harper (both published by IDG Books Worldwide, Inc.), which provide introductory to intermediate discussions on the subject. They also provide more in-depth IP filtering rules. (Hey, Paul's plugging his own books. What can we say?)

Chapter 18

Skiing the Web

- -

In This Chapter

▶ Tailoring Netscape Communicator to suit you

▶ Checking out Web pages

▶ Receiving and reading e-mail

▶ Sending your first e-mail message

- -

*O*nce upon a time, there was a company called Netscape that created a browser called Mozilla. Despite the fact that the company spelled the name *Netscape,* you were supposed to pronounce it *Mozilla.* In any case, the browser was one of the best in the world (if not *the* best), and the folks at Netscape made it even better by turning it over to the Open Source community.

Over time, Mozilla could not only ski the Web but also read e-mail, gather files using the File Transfer Protocol (FTP), run simple programs with Java, and even read Netnews (a discussion group made up of thousands of categories on the Net), all through a single graphical interface.

In this chapter, you set up Netscape Communicator for your system. Then, with the information from your ISP, you finally ski the Web, and send and receive e-mail.

Customizing Netscape Communicator

CD1 includes a copy of Netscape Communicator (or Mozilla, if you like to be confused), which Red Hat installs by default. You can activate Communicator by clicking the — you guessed it — Netscape icon on the main GNOME menu bar at the bottom of the screen.

A screen similar to Figure 18-1 appears, and Netscape is set free!

Figure 18-1:
Netscape
Communi-
cator
(Mozilla) in
its initial
invocation.

Mozilla (hereafter called Netscape Communicator) has three main screens:

✔ The Navigator screen, as shown in Figure 18-1

✔ The Mail and Discussions screen

✔ The News screen

The first thing that you want to do is to tailor Communicator to your preferences. You can do this *offline* (without connecting to the Internet), which is certainly preferable if you have only one phone line. Follow these steps to customize Communicator:

1. Choose Edit⇨Preferences.

The Preferences window appears, as shown in Figure 18-2.

Note that on the left side of the Preferences window is the Category window, which is a map of where you are in the Preferences window. You skipped over the Appearance window (it's self-explanatory) and are now concentrating on the Navigator window. The Navigator window is where you determine what initial window appears when you start Netscape Communicator; most people select either a home page or the last page they viewed.

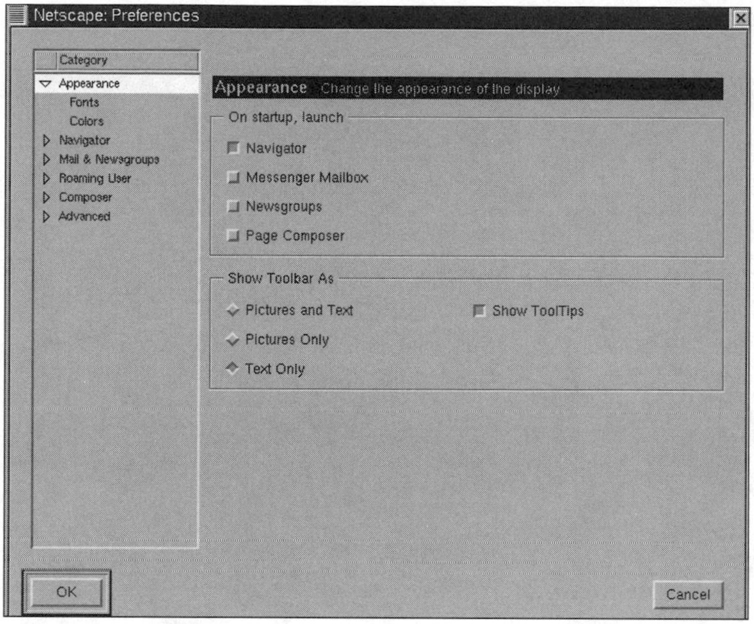

Figure 18-2:
The first
major
Preferences
window for
Communi-
cator.

2. In the Home Page area of the Navigator window, fill in the Location field.

Make sure that you fill in the home page location so you can access it by clicking the Home Page icon at the top of the Navigator screen. If you don't have a preference for a home page yet, you can always come back later and fill this in.

3. If you want, select a History number.

Communicator remembers where you have been and lets you select (and go to) a previous location. How long Communicator remembers (and how big the list becomes) depends on how many days of history you choose.

4. In the Category window, click Mail & Newsgroups and then click Identity. Fill in any necessary information.

The Identity window, shown in Figure 18-3, is where you add your e-mail address, return address, and organization name, and specify your *signature file* (the file that holds additional information included at the end of e-mail messages as a signature) if you want one.

5. In the Category window, under Mail & Newsgroups, click Messages. Then fill in any necessary information.

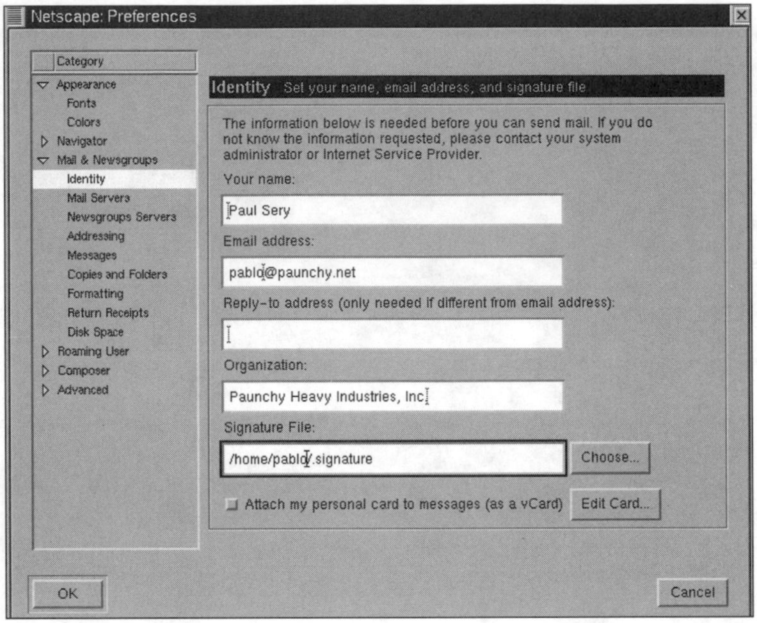

Figure 18-3:
The Identity
window in
all its glory.

The Messages window appears, as shown in Figure 18-4. You use this window to set defaults for outgoing messages, such as whether you want to send plain ASCII e-mail or encapsulate it in HTML. The latter option is fine if you know that the recipient reads e-mail with a browser rather than an ASCII e-mail reader. You can also choose to copy yourself (send yourself an automatic e-mail copy) of everything you send.

This window is also where you can select the option of automatically quoting e-mail that you reply to, which means that Communicator includes (quotes) the original message in your reply. This feature is often useful when you want to comment on what someone has written.

6. **In the Category window, under Mail & Newsgroups, click Mail Server. Fill in any necessary information.**

The Mail Server window appears, as shown in Figure 18-5. Because you are usually connected to the Internet for relatively short periods, your Internet service provider (ISP) supplies you with machines called *servers,* which send and deliver your e-mail even when you are not connected to the Internet. Then when you do connect to the Internet, your computer tells the server to deliver the e-mail or send your messages.

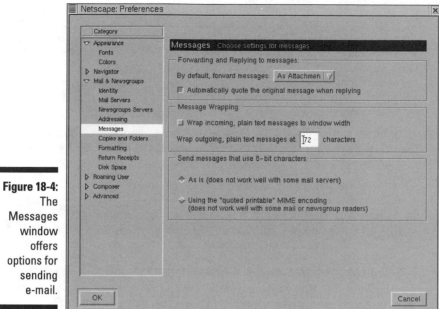

Figure 18-4:
The
Messages
window
offers
options for
sending
e-mail.

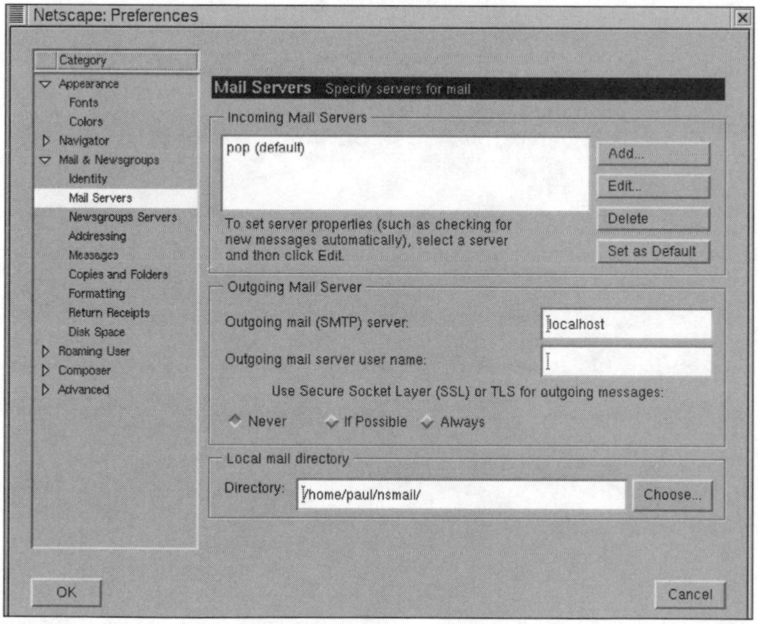

Figure 18-5:
Setting up
the e-mail
server
names and
addresses.

Your ISP gives you a login name for the mail server (usually the same as your other login name) as well as the names for both your incoming and outgoing mail server. These two names are usually the same, but if you're using a special mail service called POP (Post Office Protocol), which allows you to download e-mail to your system from the server, your ISP gives you a name for the POP server. IMAP4 is an even newer protocol for doing similar procedures as POP, and if your ISP has an IMAP4 server, it should tell you that also.

7. In the Category window, under Mail & Newsgroups, click groups Server. If you want to participate in a news server, fill in the fields.

The groups Server window appears, as shown in Figure 18-6. Communicator enables you to read Netnews, which is a series of discussion groups that have been active for many years. Discussion groups were one of the first uses of the Internet, and they have been disseminating information (and misinformation) for many years. To participate in a in a discussion group, fill in the name of your news server (provided by your ISP), as well as the working area where your messages should be downloaded for you to read. Message groups can be quite active, so fill in the last option in the window, which specifies how many messages you want to receive before being asked. These fields are shown in Figure 18-6.

8. At this point, you're all set to run Communicator and see the world, so click OK and go, go, go!

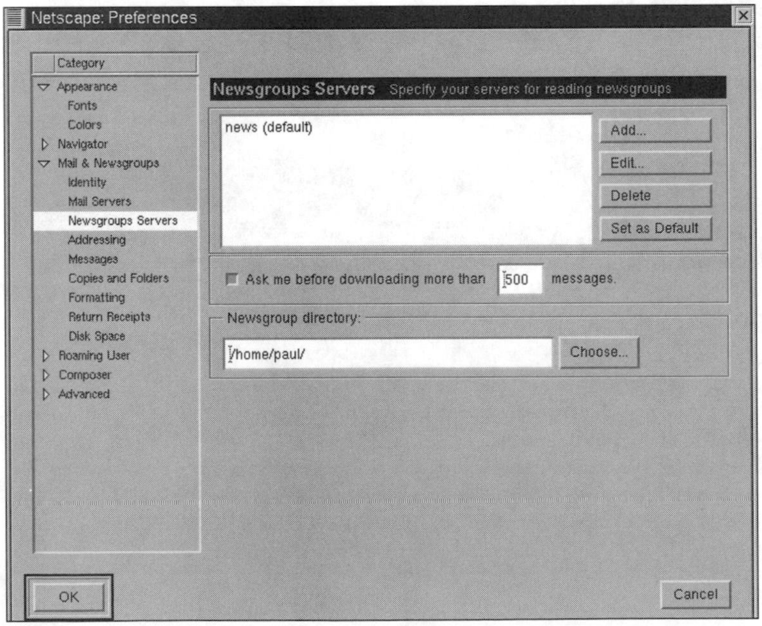

Figure 18-6:
Setting up
Netnews
server
information.

Skiing with good bindings

Before you start to ski the Web, you need the proper bindings. To navigate to a Web page, you type in or click a URL (Uniform Resource Locator). After you know one URL, you can easily go from there to other places on the Web. URLs look like this:

`http://www.li.org/`

or this:

`www.li.org/`

All major browsers let you omit the `http://`. Some browsers also allow you to omit the trailing slash (/), unless the final segment is a filename.

URLs are usually underlined on Web pages. The underline indicates that the text is a *hyperlink,* which means you can simply click the underlined text to go to that location. If your browser doesn't take you to that location, one of the following is usually the reason:

✔ The URL is old, and the page to which it is pointing no longer exists.

✔ The server system that the page is on is inoperative. You may see the message The server is down.

✔ The server system is running, but it's handling too much of a load because too many user are trying to access that page. This problem occurs, for example, when the *Sports Illustrated* server puts up the swimsuit issue.

✔ Your network connection went down, from you to your ISP or from your ISP to the requested Web site.

When skiing the Net, be patient. Even on the best days, downloading certain pages can take several minutes.

Connecting to the Internet

After you've configured your browser properly, you can connect to the Internet by typing the following in a terminal window (you start a terminal window — also known as a terminal emulator window — by clicking the icon that looks like a computer monitor on the GNOME menu bar):

```
/sbin/ifup ppp0
```

You have to wait a few seconds (or even a minute) to connect with your ISP (hearing the sound of your modem dialing is a good sign). Try pinging `gatekeeper.dec.com` to make sure that you are connected (the ping command sends out a very simple IP packet and listens for the response):

```
ping gatekeeper.dec.com
```

Now type the following:

```
netscape http://www.li.org&
```

Netscape Communicator starts and shows the URL that you just supplied (`http://www.li.org`). A screen appears, which is similar to Figure 18-7.

On the left side of the page is the <u>What is Linux?</u> link (you know it's a link because it's underlined). If you click this link, your browser takes you to a page similar to the one shown in Figure 18-8.

Note that near the top of the window is a box containing the following URL:

```
http://www.li.org/whatlinux/index.shtml
```

Use your cursor or keyboard to delete the URL and replace it with another one and then press the Return key. The browser is off to another Web page. Here are a few interesting URLs to try:

```
www.linuxtoday.com

www.theonion.com

www.ssc.com
```

Figure 18-7:
Netscape
Communi-
cator
viewing the
Linux
International
home page.

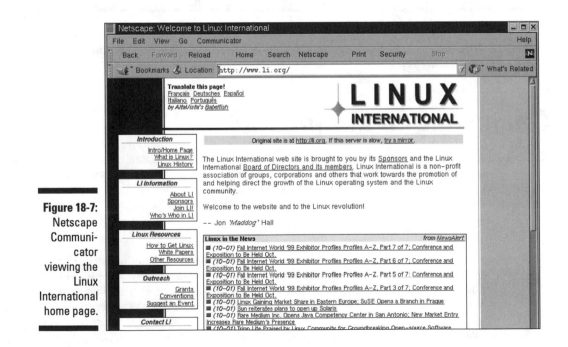

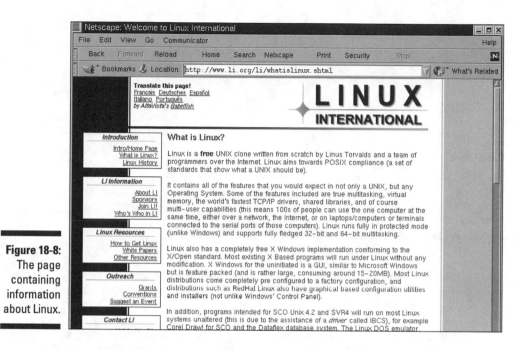

Figure 18-8:
The page
containing
information
about Linux.

Another way of opening a new Web page is to choose File⇨Open New
Location. The browser displays the Open Page dialog box, shown in Figure
18-9, where you can type the new URL and then choose whether you want to
use that URL for Navigator (most of the time) or Composer (perhaps to use
the Web page that the URL points to as part of a new Web page). You can also
use the Open Page dialog box to open a file of *HTML code* (the language that
Web pages are written in) that's local to your system, to either read that file
as documentation or to treat it as a new Web page.

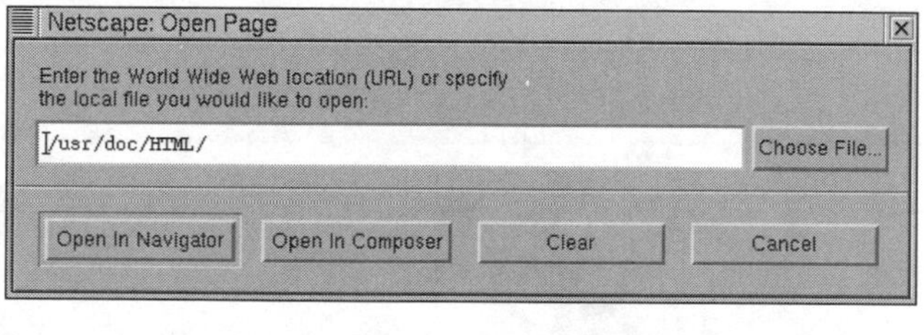

Figure 18-9:
The Open
Page
dialog box.

If you decide to load a local file and click the Choose File button, the File
Browser dialog box, shown in Figure 18-10, springs up so that you can search
the file system to find the file you want.

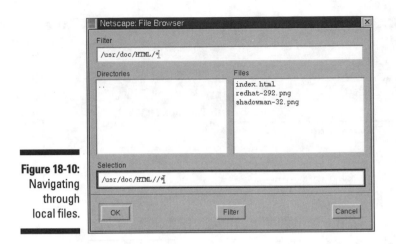

Figure 18-10:
Navigating
through
local files.

Web pages can also contain graphics, as shown in Figure 18-11. The cute penguin — the mascot of the Linux world — is going off to drink a beer while working on Linux with his notebook.

You can even send sounds through the Web (although illustrating this capability is a little difficult). Sounds are transmittable over the Internet as files, and you can play them after they reach your browser, computer, and sound card.

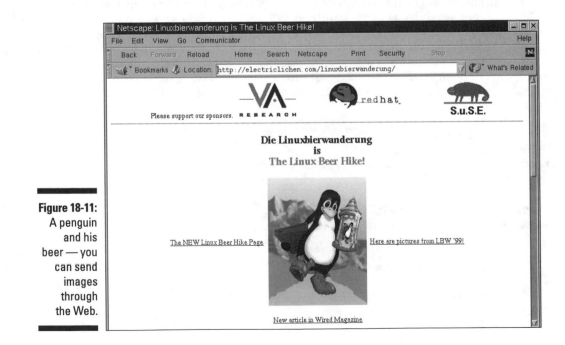

Figure 18-11:
A penguin
and his
beer — you
can send
images
through
the Web.

Getting E-mail

Now that you can ski the Net, you probably want to tell people about your adventures. Well, Communicator can send and receive e-mail, too.

Choose Communicator⇨Messenger. The browser takes you to the Netscape Mail & Newsgroups window, as shown in Figure 18-12.

To get your mail, simply click the Get Msg icon. This icon tells Communicator to make contact with your mail server and see whether any e-mail messages are waiting for you. If you have no new e-mail, a message at the bottom of the screen tells you so. If you do have e-mail, the subject and sender appear in the center of the screen, and the e-mail message itself appears at the bottom of the screen, as shown in Figure 18-13.

If you have multiple e-mail messages, you can see each one by clicking the Subject line in the middle window. You may reply to, forward, or delete a particular message by highlighting its Subject line and clicking the appropriate icon (Reply, Forward, or Delete). When you click the Reply icon, the address of the person you're replying to appears automatically in the To field of the reply. When you forward a message, a copy of the message is sent to the address you specify.

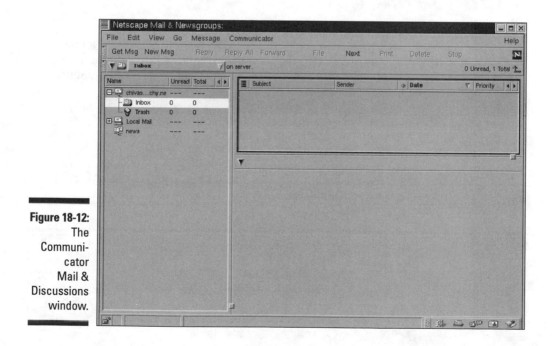

Figure 18-12:
The Communicator Mail & Discussions window.

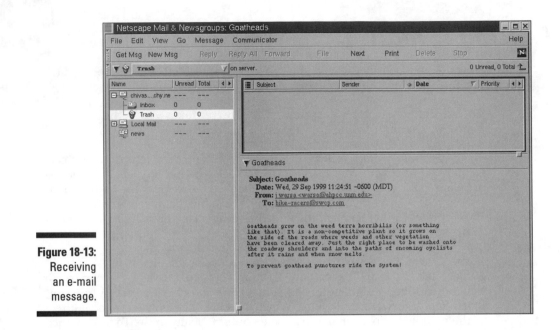

Figure 18-13:
Receiving
an e-mail
message.

Sending E-mail

To send an e-mail message, you need to know someone's e-mail address. Just as a URL consists of certain components, an e-mail address is made up of the person's e-mail name (often the same as his or her login name) and domain name. For example, to send an e-mail to the President of the United States, you address it to president@whitehouse.gov.

Your ISP should have given you an e-mail address, and you can ask your friends for their e-mail addresses. It's ironic that to get your friends' e-mail addresses, you end up spending a lot of time on the telephone.

With the Mail & Discussions window on the screen, click the New Msg icon. The Compose window, similar to Figure 18-14, appears.

It slices, it dices, it even. . . .

Netscape Communicator can do much more than what we describe in this chapter, such as get (download) files from the Internet and keep an address book. These topics are beyond the scope of this book. For more information, we recommend *Netscape Communicator 4.5 For Dummies* by Paul Hoffman (published by IDG Books Worldwide, Inc.).

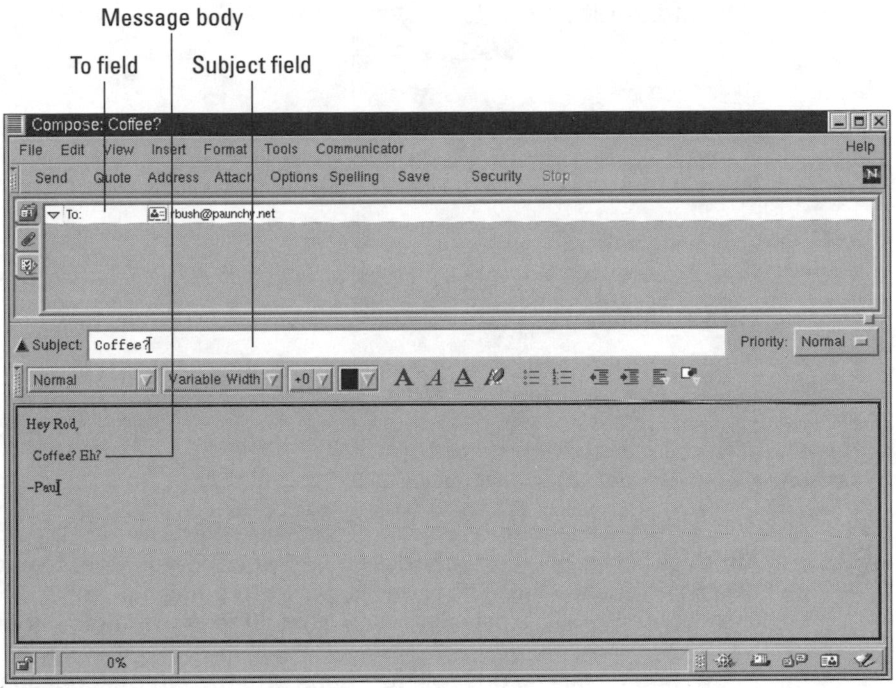

Message body

To field   Subject field

Figure 18-14:
The
Compose
window
for new
messages.

Below the row of icons, near the top of the window, is the word *To*. To the right is a white space where — after you click in it — you can type the e-mail address of the person you're trying to reach. Just for fun, try sending a letter to your own e-mail address. Then if you receive it, you'll know that you did everything correctly. Just follows these steps to do so:

1. **Click in the To field and type your own e-mail address.**

2. **Click in the Subject field and type a suitable subject.**

3. **Click in the body of the message and type your message.**

4. **Click the Send Now icon.**

    If you're sending a message to yourself, it won't appear instantaneously. It still has to travel through the telephone line, be analyzed by the server, and be sent back to you, so be patient.

You can also attach a file, an image, or even a sound to your message and send it to friends who also use Netscape Communicator (or another MIME-compliant mail reader). To attach a file to your letter, simply click the Attach icon at the top of the Compose window. The Attach File dialog box appears, shown in Figure 18-15, allowing you to search the file structure of Linux to find the file you want to send.

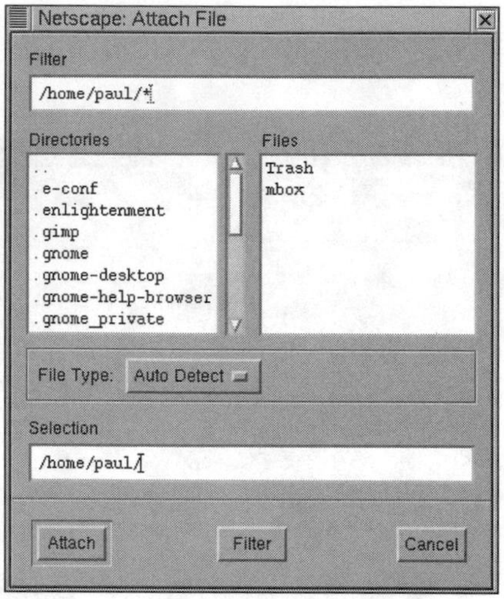

Figure 18-15:
The Attach
File dialog
box for
selecting
a file to
attach to a
message.

After you select the file, the browser asks whether you want to encode it with
Base64 or Uuencoding. Either one is fine for sending mail to most of your
friends, but Base64 is probably used most often in the Microsoft world.

At this point, you can do basic functions with the Internet, but so much more
is possible. For starters, use the Help facility in Communicator to read about
the different options. Out across the Net (despite our earlier sarcasm) is a
wealth of data to which you now have access. Remember, however, that data
can be good data or bad data, and you have to use common sense to decide
whether your data source is knowledgeable or unreliable. Happy skiing!

Part VI
The Part of Tens

The 5th Wave   By Rich Tennant

"It's called 'Linux Poker'. Everyone gets to see everyone elses cards, everythings wild, you can play off your opponents hands, and everyone wins except Bill Gates, whose face appears on the Jokers."

In this part . . .

Ah, the part you find in every *For Dummies* book: The Part of Tens. Here's where we get to rummage around and come up with ten of this and ten of that.

In Chapter 19, we list ten important places to find help. You can use some of these sources also to enhance and widen your knowledge of Linux. There's no end to the things you can find out about Linux.

In Chapter 20, we put together ten of the most frequently encountered problems after people have installed Linux. If you have trouble, turn here first.

Chapter 19

Ten Sources of Help

By now, you're probably wondering whether there is any end to the amount of information and knowledge needed to run a Linux (or UNIX) system. The answer is yes, there is an end to the knowledge that you *need* to run a system well, but not to the knowledge you can accumulate to understand how things work and interact. In this chapter, we suggest several ways to get additional training and support.

Books and More Books

When we started working with computers many years ago, the number of computer books could fill one bookshelf, and they were mostly about the electronics of the hardware itself. We hardly ever saw books on computers in the popular press bookstores. Today, thousands of books on computers are available; most describe the software and its interactions, with the hardware taking a back seat. Books like the *For Dummies* series aren't just for bookstores any more. You can find them in mass-market venues like Wal-Mart, for instance.

Perhaps you looked at other books before you bought this one and were intimidated by their use of technical terms. Or you wanted something more task-oriented. You may want to look over those books again because your knowledge level will have skyrocketed after reading this book. TCP/IP networking, compiler design, operating system theory, formal language theory, computer graphics, and systems administration training are all topics that you can study in greater depth.

Lots of books specifically about the UNIX operating system are partially or completely applicable to Linux, such as books on Perl, a comprehensive interpreter. By getting one (or more) books on Perl and sitting down with your Linux system, you have a new tool for doing your work and a new appreciation for a complete programming language. If you want to find out how to write Perl, you can just view the source code.

Linux HOWTOs

Don't forget about the Linux HOWTOs, which are on CD1. These excellent guides to Linux are covered under the Linux Documentation Project copyleft, which means you can print them. You can install them by logging in as root, mounting the CD-ROM (`mount /dev/hd{a...d} /mnt/cdrom`) and running the rpm command (`rpm -ivh /mnt/cdrom/RedHat/RPMS/howto*`). You can also read the HOWTOs with `more(1)` or `less(1)`.

School Days

Another way to find out more information about UNIX and Linux is to take a course, perhaps at a local community college. Many colleges offer courses on UNIX, and some have started using Linux to teach the UNIX courses. You can do your homework on your system at home, or if you have a notebook, you can work anywhere. (Jon typed text for the first edition of this book in a hotel in Auckland, New Zealand, and updated text for the second edition in the United Airlines lounge in Chicago.) We would have given anything in college for the chance to do our computer projects sitting in the comfort of our own pub . . . er, dorm rooms. Instead, we had to sit in a room with a bunch of punch-card machines . . . well, never mind. We would have been much more comfortable and productive with a Linux system.

Speaking like a geek

Our editors (and a darn fine ones), hate it when we say things like "fsck your file system." They want us to say "run the fsck program against the file system." We have gone along with her for the most part, but here we tell you what true UNIX (and Linux) geeks say:

- ✔ "Eff Ess Check" the file system instead of "run EF ES C K on the file system'"

- ✔ VEYE (rhymes with "eye") instead of "vee eye" when talking about the editor vi

We pointed out to editors that fsck is a noun, a verb, and an adjective:

- ✔ I ran fsck.

- ✔ I fscked the file system.

- ✔ I put the files into the fscked file system.

But this concept makes her shutter.

Geeks talk about *disks,* but editors would make us say *disk drives.* And geeks use the words X, X11, and X Window System interchangeably, whereas editors patiently interject (each and every time), "Did you mean to say X Window System?"

We also want to point out that geeks are not nerds. Geeks are people who love technical topics but also typically have a wide range of other interests. Geeks are often outgoing, and many (but not all) enjoy being with people.

One of Jon's favorite T-shirts (he has more than 3,000) reads: *It is hard being a Geek, but it is getting easier.*

So, if you really start to like the Linux operating system and want to learn more, you may well be a closet geek. Welcome to the club.

In the News

You can obtain additional information about the Linux operating system from the Internet. A facility called *Netnews* has tens of thousands of newsgroups, and each newsgroup covers a special topic. More than 30 newsgroups are devoted to Linux topics.

An ISP (Internet service provider) usually provides access to Netnews. You can use a newsreader (such as trn, tin, or pine) or one of several Web browsers (such as the Netscape browser included on CD1) to read Netnews.

User Groups

User groups are springing up all over the country. Some are more active than others are, but most hold meetings at least once a month. Some groups are Linux only; others are connected to a larger computer group — either UNIX or a more general computer user association. User groups are a great opportunity to ask questions, and they stimulate new ideas and ways of doing things.

You can find out if a Linux user group is in your area by checking with GLUE (Groups of Linux Users Everywhere), which is a service run by SSC (the publishers of the *Linux Journal*). GLUE is an automated map of user groups, and you can find it at the following address:

```
www.ssc.com
```

When you arrive at the site, click the <u>Resources</u> link, which takes you to the Linux Journal site. Then check out the Resources area there to find out where the user group closest to you meets.

No user group in your area? Then post a message at you local University or community college saying that you want to start one; then, perhaps, other people in your area will join you. Terrified at the thought of starting a user group? User group leaders often are not the most technically knowledgeable members but are simply good planners. They organize the meeting space, find (hound) speakers, send out meeting notices, locate sponsors, arrange refreshments (beer), and perform other organizational tasks. Sometimes being the leader is a thankless job, but when a meeting goes really well, it makes all the work worthwhile. So, as a newbie to Linux, you may not know a grep(1) from an awk(1), but you still may make a very good chairperson.

Bring in the Cavalry

Some people want to be able to hire people to manage or fix their systems. This is what the commercial computer world calls *support*. Often, the place where you bought your computer — whether it's a store, a value-added reseller (VAR), or the manufacturer — provides the support.

Linux is criticized for not providing that same level of support. Although the number of hardware vendors that offers support is low, more and more people are well-versed in using Linux and are willing to offer some level of support, whether it be by e-mail, telephone, or on-site services.

The first group of people that offers support is the distribution makers. Red Hat Software, Inc.; Caldera, Inc.; S.u.S.E.; and others sell support contracts for their Linux distributions. These contracts range from e-mail support to telephone support. Red Hat recently introduced round-the-clock support for a reasonable fee. Check out Red Hat's Web page (www.redhat.com) for more details.

Another group of people offering support is resellers of Linux systems. These people typically install Linux on hardware that you purchase from them. They will repair your system when it breaks and help you with knotty problems (all with a fee).

The final group of people who offer support is the independent consultants who have learned about Linux and are now in the business of offering support for the system. You can find a list of consultants in a document called the Consultants HOWTO, which is available at the following address:

```
/usr/doc/HOWTO/Consultants-HOWTO
```

Once you become familiar with the resources that Linux offers, you'll realize that it offers better support than most other proprietary systems. We find that consulting the HOWTOs or Usenet group to solve problems and answer questions is easier than going through the traditional Help Desk route.

You can find a not-as-current copy of the consultants list on CD1.

Commercial Applications

Many Linux users are frugal (we prefer that term to *cheap*) and often want or need to use only freely distributable software. And in many cases, the freely distributable software is very good and does exactly what you want it to do. Other times, though, the software you want is available only as a commercial application.

Some Linux users buy the latest and greatest hardware and want the same commercial applications on Linux that they have on their other operating systems, no matter what the price.

For commercial application vendors everywhere that may be reading this, we cannot stress this point enough: Look at Linux like *any other operating system*. You can sell your applications to a market that not only is appreciative but also believes, for various reasons, that its operating system should be *open*.

An example of functionality available from the commercial world is Applixware Office by Applix, Inc. This office suite includes a word processor, a spreadsheet, a presentation package, a mail front end, an HTML authoring program, a graphical program for drawing pictures (usually to include in your presentation or paper), an application building program, and a scripting language that allows you to tie these and other programs together.

We wrote this book with Applix Words. We chose to use Words instead of Microsoft Word because with Words, we could easily cut examples of code from the screen of our Linux systems and paste them into the text of the book. We then took those presentations to a Digital UNIX system and read them into the Applixware suite there. After we finished a chapter, we exported it to Microsoft Word 6.0 format and e-mailed it to our editor.

Likewise, we use Applixware Presentation Editor to make presentations about Linux on Linux. When we talk about Linux at a show or a convention, we can demonstrate how to use X Window System while we have the presentation slides on the screen. If we used Microsoft PowerPoint, we would have to reboot the system into Linux to do the demo, an awkward approach at best. Applixware has many of the same functions as Microsoft products. Recent versions of Applixware Office can read and create PowerPoint output, and now we can run our systems truly FAT-free.

Visit Web Sites

A variety of Web sites is available for help. Some of these sites provide technical information, some provide news about the Linux community, and others furnish a bandstand for the Linux community to voice its opinions. Here are some sites that you may want to check out:

- ✔ **Linux International:** www.li.org
- ✔ **Linux Org:** www.linux.org
- ✔ **Linux Today:** www.linuxtoday.com
- ✔ **Linux Documentation Project:** www.metalab.unc.edu/LDP/
- ✔ **Linux Now:** www.linuxnow.com
- ✔ *Linux Journal, Linux Gazette, Linux Resources:* www.ssc.com
- ✔ **Linux Focus:** www.linuxfocus.org
- ✔ *Linux Weekly News:* www.lwn.net
- ✔ **Slashdot:** www.slashdot.org
- ✔ **Freshmeat:** www.freshmeat.net
- ✔ **File Watcher:** www.filewatcher.org

This list is not exhaustive. You can find links to many more sites in some of the Web sites mentioned here.

Some of the lists offer opinions that are for mature audiences only. Most of the lists are moderated, and most of the opinions are mature, but people sometimes get carried away.

Attend Conferences

You can attend a number of conferences and trade shows to find out more information on Linux. All these shows are accurate as of the time we're writing this, but events may change. Where possible, we list the more general Web addresses for these events. You may have to do a little Web skiing to find the next upcoming event. If you get stuck, try the Linux International Web site, which has an Events page that lists new events.

Linux Kongress

Linux Kongress is the oldest Linux event. Held in Germany every year, it's a technical conference with a small trade show. The Web site is `www.linux-kongress.de`.

Linux Expo

Linux Expo is held every spring in the Raleigh/Durham area in North Carolina. It's a technical conference, trade show, and all-in-all good time. In 1998, more than 2,000 attendees and numerous vendors attended. The Web site is `www.linuxexpo.org`.

USENIX/FREENIX

USENIX, a technical organization that has long supported UNIX users, holds several technical conferences and small trade shows each year on various topics. A few years ago, a separate set of presentations, called FREENIX, was created for freely distributed operating systems such as Linux. If you're interested in a good technical conference that attracts UNIX giants (such as Dennis Ritchie) or if you're a Linux developer, you may want to look at `www.usenix.org`.

CeBIT

CeBIT, the largest computer trade show in the world, is held yearly in Hannover, Germany. It often draws more than 600,000 people. Last year, Linux International (`www.li.org`) had a booth along with several other Linux vendors and drew more than 3,000 people. CeBIT is mostly a trade show, with very little (if any) conference sessions on Linux. To find out more about CeBIT, check out `www.messe.de`.

Comdex

For the past four years, Comdex has held a Linux Pavilion, made up of an ever-growing group of vendors who try to explain Linux to over 200,000 resellers, distributors, and other vendors. Comdex is held in the spring and fall in different U.S. cities. You can check out its Web site at `www.comdex.com`.

IDG's Linux World

Linux World is a new show with conferences sponsored by IDG. Its Web site is www.linuxexpo.com.

Try to Help Others

After you've exhausted all avenues of help (or maybe even before), you should just try to figure it out yourself. Often, you'll find that the pieces fit together or that the software is not as difficult as you thought. Here are some tips:

- ✔ **If you're investigating a large software package, scan the documentation one time and then concentrate on the necessary topics.** Jon still remembers the first time he tried to learn groff(1), a powerful text-processing system. The documentation was daunting, and he thought he would never learn the package. It turns out he was right; he never learned it. But he did learn enough to do a few simple things and that was all he needed to know. With those "few simple things" (less than 2 percent of the power of the package), he could write letters, create overhead slides, and do the necessary text processing. When he needed another command, he'd look it up in a reference book.

- ✔ **Create a small sample of what you want to do.** If you're working with a new command or part of Linux, create a small example of the one part of the command or software that you don't know, and see how that works.

- ✔ **Keep it small.** A friend of Jon's named Mike Gancarz (Hi Mike!) wrote a book called *The Philosophy of Unix*. In this book, he talks about how UNIX systems were created and programmed in the early days, utilizing lots of the small, cryptic (we prefer the word *terse*) commands that lurk below the glossy interface of X Window System. With these commands, you can create powerful programs called shell scripts or just use the commands one at a time to transform your data. The main tenet of his book is to keep things small and simple.

- ✔ **Remember that Linux is only a piece of code and your computer is only a machine.** So what if you make a mistake? You're probably running Linux on a machine that has only one user, you. That's the great thing about Linux: It runs on such inexpensive machinery that you can buy an old 486 computer with enough disk and memory in it to run Linux as a practice system, all for under $50. (Jon bought such a machine at a Ham Fest. It runs Linux very nicely.) So even if you have to reinstall your system due to some mistake you made, it won't disturb anyone else on your practice machine. You now know how to install Linux, so no one has to know but you when something goes wrong.

Our other suggestion is to help someone else. "What?" you say. "How can I help someone? I'm just a beginner!"

We all started that way. No one is born with knowledge of computer science. We all pick it up over time. The way to cement a thought or an idea, however, is to explain it clearly to someone else. Helping others install Linux on their PCs helps cement some of the concepts you've discovered. Another idea is to attend a Linux Install Fest, where lots of people go (with their machines) to install Linux. Here, not only do you get to help someone else, but also you can probably learn something from other attendees.

A main tenet of Linux is the word *open*. Linux is open and is best when shared.

Chapter 20

Ten Problem Areas and Solutions

● ●

In This Chapter

▶ I can't boot Linux anymore

▶ My disk numbers have changed since installation

▶ My CD-ROM isn't detected

▶ I don't know how to remove LILO and restore my MBR

▶ I can't use LILO to boot

▶ The ls command doesn't show files in color

▶ Linux can't find a shell script (or a program)

▶ When I start X Window System, I see a gray screen

▶ I don't know how to make X Window System start at boot time

▶ I never seem to have the correct time

● ●

*I*n any complex, technical situation, people end up having problems and issues that they need help with. The problems in this chapter were taken from a database of questions and answers created after hundreds of people installed the CD-ROM. Some of these questions have been answered in the rest of the book, but because they still generate "what happened" questions, I repeat the information here.

I Can't Boot Linux Anymore

Problem: You've installed Linux and everything is fine (naturally). Then one day you make a change to your Windows or Windows NT system, and Linux stops working. You no longer see the lilo boot prompt, so you can no longer specify that you want to boot Linux.

Solution: Various operating systems tend to think that they are the only operating system on the disk or on the system. Therefore, when they are installed or updated, they write things to an area of the system called the Master Boot Record (MBR). This process overlays the Linux boot loader (called LILO) and stops you from booting Linux. The best correction requires an ounce of prevention: Make an emergency boot floppy disk, as I instruct you to do during installation. Keep this disk handy when you update your system (or during any other significant system event, such as repartitioning disks or rebuilding your kernel). Then, if you make a mistake, you can boot the floppy, which will enable you to reboot your Linux operating system. When you've rebooted your system using the floppy, just log in as root and type **lilo** on the command line. This repairs the MBR by reinstalling LILO.

If you are installing multiple operating systems on a new machine, do yourself a favor and install Linux last. Otherwise, you have to keep reinstalling LILO.

My Disk Numbers Have Changed Since Installation

Problem: Linux numbers disks each time it boots, calling SCSI disks names like sda, sdb, and sdc. Suppose that sda holds your Microsoft system, sdb holds the bulk of Linux, sdc holds your user files, and sdd holds your swap space. Now you add another disk and your user files are on sdd and your swap space is on sde. The new disk is called sdc but has nothing on it. What happened?

Solution: SCSI disks are lettered according to the SCSI IDs set on each disk. Linux names the disks using this ordering scheme. If you insert a new disk into the SCSI bus with a SCSI ID that is lower than an existing disk, you rename all disks with a SCSI ID number above the one you just installed. It's best to start installing your SCSI disks with a SCSI ID of 0, 1, 2, and so on; then put other SCSI devices at the other end of the SCSI bus (SCSI IDs 6, 5, 4, and so on). Note that most SCSI controllers are set to SCSI ID 7 by default.

IDE disks are numbered according to the IDE controller they are on and whether they are a master or a slave on that controller. Therefore, adding a new disk to a set of IDE controllers will not change the existing names, as shown here:

Controller	Disk	Linux Name
ide0	master	hda
ide0	slave	hdb
ide1	master	hdc
ide1	slave	hdd
ide2	master	hde
ide2	slave	hdf

Controller	Disk	Linux Name
ide3	master	hdg
ide3	slave	hdh

ide0 = primary controller

ide1 = secondary controller

ide2 = third controller

ide3 = fourth controller

My CD-ROM Isn't Detected

Problem: You're installing Linux, but it doesn't find your CD-ROM.

Solution: Most newer CD-ROMs are either EIDE (ATAPI) or SCSI, and most newer computer systems have enough support to see either the ATAPI CD-ROMs or the SCSI CD-ROMs, so CD-ROM support is not quite an issue as in the early days. In addition, some older systems and CD-ROMs are now supported.

Some early CD-ROMs pretended to be other devices (such as tape drives or floppies) to fool the computer system into using them, but these CD-ROMs were hidden from the detection system. If your system is one of these, don't despair: You can supply information to help Linux find your CD-ROM.

First look at the preceding section about disk numbering. This gives you an idea of the name that Linux would call your CD-ROM if Linux knew about it. If you have an EIDE/ATAPI CD-ROM, type the following line whenever you see the boot or lilo prompt while booting or installing your system:

```
linux hdX=cdrom
```

where *X* is the number that your CD-ROM would have if it could be detected.

I Don't Know How to Remove LILO and Restore My MBR

Problem: You don't know how to replace the boot record that was on your system before you started installing Linux.

Solution: You can log in to Linux as root, and then type the following command:

```
lilo -u
```

Another solution is to boot MS-DOS or Windows 3.1, 95, 98 or NT to an MS-DOS prompt and type the following:

```
fdisk /mbr
```

I Can't Use LILO to Boot

Problem: You need to put Linux on a disk or a partition that is beyond the 1023rd cylinder, the second IDE disk, or the second SCSI ID number, or you need to do something else that will make it difficult for Linux to boot using LILO. Can you boot Linux in another way?

Solution: You can use a program called LOADLIN to boot from your MS-DOS or Windows system:

1. **Copy your configured Linux kernel to the C drive of your MS-DOS or Windows system.**

   The easiest way to do this is to install Linux, log in as root, and type the following:

   ```
   grep image /etc/lilo.conf
   ```

   A line similar to the following appears:

   ```
   image=/boot/vmlinuz-2.2.10-3
   ```

   This points to your compressed kernel, which in this example is located at /boot/vmlinuz-2.2.10-3.

2. **Copy the compressed kernel to a floppy disk, as follows:**

   ```
   mcopy /boot/vmlinuz-2.2.10-3 a:\vmlinux.gz
   ```

   The kernel name vmlinuz-2.2.10-3 refers to a specific version of the Linux kernel. Except for the /boot/vmlinuz- part, which remains constant, the name might be slightly different on your system.

   Now you have to copy LOADLIN from the *Red Hat Linux For Dummies* CD1.

3. **Boot MS-DOS or Windows and put the *Red Hat Linux For Dummies* CD1 in your CD-ROM drive.**

4. **Go to the DOSUTILS directory and copy LOADLIN.EXE to your C drive.**

   If you are using MS-DOS or Windows 3.1, copy the LOADLIN16 file, which is the 16-bit version of the program.

5. **Copy the kernel image you just made on the floppy disk to your C drive.**

Now you can exit Windows and get to the MS-DOS prompt. You can then type the following (assuming your root partition is on partition /dev/hda5) to boot Linux:

```
C:\> loadlin vmlinux.gz root=/dev/hda5 ro
```

The ls Command Doesn't Show Files in Color

Problem: Using Linux from the *Red Hat Linux For Dummies* CD-ROM1, you can't get the ls command to show files in color.

Solution: You have to edit the .bashrc file in your home directory to add the following line to the end of the file:

```
alias ls ='ls --color=auto'
```

Then log off and then back on to re-execute your .bashrc file (assuming you are using the bash shell), and ls shows different file types in different colors.

Linux Can't Find a Shell Script (Or a Program)

Problem: You type a command name, but Linux can't find the command, even if it's in the current directory.

Solution: When you type a shell or binary command name, Linux looks for the name in specific places and in a specific order. To find out what directories Linux looks in, and in what order, type the following command:

```
echo $PATH
```

You see a stream similar to the following:

```
/bin:/usr/bin:/usr/local/bin
```

These are the directories Linux looks in to find the command, program, or shell you want to execute. You might see more directories depending on your distribution or how your system administrator (if you have one) set up your system.

Now suppose you create a shell or a program called flobnob, and you want to execute it (and assuming you have set the permission bits to make flobnob executable by you). You have two choices (well, you have more than two choices, but I'm listing the safest ones). One choice is to type the following on the command line:

```
./flobnob
```

This tells Linux to look in this directory (./) and execute flobnob.

Your second choice is to move flobnob to one of the directories shown in the PATH variable, such as /usr/local/bin.

When I Start X Window System, I See a Gray Screen

Problem: You configured the X Window System, but when you log in as a general user (that is, not as root) and type startx, all you get is a gray screen with a big X in the middle. You wait a long time, but nothing happens.

Solution: First, recognize that you may have to wait a long time for a slow CPU with a small amount of main memory (about 8MB). Some machines with small amounts of memory have required as long as 6 minutes to start X Window System. But assuming that you are starting X Window System on a machine with a faster CPU and more memory, you may have problems with permissions on your home directory. This is particularly true if X Window System works when you are logged on as root (that is, as superuser) but not when you are logged on as a general user.

To correct this problem, log in as root and go to the home directory of the user who is having problems. For this example, suppose that the login name of the user is lembree. After you are in the user's home directory, issue the ls -ld command to see who owns that directory and what the permissions are on that directory:

```
cd ~lembree
ls -ld .
drwxrwx-- root bin 1024 Oct 31 16:00 .
```

Note that in this example, the directory is owned by root and the group ownership is bin, which does not allow lembree to have access to the directory structure inside the directory. Because the shells and terminal emulators that X Window System needs require access to that directory structure, X Window System can't fully work.

To correct this problem, use the `chown` and `chgrp` commands to change the ownership of the lembree home directory to lembree and to change the group ownership of the lembree home directory to users:

```
chown lembree ~lembree
chgrp users ~lembree
```

Make sure you replace the lembree login name that we use in this example with the login name you are having difficulty with.

I Don't Know How to Make the X Window System Start at Boot Time

Problem: You don't want to have to log in to a command-line mode (such as DOS) and then type startx. Instead, you want to log in through X Window System.

Solution: We set up our machine so that it starts in character-cell mode and then allows me to switch to X Window System. (Many times, we want to only make a simple edit or look at something on the system, and logging in without X Window System is simply faster.) If you like to see a graphical interface from the beginning, however, do the following. In the /etc/inittab file, change this line:

```
id:3:initdefault:
```

to this:

```
id:5:initdefault:
```

Save your changes and reboot. X Window System starts at the end of the boot process, and you can then log in through the graphical interface. To go back to the old way of booting, change the line in the /etc/inittab file back to the following:

```
id:3:initdefault:
```

and reboot the machine.

I Never Seem to Have the Correct Time

Problem: When you boot Linux the time is wrong, so you set it with the `date(1)` command. Then you boot Windows and its time is wrong, so you reset it. When you reboot Linux, its time is wrong again.

Solution: Most UNIX systems keep their time using Universal Time (also known as Greenwich Mean Time, or GMT), but Microsoft systems keep their time as local time. When you set the time in either system, you set the CPU clock to that version of the time. Then when you boot the other system, it interprets what is in the CPU clock differently and reports a different time.

Linux enables you to store and think of the clock as either GMT or local time. You make this choice when you install the system. To change your choice, follow these steps:

1. **Log in as root.**

2. **Type** timeconfig.

   The Configure Timezones dialog box appears.

   Set your system clock to GMT (Greenwich Mean Time) by selecting the Hardware Clock Set To GMT option at the top of the screen.

3. **Deselect the Hardware Clock Set To GMT option.**

   Highlight the option by pressing the tab key, if necessary. (Actually, you should be there when you activate the timeconfig command.)

4. **Press the spacebar to deselect the option. Press the tab key until you reach the OK button and then press Enter.**

5. **Reset the time to the proper value using the** date **command if you reboot Linux or through the Windows system if you reboot Windows.**

Part VII
Appendixes

The 5th Wave   By Rich Tennant

MODERN MARRIAGE

WE'RE AGREED ON THE SILVER PATTERN, WALLPAPER AND CARPET SCHEME, BUT WE'RE STILL HASHING OUT THE OPERATING SYSTEM.

In this part . . .

Appendix. That useless vestige of the human anatomy certainly shouldn't be applied to the important information in this part. Appendix A keeps you glued to your seat as your read about the Linux text editor vi (visual editor). Appendix B is a real cliff-hanger, listing all of the hardware that we could find that's compatible with the latest version of Linux on accompanying CD-ROM 1 (that's Red Hat Publisher's Edition 6.1, by the way).

Here and there throughout the book, we mention man pages. In Appendix C, the excitement is turned down a notch and you discover what all those sections in a man page mean and how to find the right man page.

Your respite doesn't last long as the dangerous fdisk disk-partitioning tool is described in Appendix D. The last appendix is about installing CD-ROM 1. For those of you accustomed to short installation instructions — surprise. Appendix E refers you to the real installation instructions, which take up most of Part II.

Appendix A

Using vi

• •

*A*nyone who writes a Linux book needs a good editor. But the editor that we're talking about is a text editor — the ubiquitous vi — not the tweedy, frazzled, publishing professionals who struggle mightily with books. Text editors work with text files to give you the ability to add, delete, search, and move text — everything from thousands of lines of text right down to a single character.

Text files are usually updated with word processors, but every once in a while, you may have to go in and update a file with a text editor. In addition, text editors create small, compact files of characters, which are still the cheapest way to send e-mail and store character data on disk.

Defining Text Editors

A text editor is an essential tool for Linux. It enables you to create and modify an array of text files, including the following:

- ✔ User files, such as the logon file
- ✔ System configuration files, such as /etc/fstab, /etc/inittab, and /etc/lilo.conf
- ✔ C and C++ programs
- ✔ Shell programs
- ✔ Mail messages

Linux comes with not one but two text editors: ed and vi. The ed editor is a line-oriented text editor. It was one of the first editors for UNIX systems and traditionally is included with every UNIX and Linux system. It's also a small editor, so small distributions of UNIX and Linux can include it. You can always count on ed being there.

The second editor that comes with Linux is vi; it's included with almost every Linux distribution (some specialized distributions such as Trinux don't necessarily include it). This full-screen editor also supports the command set of a line-oriented editor named ex. The third major text editor for Linux is emacs; some people prefer to use this editor for most of their work.

In Linux, ex and vi are emulated by another text editor named vim. The commands for vi work just fine with vim. In addition, vim has more capability than vi. For instance, vim makes editing easier by allowing you to switch from command to insert mode and still move around the file with the cursor keys. On the other hand, vi forces you to continually toggle between the two modes to insert text and move around the file. Therefore, vi isn't included as a separate program with Linux systems. When you type `vi`, you're really using vim, but this fact is invisible to you.

Introducing vi

The vi editor on your Linux system is really the vim editor. With a little vim and vigor, you can invoke it by using `vi`, because a symbolic link exists between vi and vim.

Like the ed editor, the vi editor has two modes of operation and the same type of single-letter commands. To start vi, you type `vi` at the command line. The screen clears, and the left-most column displays tildes (~). You are looking at an empty, unnamed buffer in memory, into which you can enter text until you save the text to a named file.

You can start the vi editor in a number of ways, with different options, but the most common way to start vi is with only a filename as the argument, like this:

```
vi tove.and.linus
```

where `tove.and.linus` is the name of either an existing file that you want to edit or a new file that you want to create.

The vi editor has three modes of operation:

- ✔ Visual command mode
- ✔ Colon command mode
- ✔ Text mode

When you invoke vi with a filename, the editor screen appears. At the bottom-left corner is the following line:

```
"filename" [New File]
```

This status line tells you what the editor is doing. In this case, the editor has opened a buffer, and the save and quit option saves the contents of the buffer to the `filename` file. If you did indeed invoke vi with the following command:

```
vi tove.and.linus
```

the bottom-left corner displays the following line:

```
"tove.and.linus" [New File]
```

When you first invoke vi, you are in visual command mode, which is the default. You can use four special commands to either locate text or transition to more complex commands:

/   Forward search

?   Backward search

n   Continue the search in whichever direction you were currently going

:   ex command (ex is the line editor included in vi)

In command mode, the characters you type are used as commands, not as input into the file. To use commands, type the character on the command line. For the first two search commands (/ and ?), the cursor moves to the bottom of the screen, where you then type the string that you're searching for. After you press Enter, the search begins. If you want to search for an additional string, you can just press the lower-case n key to re-execute the search; to search backwards press the upper-case N key.

When you type the : command, the cursor moves to the bottom of the screen and waits for you to enter a command or a command string. You must press the Enter key to execute the command.

Given that characters you type are interpreted as commands in command mode, how do you get from command mode to text mode? Simple. Enter a command to do something in text mode, and vi takes you there. Here are some commands that you can use to switch from command mode to text mode:

i   Insert text before the cursor

a   Insert text after the cursor

I   Insert text at the beginning of the current line

A   Insert text at the end of the current line

As soon as you type any of these commands, Linux puts you in text input mode. Do not press Enter after entering the command. Any text you type after you invoke the command is placed in a buffer and echoed to the screen.

You may be asking yourself (because the directions are skimpy or you have no one else to ask), "How do I get out of text mode and back to command mode?" Again, the answer is simple. If you want out, just press the Escape (Esc) key, and you're immediately whisked back to command mode. That's pretty easy, isn't it?

If you don't know whether you're in command mode, just press Esc a few times.

Moving around in a file

After you know how to open a file in vi, you're ready to find out how to move around in it. The commands in Table A-1 move the cursor around. First, make sure that you're in command mode; otherwise, Linux places these keys in your file just like any other data.

Table A-1	Moving Around in vi
Command	*What It Does*
j	Move one line down
k	Move one line up
h	Move one character to the left
l	Move one character to the right
Ctrl+f	Scroll down a full screen
Ctrl+b	Scroll up a full screen

If you want to go to a specific line number, you use a colon command. Type a colon (:), and it appears at the bottom of the screen. Then type the line number where you want to be. Here's an example:

```
:12
```

When you press Enter, the cursor moves to the beginning of line 12.

Deleting and moving text in vi

In this section, you delete and move your text in vi. The vi editor has several commands for deleting. You can delete characters, words, or lines. The command for deleting a word is dw; this command deletes the word to the right of the cursor. You can delete more words at once by prefacing the dw command with the number of words you want deleted from the cursor position. For example, the command 6dw deletes the next six words following the cursor. Table A-2 lists additional deletion commands.

Table A-2	Deleting in vi
Command	**What It Does**
D	Deletes up to the end of the current line
dd	Deletes the current line
x	Deletes the character under the cursor (4x, 5x, and so on)

A handy command to remember is u, which is the undo command. You can immediately undo edits with this command, in the unlikely event that you make a mistake.

The business of moving text around in the file usually requires the following general steps:

1. **Position the cursor at the beginning of the first line you want to move or copy.**

2. **Type** ma, **marking that position with the letter** *a*.

3. **Position the cursor at the beginning of the last line that you want to move or copy.**

4. **Type** mb, **marking that position with the letter** *b*.

5. **Position the cursor at the line where you want to insert the text.**

6. **Type** 'a, bm. **if you want to move the text, or** 'a,bt. **if you want to copy the text.**

Note that the single quotation marks and period are required.

Controlling the environment

You can control your editing environment in vi by setting options with the
:set command. Table A-3 lists some common :set command options.

Table A-3	Everyday :set Options
Command	**What It Does**
all	Displays a list of all :set commands and their status
errorbells	Sounds the terminal bell when errors occur
ignorecase	Makes searches case insensitive
number	Displays line numbers in the leftmost column on the screen
showmode	Displays an indicator at the bottom-right of the screen, indicating which mode you are in: input mode, change mode, replace mode, and so on

Note: You can turn off :set command options by prefixing the command
with no, as in:

```
:set nonumber
```

This turns line numbering off.

Examing vi commands

Table A-4 summarizes common vi commands. We describe some of these
commands elsewhere in the book; others are new.

Table A-4	Everyday vi Commands
Command	**What It Does**
a	Inserts text after the cursor
A	Inserts text at the end of the current line
I	Inserts text at the beginning of the current line
i	Inserts text before the cursor
o	Opens a line below the current line

Command	What It Does
O	Opens a line above the current line
C	Changes up to the end of the current line
cc	Changes the current line
cw	Changes the world
J	Joins the current line with the next one
rx	Replaces the character under the cursor with x (x is any character)
~	Changes the character under the cursor to the opposite case
$	Moves to the end of the current line
^	Moves to the beginning of the current line
m	Marks the current location with the letter x
Ctrl+1	Redraws the screen
:e filename	Edits the file
:N	Moves to line N (N is a number)
:q	Quits the editor
:q!	Quits the editor without saving any changes
:r filename	Reads the file and inserts after the current line
:w filename	Writes the buffer to a file
:wq	Saves changes and exits the editor
/string	Searches forward for string
?string	Searches backward for string
n	Finds the next string
u	Undoes the last command
Esc	Ends input mode and enters visual command mode

Don't despair about the large number of options and commands. We have used vi for 19 years and have never learned — or used — more than 20 percent of them. vi is our workhorse for system administration, and it works quite well with one hand tied behind its back.

Appendix B
Hardware Compatibility

● ●

*T*he version of Linux included on the accompanying CD-ROM1 supports a wide range of hardware, but like other Linux distributions, it doesn't support all types of hardware.

If you're using Windows, you can see a list supported hardware by going to the following directory (after you put CD-ROM1 in the system) and using your favorite editor to look at the Hardware-HOWTO file:

```
<cdrom-drive-letter>:\doc\HOWTO
```

Many, if not most, computers use the D drive for the CD-ROM drive, so the command looks like this:

```
d:\doc\HOWTO
```

Or, if you're using Linux, mount the CD-ROM by using the following command:

```
mount /dev/cdrom /mnt/cdrom
```

Then go to the following directory:

```
more /mnt/cdrom/doc/HOWTO/Hardware-HOWTO
```

to view the file; press the spacebar after viewing each page.

These suggestions don't help, however, if you're in a store right now — or you don't have your system up and running yet — and are trying to determine whether Linux will run on your system. For these reasons, we provide this appendix.

We have made every attempt to present correct material in this appendix. Some equipment we've listed, however, may not work with Linux. In addition, new hardware is introduced all the time, and some of it may work with Linux but not be listed here.

The information in this appendix was taken from the Linux Hardware Compatibility HOWTO by Patrick Reijnen and the PCMCIA HOWTO by David Hinds.

After you have your system running, review some of the hardware HOWTOs to see whether it lists any other hardware that you may want to use in your Linux system.

Hardware Architectures

Linux runs on a variety of hardware architectures. These architectures are usually defined by the model name of the main CPU's manufacturer, such as the Intel architecture, the Alpha (Compaq) architecture, and the SPARC (Sun) architecture. This book and its CD-ROMs cover only the Intel architecture, which includes AMD and Cyrix CPUs from the x386 configurations and any Pentium chip.

In addition to the hardware architecture of the CPU, you have to consider the *bus structure*. A bus is made up of electrical paths, wires, and sockets that transmit electrical impulses to and from the CPU.

ISA, EISA, VLB, and PCI buses have been around a long time and are all supported in Linux. Recently, the Microchannel bus received support in the Linux kernel, but it's early code, so it may or may not work on your system. Most new systems today are PCI-based, with one or two ISA slots for backward compatibility.

In addition, although AGP is gaining acceptance as a graphics interface to replace ISA, EISA, VLB, and PCI as a throughput model for video, the number of video cards available for AGP and supported under Linux is still small. You may want to check further into compatibility by reading the latest Hardware HOWTO. Or lacking a driver for your AGP video card, you can substitute a PCI-based card instead.

The combination of the CPU architecture and the bus structure could loosely be termed the motherboard (often pronounced "muthaboard"). If Linux does not work on your system, and you suspect that the motherboard is the problem, first check with the motherboard's manufacturer to see whether it has a newer BIOS, which is the code that ties the CPU to the bus structure and devices.

Laptops

Laptops and Linux are problematic for a few reasons. First, if you want to use an older laptop for Linux, then you probably will have to fight the small hard disk. Linux requires at least 40MB of disk space for character-cell support and 120MB of main memory for X Window System. Second, most older laptops also have only 4 to 8MB of main memory, with really expensive upgrade paths to more memory (if you can find it). Third, to make laptops small and lightweight, only the newest electronic devices are used, and often in ways not expected by Linux. Fourth, many early notebooks use graphics chips from vendors who didn't give out the chips' programming specifications, making it difficult for XFree86 to provide video code that works. Finally, most early notebooks don't have a lot of peripherals inside, forcing you to use a PCMCIA card to hook up to a network or to a SCSI CD-ROM drive to get code from a CD-ROM and onto the machine's hard disk. In some cases you might have better luck putting a flea collar on a cat than getting Linux to install easily on a laptop. Our own anecdotal experience indicates that some cats are quite easy to fit while others are real bears.

Nevertheless, because prices dropped and more manufacturers cooperated with the Linux community, installing Linux on a notebook is now easier. Ideally, your notebook should have more than 8MB of main memory, more than 700MB of free disk space, and a built-in CD-ROM and floppy that can both be installed and working at the same time.

SMP Systems

The kernel on the companion CD-ROM1 supports symmetrical multiprocessors (SMPs). The Alpha and SPARC architectures also support SMP to a degree.

Memory

All memory that's typically found in PC computer systems works with Linux. When your system has large amounts of main memory, however, you must add the following to the /etc/lilo.conf file:

```
append="mem=<number of Mb>M"
```

for Linux to see all the memory you have. Jon's machine has 256MB of memory, so we added the following below the `label=linux...` line:

```
append="mem=256M"
```

Video

In character-cell mode, Linux works with all video cards. Therefore, you'll be able to get your system up and running, at a minimum. Likewise, most cards work in VGA or SVGA mode, so you'll be able to have X Window System running, although it will be a little slow and course-grained.

As a general rule, both the earliest and latest models of video cards are not supported. Early video cards were obsolete before Linux was introduced, and XFree86 (the people who provide most of the support for the video cards) never had time to retrofit support. The very latest cards are often not supported right away because getting the code ported to the video card takes time and effort. But with help from vendors, lead times are becoming shorter.

Accelerated cards and unaccelerated cards are also available. Accelerated cards typically work faster than unaccelerated cards because the software can take advantage of the hardware's ability to display the images more quickly. Some accelerated cards known to work are:

ARK Logic (ARK1000PV/VL, ARK2000PV/MT), ATI Mach8, ATI Mach32, ATI Mach64, Chips & Technologies 64200, 64300, 65520, 65525, 65530, 65535, 65540, 65545, 65546, 65548, 65550, 65554, Cirrus Logic 5420, 542x/5430, 5434, 5436, 544x, 546x, 5480, 62x5, 754x, Diamond Viper 330, Gemini P1 (ET6000 chip), IBM 8514/A, IBM XGA-I, XGA-II, IIT AGX-010/014/015/016 (16 bpp), Matrox MGA2064W (Millennium), Matrox MGA1064SG (Mystique), Number Nine Imagine I128, Oak OTI-087, S3 732 (Trio32), 764 (Trio64), Trio64V+, 801, 805, 864, 866, 868, 86C325 (ViRGE), 86C375 (ViRGE/DX), 86C385 (ViRGE/GX), 86C988 (ViRGE/VX), 911, 924, 928, 964, 968, S3 card families, SiS 86c201, 86c202, 86c205, Trident 9440, 96xx, Cyber938x, Tseng ET4000/W32/W32i/ W32p, ET6000, Weitek P9000 (16/32 bpp), Diamond Viper VLB/PCI, Orchid P9000, and Western Digital WD90C24/24A/24A2/31/33.

A variety of unaccelerated boards are available as well: Alliance AP6422, AT24, ATI VGA Wonder series, Avance Logic AL2101/2228/2301/2302/ 2308/2401, Cirrus Logic 6420/6440, 7555, Compaq AVGA, DEC 21030, Genoa GVGA, MCGA (320x200), MX MX68000/MX68010, NCR 77C22, 77C22E, 77C22E+, NVidia NV1, Oak OTI-037C, OTI-067, OTI-077, RealTek RTG3106, SGS-Thomson STG2000, Trident 8800CS, 8200LX, 8900x, 9000, 9000i, 9100B, 9200CXr, 9320LCD, 9400CXi, 9420, 9420DGi, 9430Dgi, Tseng ET3000, ET4000AX, VGA (standard VGA, 4 bit, slow), Video 7/Headland Technologies HT216-32, Western Digital/Paradise PVGA1, and WD90C00/10/11/30.

Also available are a series of boards supported by companies including S.u.S.E., Red Hat Software, and Metro Link. These boards include the following: Elsa GLoria X-Server, ELSA GLoria L, GLoria L/MX, GLoria S video cards with the Alliance Semiconductor AT3D (also AT25) chip, Hercules Stingray 128 3D, NVidia X-Server (PCI and AGP support, NV1 chipset and Riva128), ASUS 3Dexplorer, Diamond Viper 330, ELSA VICTORY Erazor, STB Velocity 128, XSuSE Matrox, Mystique, Millennium, Millennium II, Millennium II AGP, Trident, 9685 (including ClearTV) and latest Cyber chipset, XSuSE Tseng, W32, W32i ET6100, and ET6300.

Hard Drive Controllers

Linux works with standard IDE, EIDE, and SCSI disk controllers. In addition, Linux supports many SCSI controllers found on early sound cards (particularly the Sound Blaster and Media Vision cards).

We recommend that you stay away from some of the older SCSI cards and the sound-card-based SCSIs because they are slow and the booting process has difficulty determining where they are. Try to find a PCI-based SCSI controller instead.

Following are some of the supported SCSI controllers: AMI Fast Disk VLB/EISA (BusLogic compatible), Adaptec AVA-1502E (ISA/VLB) (AIC-6360), Adaptec AVA-1505/1515 (ISA) (Adaptec AHA-152x compatible), Adaptec AHA-1510/152x (ISA/VLB) (AIC-6260/6360), Adaptec AHA-154x (ISA) all models, Adaptec AHA-174x (EISA) in enhanced mode, Adaptec AHA-274x (EISA) (AIC-7771), Adaptec AHA-284x (VLB) (AIC-7770), Adaptec AHA-2920 (PCI), Adaptec AHA-2940AU (PCI) (AIC-7861), Adaptec AHA-294x/U/W/UW/D/WD (AIC-7871, AIC-7844, AIC-7881, AIC-7884), Adaptec AHA-3940/U/W (PCI) (AIC-7872, AIC-7882) (since 1.3.6), Adaptec AHA-398x/U/W (PCI) (AIC-7873, AIC-7883), Adaptec PCI controllers with AIC-7850, AIC-7855, AIC-7860, Adaptec on-board controllers with AIC-777x (EISA), AIC-785x, AIC-787x (PCI), AIC-788x (PCI), Advansys 5140 (ISA), Always IN2000, BusLogic (ISA/EISA/VLB/PCI) all models, DPT PM2001, PM2012A (EATA-PIO), DPT Smartcache/SmartRAID Plus, III, IV families (ISA/EISA/PCI), Future Domain TMC-16x0, TMC-3260 (PCI), Future Domain TMC-8xx, TMC-950, Future Domain chips TMC-1800, TMC-18C50, TMC-18C30, TMC-36C70, ICP-Vortex PCI-SCSI Disk Array Controllers (many RAID levels supported), Media Vision Pro Audio Spectrum 16 SCSI (ISA), NCR 5380 generic cards, NCR 53C400 (Trantor T130B) (use generic NCR 5380 SCSI support), NCR 53C406a (Acculogic ISApport/Media Vision Premium 3D SCSI), NCR chips 53C7x0, NCR chips 53C810, 53C815, 53C820, 53C825, 53C860, 53C875, 53C895, Qlogic/Control Concepts SCSI/IDE (FAS408) (ISA/VLB), Quantum ISA-200S, ISA-250MG, Seagate ST-01/ST-02 (ISA), SoundBlaster 16 SCSI-2 (Adaptec 152x compatible) (ISA), Tekram DC-390, DC-390W/U/F, Trantor T128/T128F/T228 (ISA), UltraStor 14F (ISA), 24F (EISA), 34F (VLB), and Western Digital WD7000 SCSI.

Boards that are not supported include SCSI adapters that fit into the parallel port and DTC boards, such as the 327x and 328x, that are not Adaptec compatible.

Serial, Parallel, and Joystick Interfaces

Any standard serial, parallel, joystick, or combo card can be used. Linux supports 8250, 16450, 16550, and 16550A UARTs.

Other Controllers (Multiport)

Some cards are used to increase the number of serial lines that a PC-style system can support above the one or two serial/parallel lines that come with it. These cards are intelligent or non-intelligent, depending on whether they or the main CPU buffer characters coming into the system can handle sending stop and start signals to the devices. Intelligent cards can cut down on the overhead of having thousands of characters coming into the system every second by taking a load off the main CPU. Some non-intelligent cards also use an IRQ for every port, which can use much of the system's resources for little gain. Try to get a card that is intelligent and uses only one IRQ.

Non-intelligent cards

Some of the non-intelligent cards are AST FourPort and clones (4 port), Accent Async-4 (4 port), Arnet Multiport-8 (8 port), Bell Technologies HUB6 (6 port), Boca BB-1004, 1008 (4, 8 port) - no DTR, DSR, and CD, Boca BB-2016 (16 port), Boca IO/AT66 (6 port), Boca IO 2x4 (4 serial/2 parallel, uses 5 IRQs), Computone ValuePort (4, 6, 8 port) (AST FourPort compatible), DigiBoard PC/X, PC/Xem, PCI/Xem, EISA/Xem, PCI/Xr (4, 8, 16 port), Comtrol Hostess 550 (4, 8 port), PC-COMM 4-port (4 port), SIIG I/O Expander 4S (4 port, uses 4 IRQs), STB 4-COM (4 port), Twincom ACI/550, and Usenet Serial Board II (4 port).

Intelligent cards

Some of the supported intelligent cards are Computone IntelliPort II (4/8/16 port), Cyclades Cyclom-8Y/16Y (8, 16 port) (ISA/PCI), DigiBoard PC/Xe (ISA), PC/Xi (EISA) and PC/Xeve, Equinox SST Intelligent serial I/O cards, Hayes ESP 1, 2 and 8 port versions, Stallion EasyIO (ISA), Stallion EasyConnection 8/32 (ISA/MCA), Stallion EasyConnection 8/64 (PCI), Stallion EasyConnection 8/64 (ISA/EISA), Stallion ONboard (ISA/EISA/MCA), and Stallion Brumby (ISA).

Network adapters

Make sure that you buy a good Ethernet card if you want one. Some of the earlier cards were flaky and would make the system stop working from time to time. Most of the new cards are both 100 Mbit/second as well as the older 10Mbit/second, so they will work now in your current environment as well as later in your newer environment.

Supported cards are 3Com 3C503, 3C505, 3C507, 3C509/3C509B (ISA), 3C579 (EISA), 3Com Etherlink III Vortex Ethercards (3C590, 3c592, 3C595, 3c597) (PCI), 3Com Etherlink XL Boomerang Ethercards (3c905) (PCI), 3Com Fast Etherlink Ethercard (3c515) (ISA), AMD LANCE (79C960)/PCnet-ISA/PCI (AT1500, HP J2405A, NE1500/NE2100), AT&T GIS WaveLAN, Allied Telesis AT1700, Allied Telesis LA100PCI-T, Ansel Communications AC3200 EISA, Apricot Xen-II/82596, Cabletron E21xx, Cogent EM110, Crystal Lan CS8920, Cs8900, Danpex EN-9400, DEC DE425 (EISA), DEC DE434, DEC DE435 (PCI), DECDE450, DECDE500 (DE4x5 driver), DEC DE450/DE500-XA (Tulip driver), DEC DEPCA and EtherWORKS, DEC EtherWORKS 3, DEC QSilver's (Tulip driver), Fujitsu FMV-181, 182, 183, 184, HP PCLAN (27245 and 27xxx series), HP PCLAN PLUS (27247B and 27252A), HP 10/100VG PCLAN (J2577, J2573, 27248B, J2585) (ISA/EISA/PCI), ICL EtherTeam 16i/32 EISA, Intel EtherExpress, Intel EtherExpress Pro, KTI ET16/P-D2, ET16/P-DC ISA (works jumperless and with hardware-configuration options), NE2000/NE1000 (be careful with clones), Netgear FA-310TX (Tulip chip), New Media Ethernet, PureData PDUC8028, PDI8023, SEEQ 8005, SMC Ultra/EtherEZ (ISA), SMC 9000 series, SMC PCI EtherPower 10/100 (Tulip driver), SMC EtherPower II (epic100.c driver), Schneider & Koch G16, Western Digital WD80x3, Zenith Z-Note, IBM's ThinkPad 300 built-in adapter, and 312 Etherarray (Tulip driver).

Sound cards

Linux supports many sound cards, including the following: 6850 UART MIDI, Adlib (OPL2), Audio Excell DSP16, Aztech Sound Galaxy NX Pro, Crystal CS4232/CS4236 (PnP) based cards, ECHO-PSS cards (Orchid SoundWave32, Cardinal DSP16), Ensoniq SoundScape, Gravis Ultrasound, Gravis Ultrasound 16-bit sampling daughterboard, Gravis Ultrasound MAX, Gravis Ultrasound ACE (no MIDI port and audio recording), Gravis Ultrasound PnP (with RAM), Logitech SoundMan Games (SBPro, 44kHz stereo support), Logitech SoundMan Wave (Jazz16/OPL4), Logitech SoundMan 16 (PAS-16 compatible), MediaTriX AudioTriX Pro, Media Vision Premium 3D (Jazz16), Media Vision Pro Sonic 16 (Jazz), Media Vision Pro Audio Spectrum 16, Media Vision Pro Audio Studio 16, Microsoft Sound System (AD1848), OAK OTI-601D (Mozart), OPTi 82C924/82C925. OPTi 82C928/82C929 (MAD16/MAD16 Pro/ISP16/Mozart), OPTi 82C931, Sound Blaster, Sound Blaster Pro, Sound Blaster 16,

Sound Blaster 32/64/AWE (configure like Sound Blaster 16), Sound Blaster AWE63/Gold and 16/32/AWE PnP, Turtle Beach Wavefront (Maui, Tropez), Wave Blaster (and other daughterboards), cards based on the ESS Technologies AudioDrive chips (688, 1688), MPU-401 MIDI, and PC speaker/parallel port DAC.

Tape Drives

When backing up your system, using a tape drive is a way to get a lot of storage on one device (2 or 4GB or even higher). Linux supports most SCSI tape drives. Other drives sometimes use the floppy controller (such as the Colorado FC-10/FC-20, Mountain Mach-2, or the Iomega Tape Controller II) or hook up to the IDE controller (Seagate TapeStor 8000 and Conner CTMA 4000 IDE ATAPI Streaming tape drive).

Note that Linux does not support tape drives that plug into the parallel port.

CD-ROM Drives

You would think that any CD-ROM device would work under Linux, and most do. Early CD-ROM drives, however, were usually attached to the sound board and used for multimedia instead of as high-capacity data drives. Linux supports most SCSI and EIDE (ATAPI) CD-ROM drives, particularly the newer ones that read data at 2x, 4x, 6x, and up to 40x speeds.

CD-Writers

Many frustrated singers, photographers, and choreographers out there would love to be able to make their own CD-ROMs, filled with music and pictures. Well, you can with Linux! Linux supports CD-writers, and a variety of software is available to instruct you on writing to write-once (WO) CDs. Programs such as cdwrite and cdrecord can be used for writing to a CD-WO, and a graphical front-end called X-CD-Roast makes the job even easier. The following CD-writers are supported: Grundig CDR 100 IPW, HP CD-Writer+ 7100, HP SureStore 4020i, HP SureStore 6020es/i, JVC XR-W2010, Mitsubishi CDRW-225, Mitsumi CR-2600TE, Olympus CDS 620E, Philips CDD 522/2000/2600/3610, Pinnacle Micro RCD-5020/5040, Plextor CDR PX-24CS, Ricoh MP 1420C, Ricoh MP 6200S/6201S, Sanyo CRD-R24S, Smart and Friendly Internal 2006 Plus 2.05, Sony CDU 920S/924/926S, Taiyo Yuden EW-50, TEAC CD-R50S, WPI (Wearnes) CDR-632P, WPI(Wearnes) CDRW-622, Yamaha CDR-100, Yamaha CDR-200/200t/200tx, and Yamaha CDR-400t/400tx.

Modems

Modems are simple things on the surface. They are either external to your system and plug into an existing serial line, or they are internal to the system and look like another serial line to the system. Alas, some modems are made for only Windows and therefore do not work with Linux. These modems are generally known as WinModems or Windows modems. Keep clear of them.

Mice

Here is another case where you might say "Surely I shouldn't have any mice issues to worry about because they're so simple." Well, when we start thinking of the vagaries of mice and men, we know that nothing is simple. Linux supports the following mice: Microsoft serial mouse, Mouse Systems serial mouse, Logitech Mouseman serial mouse, Logitech serial mouse, ATI XL Inport bus mouse, C&T 82C710 (QuickPort) (Toshiba, TI Travelmate), Microsoft bus mouse, Logitech bus mouse, PS/2 (auxiliary device) mouse, and Alps Glidepoint.

Printers and Plotters

All printers and plotters connected to the parallel or serial port should work — except those printers made to work with only Microsoft products. Do you see a pattern here?

Many Linux programs output PostScript files. Non-PostScript printers can emulate PostScript Level 2 using Ghostscript, particularly: Apple Imagewriter, Itoh M8510, Canon BubbleJet BJ10e (bj10e), Canon BubbleJet BJ200, BJC-210 (B/W only), BJC-240 (B/W only) (bj200), Canon BubbleJet BJC-600, BJC-610, BJC-4000, BJC-4100, BJC-450, MultiPASS C2500, BJC-240, BJC-70 (bjc600), Canon BubbleJet BJC-800 (bjc800), Canon LBP-8II, LIPS III, DEC LA50/70/ 75/75plus, DEC LN03, LJ250, Epson 9 pin, 24 pin, LQ series, AP3250, Epson Stylus Color/Color II/500/800 (stcolor), HP 2563B, HP DesignJet 650C, HP DeskJet, Deskjet Plus (deskjet), HP Deskjet 500, Deskjet Portable (djet500), HP DeskJet 400/500C/540C/690C/693C (cdj500), HP DeskJet 550C/560C/ 600/660C/682C/683C/693C/850/870Cse (cdj550), HP DeskJet 850/870Cse/ 870Cxi/680 (cdj850), HP DeskJet 500C/510/520/5540C/693C printing black only (cdjmono), HP DeskJet 600 (lj4dith), HP DeskJet 600/870Cse, LaserJet 5/5L (ljet4), HP Deskjet 500/500C/510/520/540/550C/560C/850C/855C, HP Deskjet 720, 820 and 1000 series, HP PaintJet XL300, Deskjet 600/1200C/1600C (pjxl300), HP LaserJet/Plus/II/III/4, HP PaintJet/XL, IBM Jetprinter color, IBM Proprinter, Imagen ImPress, Mitsubishi CP50 color, NEC P6/P6+/P60, Oki

OL410ex LED (ljet4), Okidata MicroLine 182, Ricoh 4081/6000 (r4081), SPARCprinter, StarJet 48 inkjet printer, Tektronix 4693d color 2/4/8 bit, Tektronix 4695/4696 inkjet plotter, and Xerox XES printers (2700, 3700, 4045, and so on).

Scanners

Scanners are our second-most-favorite piece of hardware because they enable us to scan all types of pictures and then manipulate them with gimp(1), an image manipulation program that's comparable to Adobe PhotoShop. Linux has an interface called SANE that enables you to attach and control many types of scanners. The scanners currently supported are A4 Tech AC 4096/AS 8000P, Adara Image Star I, Conrad Personal Scanner 64, P105 handheld scanners, Epson GT6000, Fujitsu SCSI-2 scanners, Genius ColorPage-SP2, Genius GS-B105G handheld scanner, Genius GeniScan GS4500, GS4500A handheld scanners, HighScreen Greyscan 256 handheld scanner, HP ScanJet II series SCSI, HP ScanJet IIc, IIcx, IIp, 3c, 4c, 4p, 5p, 5pse, plus, Logitech Scanman+, Scanman 32, Scanman 256 handheld scanners, Microtek ScanMaker E3, E6, II, IIXE, III and 35t models, Mustek M105 handheld scanner, Mustek HT800 Turbo, Matador 105, Matador 256 handheld scanners, Mustek Paragon 6000CX, Nikon Coolscan SCSI 35mm film scanner, Pearl 256 handheld scanner, and UMAX SCSI scanners.

Touch Screens

As if you don't have enough stuff to spend money on, the Metro Link X-server supports the following touch screen controllers: Carrol Touch serial touch screen, EloGraphics, Lucas Deeco, and MicroTouch.

Video Capture Boards, Frame Grabbers, and TV Tuners

Our favorite hardware categories are video capture boards, frame grabbers, and TV tuners. These devices enable you to capture images and send them over the wire, only in real time. A few programs are available that support TV tuners: BTTV (http://www.thp.Uni-Koeln.DE/~rjkm/linux/bttv.html), Xawtv and Xtvscreen. The CMOS Video Conferencing Kit comes with a video capture card and a CCD camera. Other boards that are supported are Data Translation DT2803, Data Translation DT2851 Frame Grabber, Data Translation DT3155, Diamond DTV2000 (based on BT848), Dipix XPG1000/FPG/PPMAPA (based on TI C40 DSP), Epix SVM, Epix Silicon Video

MUX series of video frame grabbing boards, FAST Screen Machine II, Hauppage Wincast TV PCI (based on BT848), Imaging Technology ITI/IC-PCI, ImageNation Cortex I, ImageNation CX100, Imaging Technology IC-PCI frame grabber board, Matrox Meteor, Matrox PIP-1024, MaxiTV/PCI (based on ZR36120), Miro PCTV (based on BT848), MuTech MV1000 PCI, MuTech MV200, Pro Movie Studio, WinVision B&W video capture card, Quickcam, Sensus 700, Smart Video Recoder III (based on BT848), STB TV PCI Television Tuner (based on BT848), Tekram C210 (based on ZR36120), Video Blaster, Rombo Media Pro+, and VT1500 TV cards.

UPS and Miscellaneous Devices

Many people have little surge protectors on the power to their computer systems. Although it's better than nothing, that surge protector offers only so much protection from surges and no protection from brownouts or blackouts. As you will come to know, Linux systems just hate having their power turned off before completing a nice, orderly shutdown of services. And when the system does come back up, you're in for a long wait while Linux checks to see whether the file system was corrupted. An uninterruptable power supply (UPS) uses batteries to provide power to the computer system, allowing the computer system to shut down in an orderly way if the power starts to fail. Good ones also give you the ability to tie the computer into your UPS, and therefore have the UPS judge when it should go to complete shutdown. Some of the UPS units mentioned are APC SmartUPS, APC-BackUPS 400/600, APC-SmartUPS SU700/1400RM, UPS with RS-232 monitoring port (genpower package), and MGE UPS.

Many more hardware devices are supported, and some do not fit into any other category than *strange* . . . er, . . . *miscellaneous.* They include Mattel Powerglove, AIMS Labs RadioTrack FM radio card, Reveal FM Radio card, and Videotext.

PCMCIA Cards

PCMCIA cards are used to get extra features into very small places. We own several modems and Ethernet controllers, a SCSI interface, and a sound card. All are PCMCIA cards, and all have support under Linux.

Here are some Ethernet cards that work under Linux: 3Com 3c589, 3c589B, 3c589C, 3c589D, Farallon EtherWave, EtherMac, CONTEC C-NET(PC)C, Eagle NE200 Ethernet, Labs EPX-10BT, EPX-ET 10BT, Fujitsu FMV-J181, FMV-J182, FMV-J182A, Towa LA501, Hitachi HT-4840-11 EtherCard, NextCom NC5310, RATOC REX-9822, REX-5588A/W, TDK LAC-CD02x, LAK-CD021, LAK-CD022A, LAK-CD021AX Ethernet, New Media EthernetLAN, Accton EN2212, EN2216

EtherCard, Addtron Ethernet, Allied Telesis CentreCOM CE6001, LA-PCM, AmbiCom AMB8002, Apollo RE450CT, Asante FriendlyNet, Billionton LNT-10TB, California Access LAN Adapter, CeLAN EPCMCIA, CNet CN30BC, CN40BC Ethernet, Compex/ReadyLINK Ethernet Combo, Compex LinkPort Ethernet, Connectware LANdingGear Adapter, Danpex EN-6200P2 Ethernet, Datatrek NetCard, Dayna Communications CommuniCard E, Digital DEPCM-AA, PCP78-AC Ethernet, Digital EtherWORKS Turbo Ethernet, D-Link DE-650, DE-660, DynaLink L10C Ethernet, Edimax Technology Ethernet Combo, EFA InfoExpress 205, 207 Combo, Labs EPX-ET10T2 Combo, ELECOM Laneed LD-CDWA, LD-CDX, LD-CDNIA, LD-CDY, EP-210 Ethernet, Epson Ethernet, EtherPRIME Ethernet, Explorer NE-10000 Ethernet, 4109 Ethernet, Fiberline FL-4680, Gateway 2000 Ethernet, Genius ME3000II Ethernet, Grey Cell Ethernet, GVC NIC-2000P Ethernet Combo, Hypertec HyperEnet, IBM CreditCard Ethernet Adapter, IC-Card Ethernet, Infotel IN650ct Ethernet, I-O Data PCLA/T, Katron PE-520 Ethernet, KingMax Technology EN10-T2 Ethernet, Kingston KNE-PCM/M, KNE-PC2, KTI PE-520 Plus, LANEED Ethernet, LanPro EP4000A, Lantech Ethernet, Linksys EtherCard, Logitec LPM-LN10T, LPM-LN10BA Ethernet, Longshine ShineNet LCS-8534TB Ethernet, Macnica ME-1 Ethernet, Maxtech PCN2000 Ethernet, Melco LPC-TJ, LPC-TS, Micronet EtherFast Adapter, NDC Instant-Link, Network General Sniffer, /National NE4100 InfoMover, OvisLink Ethernet, Panasonic CF-VEL211P-B, Planet SmartCOM 2000, 3500, Pretec Ethernet, PreMax PE-200 Ethernet, Proteon Ethernet, Relia RE2408T Ethernet, Reliasys 2400A Ethernet, RPTI EP400, EP401 Ethernet, SCM Ethernet, Sky Link Express, Socket Communications Socket EA LAN Adapter, SuperSocket RE450T, Surecom Ethernet, SVEC PN605C, -Conrad Ethernet, Trust Ethernet Combo, Volktek NPL-402CT Ethernet, Megahertz XJ10BT, XJ10BC, CC10BT Ethernet, New Media BASICS Ethernet, Ositech Four of Diamonds, Compaq Ethernet Adapter, Xircom CreditCard CE2, D-Link DFE-650, Linksys EtherFast 10/100, NetGear FA410TXC, Compaq Netelligent 10/100, Intel EtherExpress PRO/100, and Xircom CreditCard CE3.

Wireless network adapters are neat. They enable you to roam about but still be connected with your other systems. Linux supports the following wireless network adapters: AT&T GIS/NCR WaveLAN version 2.0, DEC RoamAbout/DS, and Xircom CreditCard Netwave.

Most modem and serial cards should work. Unfortunately, some manufacturers have made cards that work with only Microsoft software. These are typically called WinModems, and you probably should avoid them.

SCSI adapters enable you to attach any number of SCSI devices (disks, tapes, scanners, CD-ROMS, and CD-Writers) to your notebook. Supported controllers are Adaptec APA-1460, APA-1450A, APA-1460A, APA-1460B SlimSCSI, Iomega Zip and Jaz Cards, New Media Bus Toaster SCSI, New Media Toast 'n Jam (SCSI only), Noteworthy Bus Toaster SCSI, Sony CD-ROM Discman PRD-250, Future Domain SCSI2GO, IBM SCSI, Simple Technologies SCSI, Eiger Labs SCSI, MACNICA mPS110, mPS110-LP SCSI, NEC PC-9801N-J03R, Qlogic FastSCSI, Panasonic KXL-D740, KXL-DN740A, KXL-DN740A-NB 4X CD-ROM,

Raven CD-Note 4X, RATOC REX-9530 SCSI-2, Toshiba NWB0107ABK, SCSC200B, Digital SCSI II adapter, IO-DATA PCSC-II, PCSC-II-L, IO-DATA CDG-PX44/PCSC CD-ROM, Logitec LPM-SCSI2, Logitec LCD-601 CD-ROM, Melco IFC-SC2, IFC-DC, Pioneer PCP-PR1W CD-ROM, and Taxan ICD-400PN.

Supported ATA/IDE CD-ROM adapters include the following: Argosy EIDE CD-ROM, Caravelle CD-36N, Creative Technology CD-ROM, Digital Mobile Media CD-ROM, EXP Traveler 620 CD-ROM, H45 Technologies Quick 2X CD-ROM, H45 Technologies QuickCD 16X, IO-DATA CDP-TX4/PCIDE, CDP-TX6/PCIDE, CDV-HDN6/PCIDE, IO-DATA CDP-TX10/PCIDE, MOP-230/PCIDE, and TEAC IDE Card/II.

The following multifunction cards are supported: 3Com 3c562, 3c562B/C/D, 3c563B/C/D, 3Com 3CCEM556, 3CXEM556, Motorola Marquis, D-Link DME336T, Grey Cell GCS3400, IBM Home and Away, IBM Home and Away 28.8, Linksys LANmodem 28.8, 33.6, Gateway Telepath Combo, Megahertz/U.S. Robotics EM1144, EM3288, EM3336, Motorola Mariner, Ositech Jack of Diamonds, and Xircom CreditCard CEM28, CEM33, and CEM56.

Appendix C

The Linux man Pages

● ●

In This Appendix

▶ Starting the man command

▶ Reading the man pages

▶ Finding commands

● ●

*U*NIX and Linux systems are largely made up of small, terse commands executed on the command line. Typically, each command is associated with at least one man page. The Linux man pages have nothing to do with gender: The *man* stands for *manual*.

At one time, the man pages were the only documentation that came with UNIX systems. Somewhere we still have the thin book we received as first-time UNIX users and systems administrators. All that it contained was the man pages, and from that, we were supposed to install a UNIX system. Many years later, we still look at the man pages first to get a quick idea of what a command should do, and what arguments to use on the command line or what values to set.

This appendix shows you how to use the man(1) command, how to read and understand the man pages, and how to locate other man pages that may help you understand the Linux command you're investigating.

Using the man Command

To get started using the man pages, follow these steps:

1. **With Linux up and running, log in as a user (either a general user or root).**

2. **Type the** man **command.**

   The system asks what manual page you want. The syntax of the man command (like many other commands) requires at least one argument.

3. **Supply an argument by typing** man man.

The first man is the command name, and the second man tells Linux that you want information on the manual program itself. The system may tell you to wait a moment while it formats the page to your screen, and then it displays the reference page for the man command.

4. **If a colon (:) appears at the bottom of the screen, press the spacebar to see the next page, or use the arrow keys to maneuver around the pages.**

5. **To quit the program, press the q key.**

Sections in the man Pages

You can usually find the man pages in several directories throughout the system:

- ✔ /usr/man
- ✔ /usr/local/man
- ✔ /usr/X11/man
- ✔ /usr/lib/perl5/man

Each directory is broken up into subdirectories representing sections of the manual, as follows:

- ✔ **man1:** User commands
- ✔ **man2:** System calls
- ✔ **man3:** Library functions
- ✔ **man4:** Special files
- ✔ **man5:** File formats
- ✔ **man6:** Games (look at everyone going to that section!)
- ✔ **man7:** Miscellany
- ✔ **man8:** System administration commands
- ✔ **mann:** nroff, troff, and groff (and now tk) macros

Note that most directories have more than one section.

Two sections may have entries for a command of the same name. For example, section 1 has an open command, and section 2 has an open system call. To make sure that you're reading about the right one, you can specify the command on the man command line. For example:

```
[maddog@doghouse maddog]$ man 2 open
```

Most sections of the man database (because that's basically what it is) have two parts:

- ✔ An intro page represented by a file called intro.*n,* where the *n* is a number that corresponds to the section number.

- ✔ All commands, calls, library names, and filenames, represented by files with the name command.*n,* where *n* is the section number name.

  If you use cd to change to the /usr/man/man1 directory and issue the ls command, you see files such as cat.1 and grep.1. Oddly, you don't find a file called cd.1, because the cd command is built into the different shells, and its documentation is covered in the bash.1 file, or the csh.1 file.

If you're using bash as a shell, you can get information about the rest of the built-ins as follows:

```
[maddog@doghouse maddog]$ help
```

The intro page briefly describes that section of the manual and indicates whether you need to know anything special about that section. Printing an intro page is simple. For example:

```
[maddog@doghouse maddog]$ man 2 intro
```

or

```
[maddog@doghouse maddog]$ man 3 intro
```

Topics in the man Pages

Each man page is made up of several sections. Here, we list the sections that we think are most important in your quest to figure out how to read man pages. Note that some man pages don't contain all these sections, and other pages contain more sections than those outlined here.

Name

The name is usually the command name, followed by a hyphen, followed by a one-line description of the command's functionality; this is usually what you see if you execute a man -k command or an apropos command. Either of these commands, when followed by a word, lists the name field from every manual page that contains that word. Type the following:

```
[maddog@doghouse maddog]$ apropos cat
```

Your `apropos` command may produce few or no commands. Perhaps no one has generated the database made up of command names and descriptions. To do this, either you or your systems administrator has to become superuser or root and then execute the following command line:

```
/usr/sbin/makewhatis
```

Synopsis

The synopsis is a shorthand way to describe what the command is looking for in terms of an argument list. For example:

```
lpq [-l] [-Pprinter] [job # ...] [user ...]
```

is the synopsis for the `lpq` command (whose job is to show what is in the print queue). The command name (`lpq`) is first, followed by a series of bracketed arguments. If an argument is enclosed in square brackets, the argument is optional, meaning the `lpq` command needs no arguments. If you type:

```
[maddog@doghouse maddog]$ lpq
```

you probably get a `no entries` message — which means nothing is waiting to be printed — or a list of people's jobs waiting to be printed on the default printer.

If you want to see what is waiting to be printed on another printer, you use the optional argument `-P` followed by the name of the printer. For example:

```
[maddog@doghouse maddog]$ lpq -Pzklpsa
```

Now if you type this command, you probably get a message like `lpq: zklpsa: unknown printer`, indicating that your system does not know about a printer named `zklpsa`. If you get something else, please let us know because that may explain where our print jobs are going . . . no, no, just kidding.

If, however, you have a printer called hp5l, then you can enter the following command to find out its status:

```
[maddog@doghouse maddog]$ lpq -Php5l
```

In any case, the purpose of this section is not to show you all the functionality of the `lpq` command. Rather, the synopsis section shows in a shorthand way how you should use the command, including which arguments are optional.

Another confusing thing you may see is the . . . notation. Looking back at the
lpq command synopsis, you see it twice, once following the job # argument
and once following the user argument. This notation tells you that you can
list as many job numbers on the line as you want, separated by spaces, and
as many user names as you want, separated by spaces.

Sometimes you see a command argument that begins with one hyphen (-) or
two (--). These characters are technically known as *options,* whereas job #
and user of the lpq command are *arguments.* Options tell the command how
to manipulate arguments. You may see an option line that looks like this:

```
cat   [-benstuvAET]
```

or even:

```
ls [-abcdfgiklmnpqrstuxABCFGLNQRSUX1]
```

Don't be overwhelmed. If you deal with the options one at a time, you'll be
able to understand how the command works. Take heart in the fact that most
of the time, people use only one or two options.

If you issue the man ls command, you see that ls has many more options.
That's why ls has been described as "a command that went bad with good
intentions."

Description

The description section is a brief introduction to the command's functionality, which is then expanded on by what the options specify the command to
do. A good example of a description is the manual page for man itself.

Options

The options section tells how the command treats data in the arguments.
Each option modifies the command's actions, drastically or subtly. The
options can also pass information to the command about where to find files.
The three types of options are:

- ✔ No argument
- ✔ Attached argument
- ✔ Positional argument

No argument means the option has a hyphen, followed by one or more single-character options. For example:

```
[maddog@doghouse maddog]$ ps -ax
```

The a and the x do not have any other values that they have to look at. However, in the following command:

```
[maddog@doghouse maddog]$ lpq -Pzklpsa
```

the -P option needs you to supply an argument, in this example, zklpsa.

Environmental variables

Sometimes, to cut down on the information you have to give the command, you can set an *environmental variable*. Each shell (or command interpreter) has an *environment* that it works in. This environment (when it is created) consists of certain files that are open, some memory, and almost always some environmental variables.

Using the bash shell, type the following (if you're not sure that you're using the bash shell, type bash at the command prompt and then continue with the example):

```
[maddog@doghouse maddog]$ printenv
```

You see something like this:

```
USEºE=
COLORTERM=gnome-terminal
HISTSIZE=1000
HOSTNAME=atlas.paunchy.net
LOGNAME=maddog
HISTFILESIZE=1000
INIT_VERSION=sysvinit-2.74
MAIL=/var/spool/mail/maddog
LD_LIBRARY_PATH=/usr/local/applixware/axdata/axshlib/lib
TERM=xterm
HOSTTYPE=i386
PATH=/usr/bin:/usr/bin:/usr/local/bin:/usr/X11R6/bin:/bin:
 /usr/X11R6/bin:/usr/local/netscape:
 /home/maddog/bin:/usr/X11R6/bin:
 /usr/local/netscape:/home/maddog/bin
CONSOLE=/dev/console
KDEDIR=/usr
HOME=/home/maddog
INPUTRC=/etc/inputrc
PREVLEVEL=N
RUNLEVEL=5
```

```
SHELL=/bin/bash
XAUTHORITY=/home/maddog/.Xauthority
USER=maddog
PGDATA=/var/lib/pgsql
BASH_ENV=/home/maddog/.bashrc
BOOT_IMAGE=linux
DISPLAY=:0
SESSION_MANAGER=local/atlas.paunchy.net:/tmp/.ICEunix/7376,
          tcp/atlas.paunchy.net:1371
OSTYPE=Linux
WINDOWID=62914566
GDMSESSION=Default
LD_PRELOAD=/usr/local/lib/open.so
SHLVL=3
_=/usr/bin/printenv
```

This list includes lots of environmental variables, but we don't have the space to describe them all. So, here are the most important ones:

- **PATH** tells the shell all the places to look for commands

- **HOME** tells cd where to go when you don't supply any arguments

- **OSTYPE** tells the shell and programs what operating system they're on

Different shells have different ways to set these variables (and create and set others) to tell the commands what to do.

Note that a variable not being set to some value (null) is different than a variable that doesn't exist (unset), and these differences vary from command to command. For example, in the preceding listing, the first variable, USERNAME, is set to NULL. The fact that it's there at all is significant. The fact that it is set to NULL instead of some other value is also significant to various programs.

Diagnostics

Error messages or exit codes indicate that something has gone wrong in the program or the shell. Normally, UNIX error messages are terse. Sometimes things may seem to be wrong when they really are okay. For example, most new UNIX users think that when they issue an ls command in an empty directory, they should get an error message such as directory empty or file not found. The problem? The command ls by itself can display the filenames in any order (as opposed to ls *, which displays the files in alphabetical order). Therefore, if you have a directory with three files in it named *file, not,* and *found* — which happen to print in that order — you can't determine whether the directory is empty or not. Granted, this is a contrived example, but the developers of UNIX thought that less was better than more (we're not talking about the command names less and more) and that silence is golden (which means something if you've ever heard those old, noisy, hard-copy terminals).

Most programs display an *exit code,* which you normally don't see unless it's a non-zero code, which means the program ended unsuccessfully. If you're a programmer, you can test for this, and if you do programming or shell script writing, we encourage you to set and test exit codes.

Bugs/deficiencies

Yes, all programs have bugs, and most Linux people are good about correcting them. But some bugs are so arcane that they affect only one in a million people, and to try and correct them would mean redesigning the entire program. Therefore, this type of bug is regarded as a deficiency or a limitation and is listed in the man page.

Compatibility issues

When a new version of a command or a program comes out, it may work slightly differently than the old command or program. This modification can cause a *compatibility issue* with shell scripts that have been written to use the old command or program. If the author of the command or program thinks a problem may occur, it should be documented here.

Caveats

Caveats are warnings that the programmer wants to give to the user of the command or program. Caveats may include things to think about before executing the command or program, security issues, or how much file system space the program uses on large applications.

Disclaimers

Disclaimers are usually legal statements included at the insistence of the author's employer or the employer's lawyers, telling you that if you use this program and it harms someone, don't come back to them. All programs in all operating systems have disclaimers someplace.

Authors

The authors are simply the people who wrote the command or program that the manual page is describing. Often, this section also explains how to report bugs or discuss new features you may want to see.

Acknowledgments

The acknowledgments section, which is much more pleasant than the disclaimers section, recognizes the previous work put into a program that the author has built on. Allowing and encouraging people to build on the work of others is the essence of Linux and the GNU Public License.

Debugging options

Some programs, such as sendmail, have the capability to diagnose problems. If the manual page has a debugging options section, you can find information on setting and using these options to debug the program.

Configuration files

Along with options and environmental variables, another way to determine what program the manual page is describing is through *configuration files,* sometimes known as *startup files.* These files may be in your home directory, a systemwide directory, or a sitewide directory. Often, Linux looks for them in a certain order: Sitewide files have the strongest influence, and systemwide files and local user (your startup) files have the second and third strongest influence, respectively. The systems administrator can use those files to set policies across companies and systems, while allowing you to tailor the program to your needs.

Two examples of startup files are the .bashrc file, which is probably in your home directory, and the /etc/bashrc file in the /etc directory. Note that the file in your home directory starts with a period. This type of file is called a *hidden,* or *dot,* file. You don't normally see hidden files when you list your directory, unless you issue the ls -a or ls .* command.

Copyrights

Many people mistakenly believe that Linux code or other freeware code is not copyrighted. The authors of the code often take great care to copyright their code because they want to receive credit for their work.

Copying permissions/distribution policy

The copyright holder gives away most Linux code through the GNU Public License, or what is commonly called *copyleft.* The copyleft stipulates that those holding a copy of the code can use it for whatever purpose they want, as long as they make the code freely available to anyone who wants it. If they change the code, they must make the changed code (including the source code) freely available to those who want it.

Sometimes, other copying and distribution policies are associated with the command or program that the manual page is describing. These policies can include the following types of permissions, where you may:

- ✔ Use but not redistribute the code
- ✔ Use the code, but no source code is available
- ✔ Use and distribute the code as shareware, by paying a fee for continued use
- ✔ Have limited use, such as educational or personal (but not commercial) use
- ✔ Use the code on one machine only

If you bought the operating system, or a *layered product distribution* (a distribution that includes both the operating system and a commercial application), or both from a CD-ROM vendor, then the overall distribution policy on the CD-ROM is usually the most strict (that is, you're limited to installing it on one machine because of its licensed software), so you don't have to worry as long as you follow its overall licensing.

POSIX compatibility/standards conformance

In the dark days of computer science, each vendor went off to develop its own operating system, with its own set of commands and programming interfaces. This way of thinking created a Tower of Babel (not to be confused with the Tower of Hanoi, which is a puzzle game) among computer users and programmers. When UNIX systems first appeared, however, they were portable across different types of hardware, and you could have the same operating system, commands, and programming interfaces whether you were programming a Digital Equipment Corporation system, a Sun Microsystems computer, an IBM computer, or others. Unfortunately, this approach lasted about ten minutes in the scope of UNIX's life, because as UNIX escaped from Bell Labs, it went to the University of California, Berkeley, and *poof:* Two different UNIX systems were now in existence!

A little later, vendors started introducing their versions of UNIX, some using System V as a basis, others using BSD (as the Berkeley version was called). Some vendors, such as Sun Microsystems, started out with BSD and then switched to System V (to the chagrin of its users).

In 1988, the IEEE developed the POSIX standard for operating systems. The IEEE is a great organization, and probably the best thing that it did was to build on UNIX rather than start over from scratch. It took the interfaces from the existing System V and Berkeley versions of UNIX.

If an operating system is POSIX-compatible and a program is written to POSIX standards, the program should run on the operating system with no problems, and users should be able to use that operating system with little or no retraining from the last POSIX operating system they learned.

Although much work still has to be accomplished both in defining what POSIX is and in vendors implementing POSIX, POSIX compliance and certification are worthy goals.

Other standards should be implemented and met by manufacturers, distribution makers, and developers (not necessarily in that order) — standards for network communication, for the way data is put on the CD-ROM, and so on. Both formal standards and informal defacto standards exist, both of which help your system work better with the next system.

Linux was built with POSIX compatibility as a goal, and it follows many of the other standards. This makes it easy to port code from one set of POSIX-compatible interfaces to another and from one POSIX-compatible operating system to another. It also allows Linux to interoperate with other operating systems. Many Linux people are active in standards bodies, and the movement toward standards is generally supported in the Linux community.

Files

In addition to the startup or configuration files mentioned previously, sometimes the command or program that the manual page is describing uses other files in the system and temporary files for holding intermediate work. Such files are listed in this section of the man page. If a command does not work, perhaps one of these files is missing, has the wrong file permissions (or the directories they are in have the wrong permissions), is owned by the wrong person, or has corrupt data.

Future work

The future work section lists the author's plans for the command or program that the manual page is describing, often in an attempt to generate interest and help from other people.

Other places to look for help

You can find help in several other places on the system. One place is the /usr/doc directory.

Note: Some system administrators conserve disk space by not loading /usr/doc on their systems. With the abundance of inexpensive disks, this is usually penny wise, pound foolish. Documentation such as that found in /usr/doc can be put on one system and then made available to everyone through the magic of the Network File System (NFS). Tell your system administrator to do that. If you are your own system administrator, go into a closet and give yourself a lecture!

See also/related software

The see also/related software section lists programs associated with the command or program that the manual page is describing. Often, several programs make up a system of programs to do a particular task. Some programs have similar capabilities but are not quite the same. Some programs are the antithesis of the program you're looking at (for example, cut and paste). The *see also* often gives you an overall picture of what the program is supposed to do or leads you to the right program for the job.

Finding the Right man Page

If you don't know what command you're looking for, use the `apropos` command followed by the word you're interested in. The `apropos` command searches all the man pages looking for that word, and lists the man command names along with one-line descriptions of all the commands that contain that word. You should probably pipe the output of the `apropos` command into the `more` command:

```
[maddog@doghouse maddog]$ apropos print | more
```

Note that `apropos` matches on partial words (called *strings*), which is why we suggested `print` instead of `printer`. The shorter your *keyword*, the more matches the command finds.

Second, after you have the pages you want to look at, execute the `man` command for each one. From the one-line description, you can probably decide which commands fit your needs.

Third, look at the description field, which gives you a better idea of what the command can do. If you're still not sure about the command's basic functionality, look at the see also section, to see whether any other commands fit the bill.

After that, skip the synopsis section — it's usually a reminder of how to type the command — and go directly to the options section. Read through the options section, trying to apply the options to the basic description of the command.

After you've read several man pages, you'll notice that the same options appear for similar commands.

This is all pretty much passive work. To find out what a command really does, you should try it out. Create a small test file by using an editor, or use an existing file, such as the /etc/passwd file, as input. (It's better not to practice while logged in as root as you could accidentally damage a file or directory.)

From time to time, we read all the man pages in the system, concentrating on the command descriptions. we do this to become familiar with new commands. Also, our memories are not what they used to be. But to be fair to our failing memories, the system does have close to 1,200 general-user commands and about 260 system administration commands.

Appendix D
Making Life Difficult with fdisk

● ●

*B*ack in the bad 'ol days before Disk Druid (see Chapter 5 for more on Disk Druid), you had to walk five miles through hip-deep snow to partition Linux disks. Back then, fdisk was the only way to set up a hard drive to install Linux. Just in case you want to experience life as it was, in this appendix, we describe how to use fdisk. Have fun.

Starting fdisk

If for some reason you can't or won't use Disk Druid, the fdisk program is still available. During the installation process, Linux asks you to choose whether you want to partition your disk with Disk Druid or fdisk (see Chapter 5). Your first action is easy — simply choose fdisk. When you do so, the screen in Figure D-1 appears. From there, follow these steps:

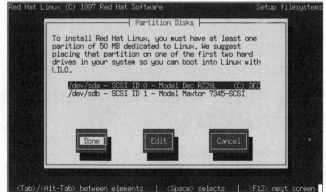

Figure D-1: Selecting the disk that you want fdisk to partition.

1. **Specify which of your disks you want fdisk to partition.**

2. **Press the Tab key until you reach the Done button and then press Enter.**

   The fdisk program starts. The first screen of fdisk appears, as shown in Figure D-2.

Figure D-2:
The first
fdisk
screen.

```
This is the fdisk program for partitioning your drive. It is running
on /dev/sda.

Command (m for help): []
```

3. Type m.

A listing of fdisk commands appears, as shown in Figure D-3.

```
This is the fdisk program for partitioning your drive. It is running
on /dev/sda.

Command (m for help): m
Command action
   a    toggle a bootable flag
   b    edit bsd disklabel
   c    toggle the dos compatibility flag
   d    delete a partition
   l    list known partition types
   m    print this menu
   n    add a new partition
   p    print the partition table
   q    quit without saving changes
   t    change a partition's system id
   u    change display/entry units
   v    verify the partition table
   w    write table to disk and exit
   x    extra functionality (experts only)

Command (m for help): []
```

Figure D-3:
A list of
commands
in fdisk.

Viewing partitions

Before you start creating a partition with fdisk, you need to see what partitions (if any) exist. Type p to list the current partition table, which probably looks a lot like the one shown in Figure D-4.

If you kept the Microsoft operating system on your hard disk and used FIPS to make your Microsoft operating system partition smaller, you probably have a second partition using up all the additional space on the disk. The first thing you have to do with fdisk is remove that partition.

Figure D-4:
The p
command
produces a
listing of
partitions.

```
Command (m for help): p

Disk /dev/sda: 33 heads, 61 sectors, 1018 cylinders
Units = cylinders of 2013 * 512 bytes

   Device Boot   Begin   Start    End   Blocks  Id  System
/dev/sda1    *       1       1    300  301919+   6  DOS 16-bit >=32M
/dev/sda2          301     301   1018  722667    6  DOS 16-bit >=32M

Command (m for help):
```

Deleting partitions

Look at the partitions printed by the p command. The first one (probably designated by hda1 if it is an IDE disk or sda1 if it is a SCSI disk) is known to fdisk as partition 1, and it's probably the Microsoft operating system (such as Windows or MS-DOS), if you have one. The second partition is partition 2; this is probably the partition created by FIPS and is therefore empty. To delete the empty partition, follow these steps:

1. **Type** d.

   The screen shown in Figure D-5 appears.

Figure D-5:
Typing the d
command in
fdisk.

```
Disk /dev/sda: 33 heads, 61 sectors, 1018 cylinders
Units = cylinders of 2013 * 512 bytes

   Device Boot   Begin   Start    End   Blocks  Id  System
/dev/sda1    *       1       1    300  301919+   6  DOS 16-bit >=32M
/dev/sda2          301     301   1018  722667    6  DOS 16-bit >=32M

Command (m for help): d
Partition number (1-4):
```

2. **Enter the number of the partition you want to delete.**

   This number is probably 2.

3. **Type** p **to display the partition table again.**

   In this way, you confirm what you just did. A screen similar to the one shown in Figure D-6 appears.

```
Command (m for help): p

Disk /dev/sda: 33 heads, 61 sectors, 1018 cylinders
Units = cylinders of 2013 * 512 bytes

   Device Boot    Begin    Start      End    Blocks   Id  System
/dev/sda1    *        1        1      300   301919+    6  DOS 16-bit >=32M
/dev/sda2           301      301     1018   722667     6  DOS 16-bit >=32M

Command (m for help): d
Partition number (1-4): 2

Command (m for help): p

Disk /dev/sda: 33 heads, 61 sectors, 1018 cylinders
Units = cylinders of 2013 * 512 bytes

   Device Boot    Begin    Start      End    Blocks   Id  System
/dev/sda1    *        1        1      300   301919+    6  DOS 16-bit >=32M

Command (m for help): ▊
```

Figure D-6:
Specifying
the number
of the
partition you
want to
delete and
then typing
the p
command.

Creating a partition

Now you come to the big part, the part you've been waiting for, the actual creation of the new partition (or partitions if you'll have more than one).

After you tell the fdisk program that you want to create a partition, you then tell the program the following:

- ✔ The type of partition you want to create
- ✔ Which partition you want to create
- ✔ Where the partition should start on your disk
- ✔ How big the partition should be

After that, you display the partition table one more time to make sure that everything is okay.

If you think that we recommend displaying the partition table a lot, you're right. We display the partition table all the time when we're doing this type of disk work. You can't be too careful when changing your hard disk partitions. Displaying the partition table is so fast and easy with fdisk that if you don't do it between steps, you're asking for trouble.

Now you make that new partition. We show you all the steps that we took in Figure D-7. To follow along with this figure, follow these steps:

```
Command (m for help): n
Command action
   e   extended
   p   primary partition (1-4)
p
Partition number (1-4): 2
First cylinder (301-1018): 301
Last cylinder or +size or +sizeM or +sizeK ([301]-1018): 1018

Command (m for help): p

Disk /dev/sda: 33 heads, 61 sectors, 1018 cylinders
Units = cylinders of 2013 * 512 bytes

   Device Boot    Begin    Start      End   Blocks   Id  System
/dev/sda1   *        1        1      300   301919+    6  DOS 16-bit >=32M
/dev/sda2          301      301     1018   722667    83  Linux native

Command (m for help):
```

Figure D-7:
The process
of creating a
partition.

1. **Type** n **for new partition.**

2. **Type** p **for primary partition.**

3. **Type the partition number that you want to create.**

   The partition number is probably 2.

4. **Type the number of the first cylinder of the partition.**

   Note that you *can* use a number other than the default, and leave a space between the first partition and the second partition. Some people use this feature when they want to leave room on the hard disk for the growth of a partition or when they want to place partitions in specific sections of the hard disk. For now, use the suggested default.

5. **Type the size, or ending point, of the partition.**

   You can enter the size in four ways:

   - With a plus sign, followed by the size specified in bytes

   - With a plus sign, followed by the size specified in megabytes, followed immediately by M

   - With a plus sign, followed by the size specified in kilobytes, followed immediately by K

   - By specifying the ending cylinder (without the plus sign)

   The first three are particularly useful in setting aside areas of the disk that are large enough to hold your Linux distribution, your /home directory, your swap space, or other areas. The last option, specifying the ending cylinder, is useful when allocating all the remaining space to the file system you're defining. We typed **1018**, which is the end of the disk. This means we can't put any more partitions on that disk, and all our Linux files have to go into that one partition (unless we have another disk).

6. **Type — you guessed it —** p **to display the partition table again.**

Creating multiple partitions

Just for grins, in this section, we go back and create multiple partitions on the hard disk to illustrate having several partitions just for Linux. First, we delete the large partition 2, which we created in the preceding section, by typing d and then 2.

Now look at Figure D-8. We make several partitions on the disk — using the same series of steps that we went through in the preceding section — but we use the size specification for the first two partitions and then use the cylinder specification for the last one. We show you all this in one example, so just follow along with Figure D-8.

Now we have one DOS partition for our Microsoft operating system and three partitions for Linux. Partition 2 is small for Linux, but we wanted to create all four partitions on one hard disk, so the 200MB size is used only for illustration. The recommended value is 700MB for all the programs on the companion CD2.

```
Command (m for help): n
Command action
   e   extended
   p   primary partition (1-4)
p
Partition number (1-4): 2
First cylinder (301-1018): 301
Last cylinder or +size or +sizeM or +sizeK ([301]-1018): +200M

Command (m for help): p

Disk /dev/sda: 33 heads, 61 sectors, 1018 cylinders
Units = cylinders of 2013 * 512 bytes

   Device Boot    Begin    Start    End    Blocks    Id  System
/dev/sda1    *        1        1    300    301919+    6  DOS 16-bit >=32M
/dev/sda2            301      301    504    205326    83  Linux native

Command (m for help): n
Command action
   e   extended
   p   primary partition (1-4)
p
Partition number (1-4): 3
First cylinder (505-1018): 505
Last cylinder or +size or +sizeM or +sizeK ([505]-1018): +128M

Command (m for help): p

Disk /dev/sda: 33 heads, 61 sectors, 1018 cylinders
Units = cylinders of 2013 * 512 bytes

   Device Boot    Begin    Start    End    Blocks    Id  System
/dev/sda1    *        1        1    300    301919+    6  DOS 16-bit >=32M
/dev/sda2            301      301    504    205326    83  Linux native
/dev/sda3            505      505    635    131851+   83  Linux native

Command (m for help): n
Command action
   e   extended
   p   primary partition (1-4)
p
Partition number (1-4): 4
First cylinder (636-1018): 636
Last cylinder or +size or +sizeM or +sizeK ([636]-1018): 1018

Command (m for help): █
```

Figure D-8:
Creating multiple partitions by using size specifications for the first and the ending cylinder specification for the last partition.

Finally, Figure D-9 shows a final display of the partition table, to show you how the four partitions appear.

```
Command (m for help): p

Disk /dev/sda: 33 heads, 61 sectors, 1018 cylinders
Units = cylinders of 2013 * 512 bytes

   Device Boot    Begin    Start      End   Blocks   Id  System
/dev/sda1   *        1        1      300  301919+    6  DOS 16-bit >=32M
/dev/sda2            301      301      504  205326    83  Linux native
/dev/sda3            505      505      635  131851+   83  Linux native
/dev/sda4            636      636     1018  385489+   83  Linux native

Command (m for help):
```

Changing partition types

When Linux fdisk creates partitions, it creates Linux native partitions by default. Many styles of file systems are available. The file system that you choose determines the way the operating system puts data on the disk partition, the maximum size of directories, the length of file names, and how many files can be in any one partition.

One of the non-native file systems you may want to create is a *swap partition*. In the preceding section, we created one swap partition: disk partition 3, set up for 127MB, which is the maximum size of any one swap partition in Linux. Linux systems can handle up to 16 swap partitions, so the size limitation is not that crucial.

Linux is stingy with memory space, and a swap partition is not always necessary. Adding one at this time, however, allows you to run many programs as well as large programs without repartitioning your disk. We recommend 127MB to start, assuming you have enough hard disk space for that amount.

When you create the swap partition, you must remember to use the t command to change it to a swap partition, which brings us to the point of this section. In Figure D-10, we show you the steps for switching the file system type from Linux native to swap. To follow along:

```
Command (m for help): L

0   Empty              9   AIX bootable    75  PC/IX          b7  BSDI fs
1   DOS 12-hit FAT     a   OS/2 Boot Manag 80  Old MINIX      b8  BSDI swap
2   XENIX root         b   Win95 FAT32     81  Linux/MINIX    c7  Syrinx
3   XENIX usr          40  Venix 80286     82  Linux swap     db  CP/M
4   DOS 16-bit <32M    51  Novell?         83  Linux native   e1  DOS access
5   Extended           52  Microport       93  Amoeba         e3  DOS R/O
6   DOS 16-bit >=32    63  GNU HURD        94  Amoeba BBT     f2  DOS secondary
7   OS/2 HPFS          64  Novell Netware  a5  BSD/386        ff  BBT
8   AIX                65  Novell Netware

Command (m for help):
```

1. **Type** p.

   This command displays the partition table and enables you to choose which partition you want to make a swap partition.

2. **Type** t.

   The t command tells fdisk that you want to change the type of a partition.

3. **Type the number of the partition you want to change.**

   In this example, we typed **3**.

4. **Type** L **to list the file codes, if you want.**

5. **Type the numerical file code that represents the file system/partition type that you want.**

   Because we want a swap partition, we typed **82**.

   Remember to write down which partitions (such as /dev/hda2 or /dev/sdb3) are used for which file systems (such as /usr or /tmp) as you create the partitions and as you select the partitions later for various file systems.

6. **Type** p **to display the partition table and review the results.**

7. **If you want to define more swap partitions, repeat Steps 2 through 6.**

   At this point, however, you may be finished with changing file system types because most of the other file systems can remain as Linux native.

Changing the boot designation

You need tweak the disk one more time before you go on with the installation. You need to set at least one partition as the partition for the computer to boot. Normally, this is the first partition. Sometimes, the first partition is already set to boot; look at the second column of the partition table and see whether an asterisk (*) appears in the boot column. If it does, you can go to the next section.

If no asterisk appears in that column, or if the asterisk is on a disk partition other than partition 1, you have to change it. In the example in Figure D-11, we first negated, or cleared, the boot designator for partition 1, just to show you that you use the same steps to clear or set a boot designator.

```
Command (m for help): p

Disk /dev/sda: 33 heads, 61 sectors, 1018 cylinders
Units = cylinders of 2013 * 512 bytes

    Device Boot    Begin    Start    End    Blocks    Id    System
/dev/sda1     *       1        1      300    301919+    6    DOS 16-bit >=32M
/dev/sda2           301      301      504    205326    83    Linux native
/dev/sda3           505      505      635    131851+   82    Linux swap
/dev/sda4           636      636     1018    385489+   83    Linux native

Command (m for help): a
Partition number (1-4): 1

Command (m for help): p

Disk /dev/sda: 33 heads, 61 sectors, 1018 cylinders
Units = cylinders of 2013 * 512 bytes

    Device Boot    Begin    Start    End    Blocks    Id    System
/dev/sda1             1        1      300    301919+    6    DOS 16-bit >=32M
/dev/sda2           301      301      504    205326    83    Linux native
/dev/sda3           505      505      635    131851+   82    Linux swap
/dev/sda4           636      636     1018    385489+   83    Linux native

Command (m for help): a
Partition number (1-4): 1

Command (m for help): p

Disk /dev/sda: 33 heads, 61 sectors, 1018 cylinders
Units = cylinders of 2013 * 512 bytes

    Device Boot    Begin    Start    End    Blocks    Id    System
/dev/sda1     *       1        1      300    301919+    6    DOS 16-bit >=32M
/dev/sda2           301      301      504    205326    83    Linux native
/dev/sda3           505      505      635    131851+   82    Linux swap
/dev/sda4           636      636     1018    385489+   83    Linux native

Command (m for help): █
```

Figure D-11:
Changing
the boot
partition.

Follow these steps to change the boot designator:

1. **Type** p **to display the partition table.**

2. **Type** a.

   The a command tells fdisk that you want to change the boot designator.

3. **Type the partition number you want to change.**

   Remember, you follow the same process if you need to clear a boot indicator or set one.

4. **Type** p **to verify the change.**

Saving the partition table and exiting fdisk

The changes you make do not have any effect until you save them. If you want to quit fdisk at any time without saving changes, use the q command. If you're satisfied with the changes, however, do the following at the fdisk command prompt:

1. **Type** w **to write the disk partition back to the disk.**

2. **Type** q**.**

   The fdisk programs terminates, and you return to the Red Hat installation screen.

3. **You've finished partitioning your hard disk, so select the Done button.**

4. **If the system tells you to reboot, select the Ok button.**

   You may see the reboot message if you changed the partition table by adding or deleting partitions, as shown in Figure D-12. This is a normal occurrence.

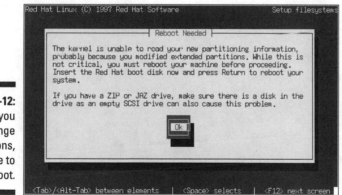

Figure D-12:
When you
change
partitions,
you have to
reboot.

5. **Follow the same steps that you performed from the time you booted the floppy disk in the "Beginning the Installation" section, in Chapter 5, until the installation program again gives you the choice of partitioning your disks — but because your disks are now partitioned properly, select the Done button.**

Appendix E

About the CD-ROMs

● ●

*T*he CD-ROMs that comes with this book contain the full freeware distribution of Red Hat Linux 6.1, sourcecode, as well as Netscape Communicator. CD2 contains source code, CD1 contains everything else.

System Requirements

Make sure that your computer meets the minimum system requirements listed here. If your computer doesn't match up to most of these requirements, you may have problems using the contents of the CDs:

- ✔ A PC with a 486 or faster processor.
- ✔ At least 8MB of total RAM installed on your computer. For the best performance, we recommend that people who want to use X Window System have at least 16MB and preferably 32MB of main memory.
- ✔ At least 800MB of hard drive space available to install all the software from the CD. You'll need less space if you don't install every program. For example, if you want to install only the smallest subset of the base system and X Window System, you can do that in about 180 bytes.
- ✔ A CD-ROM drive.
- ✔ A 3¼-inch floppy disk drive and a blank 3¼-inch disk.
- ✔ A monitor capable of displaying at least 256 colors or grayscale.
- ✔ An IDE or a SCSI disk.
- ✔ A keyboard and a mouse.
- ✔ A modem with a speed of at least 14,400 bps if you want to go online.

Appendix B lists all the hardware compatible with Linux.

Using the CDs

The instructions for installing CD1 are detailed in Part II. After you install the software, return the CD to its plastic jacket for safekeeping.

What You'll Find

CD1 contains the freely distributable parts of Red Hat Linux Publisher's Edition Version 6.1. You may view a lot of the documentation on this CD through an HTML viewer such as Netscape, which is also included on CD1, or you may print it out. You can also view most of this documentation from other operating systems such as DOS, Windows, or UNIX.

We recommend that you look at the "The Official Red Hat Linux Installation Guide," which is in the following directory:

```
[Your CD-ROM drive number]:\doc\rhmanual\manual\index.htm
```

The guide is included in HTML format, so you can view it with a Web browser.

Because CD1 has a full implementation of Linux, to list all the accompanying tools and utilities would take too much room. Briefly, the CD includes most of the software that you need to access the Internet; write programs in several computer languages; create and manipulate images; create, manipulate, and play back sounds (if you have a sound board); play certain games; and work with electrical design. And of course, all the source code is included — CD2 includes additional source code for Linux.

If You Have Problems (Of the CD Kind)

We tried our best to test various computers with the minimum system requirements. Alas, your computer may differ, and Linux may not install or work as stated.

The two likeliest problems are that you don't have enough RAM for the programs you want to use, or you have some hardware that Linux doesn't support. Luckily, the latter problem occurs less frequently each day as more hardware is supported under Linux. (Check out Appendix B for a list of compatible hardware.)

You may also have SCSI disks that use a controller not supported by Linux or a controller that is simply too new for the Linux development team to have given it the proper support at the time the CDs were pressed.

If you have trouble with corrupt files on either of the CDs, please call the IDG Books Worldwide Customer Service phone number: 800-762-2974 (outside the United States: 317-596-5430). Customer service won't be able to help with complications relating to the program or how it works. Please see the Installation Instructions at the end of this book.

Index

• L •

IDG BOOKS WORLDWIDE
BOOK REGISTRATION

Register This Book and Win!

We want to hear from you!

Visit **http://my2cents.dummies.com** to register this book and tell us how you liked it!

- ✔ Get entered in our monthly prize giveaway.

- ✔ Give us feedback about this book — tell us what you like best, what you like least, or maybe what you'd like to ask the author and us to change!

- ✔ Let us know any other ...*For Dummies*® topics that interest you.

Your feedback helps us determine what books to publish, tells us what coverage to add as we revise our books, and lets us know whether we're meeting your needs as a ...*For Dummies* reader. You're our most valuable resource, and what you have to say is important to us!

Not on the Web yet? It's easy to get started with *Dummies 101*®: *The Internet For Windows*® *98* or *The Internet For Dummies*, 6th Edition, at local retailers everywhere.

Or let us know what you think by sending us a letter at the following address:

...*For Dummies* Book Registration
Dummies Press
7260 Shadeland Station, Suite 100
Indianapolis, IN 46256-3917
Fax 317-596-5498

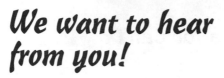

...FOR DUMMIES™
BESTSELLING
BOOK SERIES

redhat®

The Revolution of Choice

GNU GENERAL PUBLIC LICENSE

Version 2, June 1991

Preamble

The licenses for most software are designed to take away your freedom to share and change it. By contrast, the GNU General Public License is intended to guarantee your freedom to share and change free software—to make sure the software is free for all its users. This General Public License applies to most of the Free Software Foundation's software and to any other program whose authors commit to using it. (Some other Free Software Foundation software is covered by the GNU Library General Public License instead.) You can apply it to your programs, too.

When we speak of free software, we are referring to freedom, not price. Our General Public Licenses are designed to make sure that you have the freedom to distribute copies of free software (and charge for this service if you wish), that you receive source code or can get it if you want it, that you can change the software or use pieces of it in new free programs; and that you know you can do these things.

To protect your rights, we need to make restrictions that forbid anyone to deny you these rights or to ask you to surrender the rights. These restrictions translate to certain responsibilities for you if you distribute copies of the software, or if you modify it.

For example, if you distribute copies of such a program, whether gratis or for a fee, you must give the recipients all the rights that you have. You must make sure that they, too, receive or can get the source code. And you must show them these terms so they know their rights.

We protect your rights with two steps: (1) copyright the software, and (2) offer you this license which gives you legal permission to copy, distribute and/or modify the software.

Also, for each author's protection and ours, we want to make certain that everyone understands that there is no warranty for this free software. If the software is modified by someone else and passed on, we want its recipients to know that what they have is not the original, so that any problems introduced by others will not reflect on the original authors' reputations.

Finally, any free program is threatened constantly by software patents. We wish to avoid the danger that redistributors of a free program will individually obtain patent licenses, in effect making the program proprietary. To prevent this, we have made it clear that any patent must be licensed for everyone's free use or not licensed at all.

The precise terms and conditions for copying, distribution and modification follow.

TERMS AND CONDITIONS FOR COPYING, DISTRIBUTION AND MODIFICATION

This License applies to any program or other work which contains a notice placed by the copyright holder saying it may be distributed under the terms of this General Public License. The "Program", below, refers to any such program or work, and a "work based on the Program" means either the Program or any derivative work under copyright law: that is to say, a work containing the Program or a portion of it, either verbatim or with modifications and/or translated into another language. (Hereinafter, translation is included without limitation in the term "modification".) Each licensee is addressed as "you".

Activities other than copying, distribution and modification are not covered by this License; they are outside its scope. The act of running the Program is not restricted, and the output from the Program is covered only if its contents constitute a work based on the Program (independent of having been made by running the Program). Whether that is true depends on what the Program does.

1. You may copy and distribute verbatim copies of the Program's source code as you receive it, in any medium, provided that you conspicuously and appropriately publish on each copy an appropriate copyright notice and disclaimer of warranty; keep intact all the notices that refer to this License and to the absence of any warranty; and give any other recipients of the Program a copy of this License along with the Program.

   You may charge a fee for the physical act of transferring a copy, and you may at your option offer warranty protection in exchange for a fee.

2. You may modify your copy or copies of the Program or any portion of it, thus forming a work based on the Program, and copy and distribute such modifications or work under the terms of Section 1 above, provided that you also meet all of these conditions:

   (a) You must cause the modified files to carry prominent notices stating that you changed the files and the date of any change.

   (b) You must cause any work that you distribute or publish, that in whole or in part contains or is derived from the Program or any part thereof, to be licensed as a whole at no charge to all third parties under the terms of this License.

   (c) If the modified program normally reads commands interactively when run, you must cause it, when started running for such interactive use in the most ordinary way, to print or display an announcement including an appropriate copyright notice and a notice that there is no warranty (or else, saying that you provide a warranty) and that users may redistribute the program under these conditions, and telling the user how to view a copy of this License. (Exception: if the Program itself is interactive but does not normally print such an announcement, your work based on the Program is not required to print an announcement.)

   These requirements apply to the modified work as a whole. If identifiable sections of that work are not derived from the Program, and can be reasonably considered independent and separate works in themselves, then this License, and its terms, do not apply to those sections when you distribute them as separate works. But when you distribute the same sections as part of a whole which is a work based on the Program, the distribution of the whole must be on the terms of this License, whose permissions for other licensees extend to the entire whole, and thus to each and every part regardless of who wrote it.

Thus, it is not the intent of this section to claim rights or contest your rights to work written entirely by you; rather, the intent is to exercise the right to control the distribution of derivative or collective works based on the Program. In addition, mere aggregation of another work not based on the Program with the Program (or with a work based on the Program) on a volume of a storage or distribution medium does not bring the other work under the scope of this License.

3. You may copy and distribute the Program (or a work based on it, under Section 2) in object code or executable form under the terms of Sections 1 and 2 above provided that you also do one of the following:

   (a) Accompany it with the complete corresponding machine-readable source code, which must be distributed under the terms of Sections 1 and 2 above on a medium customarily used for software interchange; or,

   (b) Accompany it with a written offer, valid for at least three years, to give any third party, for a charge no more than your cost of physically performing source distribution, a complete machine-readable copy of the corresponding source code, to be distributed under the terms of Sections 1 and 2 above on a medium customarily used for software interchange; or,

   (c) Accompany it with the information you received as to the offer to distribute corresponding source code. (This alternative is allowed only for noncommercial distribution and only if you received the program in object code or executable form with such an offer, in accord with Subsection b above.)

The source code for a work means the preferred form of the work for making modifications to it. For an executable work, complete source code means all the source code for all modules it contains, plus any associated interface definition files, plus the scripts used to control compilation and installation of the executable. However, as a special exception, the source code distributed need not include anything that is normally distributed (in either source or binary form) with the major components (compiler, kernel, and so on) of the operating system on which the executable runs, unless that component itself accompanies the executable.

If distribution of executable or object code is made by offering access to copy from a designated place, then offering equivalent access to copy the source code from the same place counts as distribution of the source code, even though third parties are not compelled to copy the source along with the object code.

4. You may not copy, modify, sublicense, or distribute the Program except as expressly provided under this License. Any attempt otherwise to copy, modify, sublicense or distribute the Program is void, and will automatically terminate your rights under this License. However, parties who have received copies, or rights, from you under this License will not have their licenses terminated so long as such parties remain in full compliance.

5. You are not required to accept this License, since you have not signed it. However, nothing else grants you permission to modify or distribute the Program or its derivative works. These actions are prohibited by law if you do not accept this License. Therefore, by modifying or distributing the Program (or any work based on the Program), you indicate your acceptance of this License to do so, and all its terms and conditions for copying, distributing or modifying the Program or works based on it.

6. Each time you redistribute the Program (or any work based on the Program), the recipient automatically receives a license from the original licensor to copy, distribute or modify the Program subject to these terms and conditions. You may not impose any further restrictions on the recipients' exercise of the rights granted herein. You are not responsible for enforcing compliance by third parties to this License.

7. If, as a consequence of a court judgment or allegation of patent infringement or for any other reason (not limited to patent issues), conditions are imposed on you (whether by court order, agreement or otherwise) that contradict the conditions of this License, they do not excuse you from the conditions of this License. If you cannot distribute so as to satisfy simultaneously your obligations under this License and any other pertinent obligations, then as a consequence you may not distribute the Program at all. For example, if a patent license would not permit royalty-free redistribution of the Program by all those who receive copies directly or indirectly through you, then the only way you could satisfy both it and this License would be to refrain entirely from distribution of the Program.

   If any portion of this section is held invalid or unenforceable under any particular circumstance, the balance of the section is intended to apply and the section as a whole is intended to apply in other circumstances.

   It is not the purpose of this section to induce you to infringe any patents or other property right claims or to contest validity of any such claims; this section has the sole purpose of protecting the integrity of the free software distribution system, which is implemented by public license practices. Many people have made generous contributions to the wide range of software distributed through that system in reliance on consistent application of that system; it is up to the author/donor to decide if he or she is willing to distribute software through any other system and a licensee cannot impose that choice.

   This section is intended to make thoroughly clear what is believed to be a consequence of the rest of this License.

8. If the distribution and/or use of the Program is restricted in certain countries either by patents or by copyrighted interfaces, the original copyright holder who places the Program under this License may add an explicit geographical distribution limitation excluding those countries, so that distribution is permitted only in or among countries not thus excluded. In such case, this License incorporates the limitation as if written in the body of this License.

9. The Free Software Foundation may publish revised and/or new versions of the General Public License from time to time. Such new versions will be similar in spirit to the present version, but may differ in detail to address new problems or concerns.

   Each version is given a distinguishing version number. If the Program specifies a version number of this License which applies to it and "any later version", you have the option of following the terms and conditions either of that version or of any later version published by the Free Software Foundation. If the Program does not specify a version number of this License, you may choose any version ever published by the Free Software Foundation.

10. If you wish to incorporate parts of the Program into other free programs whose distribution conditions are different, write to the author to ask for permission. For software which is copyrighted by the Free Software Foundation, write to the Free Software Foundation; we sometimes make exceptions for this. Our decision will be guided by the two goals of preserving the free status of all derivatives of our free software and of promoting the sharing and reuse of software generally.

If the program is interactive, make it output a short notice like this when it starts in an interactive mode:

Gnomovision version 69, Copyright (C) 19yy name of author

Gnomovision comes with ABSOLUTELY NO WARRANTY; for details type `show w'.

This is free software, and you are welcome to redistribute it under certain conditions; type `show c' for details.

The hypothetical commands `show w' and `show c' should show the appropriate parts of the General Public License. Of course, the commands you use may be called something other than `show w' and `show c'; they could even be mouse-clicks or menu whatever suits your program.

You should also get your employer (if you work as a programmer) or your school, if any, to sign a "copyright disclaimer" for the program, if necessary. Here is a sample; alter the names:

Yoyodyne, Inc., hereby disclaims all copyright interest in the program

`Gnomovision' (which makes passes at compilers) written by James Hacker.

<signature of Ty Coon>, 1 April 1989

Ty Coon, President of Vice

This General Public License does not permit incorporating your program into proprietary programs. If your program is a subroutine library, you may consider it more useful to permit linking proprietary applications with the library. If this is what you want to do, use the GNU Library General Public License instead of this License.

Installation Instructions

Red Hat Linux For Dummies CD-ROM1 contains the full freeware distribution of Red Hat Linux Publisher's Edition 6.1. CD-ROM2 contains source code for the distribution.

Important Information About Using Linux: Linux supports many IBM-compatible PCs, but some PCs and components aren't supported. Appendix B lists the hardware compatible with Linux. Please review the appendix before attempting to install Linux from *Red Hat Linux For Dummies* CD-ROM 1.

The Linux operating system and its applications are collaborative products of a worldwide community of independent users. IDG Books Worldwide, Inc., doesn't guarantee the fitness of the Linux operating system, Linux applications, or the *Red Hat Linux For Dummies* CD-ROMs for any computer system or purpose. IDG Books Worldwide, Inc., doesn't provide additional installation support or technical support for the Linux operating system, Linux applications, or the *Red Hat Linux For Dummies* CD-ROMs.

Part II of this book describes the installation process for Linux.

Limited Warranty